THOUGHTS ON A WINE CELLAR

A Love Song

by

Henry Goulding

"Drink to me, drink to my health, you know I can't drink anymore."

Pablo Picasso

To Lucy, my love,
to Emily, Gus and Claudia, my little ones
and
to James D'Albiac, a generous spirit
who introduced me to the poetry that is wine.

FOREWORD

France. Normandy. Carteret. La Cale Marine. August.

We sit, as we have always sat, around a wooden table in a wood-panelled room, and look, as we have always looked, across a room of ships and out through the windows across the tide-pulled harbour to the disappearing coast. We eat as we have always eaten. Moules marinières. And chips. And, for Emily, steak. And chips. Bowls of chips crowd the middle of the table, vying for space with the steel bowls into which the discarded shells clatter. The children chatter and we shepherd them on, through conversation, through dropped forks, through more ketchup, through hurry up, through ice cream and then, afterwards, across the road, into the car and down to the beach.

We do as we always have done and I look at the scene and wish it might last forever. Or at least as long as there remains wine in the bottle and Muscadet in my glass. Beads condense on the outside of the tumbler, its scalloped sides finding comfort in my fingers. Edges smoothe and time slips. In that moment all existence passes through the prism of the pale wine: the noise of the restaurant, the cry of the gulls outside, the brine of the tide-exposed mud, the muted converse of the sailors beneath the harbour wall, the wind in the fescue beyond, the wash of the breaking shore, the brightness of this August afternoon, the corrupted heat rising off the tarmac, the sweat on my skin, the tiredness beneath my eyes, the blessedness of this God-given moment.

I stare at my tumbler and listen to the conversation. This glass of near-tasteless near-perfect wine has opened this window for me, has paused time and left me this quiet reflective space in which to recognise the near-perfection of this stolen instant.

I fill your glass and then mine and I give silent thanks for the power of Muscadet.

Whisper the words gently, my love, but, if the doctors are to be believed, there is a chance that we shall not grow old together. They say it might be a matter of...a matter of X. How long is X? Who knows? Clearly no one. As you yourself say, it might only be "might". It might only be X. But it might be Y. As with all of us, it will ultimately be something but, until then, it might only be anything.

Which plays havoc with my mind. I ignore it and at the same time I think of it all the time. Binary planets in perpetual motion. I ignore it to focus on life and to live in the present; I think of it all the time because ignoring it might suggest I am taking life for granted and not appreciating the present.

Contradicting myself out of all sense and losing all supports of my own, I fall back on love, the one constant and the one truth which pervades all that I am, do, see. I lean on love. I lean on the love of friends, old and new, whose gentleness and care never cease to astonish. I lean on the love of work colleagues which is no less love for being disguised in the formality of work. I lean on the love of Father Gianni who teaches me of God's love, as much a support on this planet as beyond. I lean on the love of Orrin who teaches me of the perpetual balance of the universe and the ultimate peace that suffuses all. I lean on the love of family (I was once so small!). I lean on the love of the little ones who teach me the blessings of my 49 years. And you, my love, above all I lean on the love of you which needs no words.

Who knows? The very words. They are a statement of fact as much as a question. A question wrapped in uncertainty and so a statement in no uncertain terms: a pillar of support for the present and the promise of a future to come.

All of which has little to do with wine.

1,100 bottles or thereabouts. That's about the size of it. 20 years or so work, 20 years or so dreaming, 20 years or so love affair. 1,100 bottles. Maybe 1,200. I was once told the perfect size for a wine collection is 1,000 bottles or so. Large enough to develop a tail so that you are always drinking a wide variety of wines at full maturity, small enough that you stand a chance of drinking it all and are not obliged to sell or give large parts of it away.

My father had a small wine collection and my parents used to joke about it.

"We have all this wine," they said "will we ever have the time to drink it?"

How we all laughed.

The fates whispered and the fates conspired and no, they did not, not together in any event.

Have they planned the same for us, my love, for you and me? Yes or no is unknown. But what is the alternative? Do nothing? Concede defeat before battle is even engaged? Out of the question. Wine represents for me so many things that I hold dear about life; to do without it would be to do without oxygen. It is a key to friendship, camaraderie, shared experience. It is a key to conversation and the exchange of ideas. It is a key to time and place, both what is in the bottle and what is released when the cork is pulled. It is a key to memory. It is a key to plurality, variety and difference. It is a celebration of the infinite. It is a season to food, it is a reason for water. Even now I cannot help but plan for the future, cannot help but buy the odd half-case or two and invest in what might be. It is a habit I am reluctant to leave behind. It is a habit that celebrates life in so many wonderful ways.

I can still recall the thrill of laying down that first case in 1996, the year after we were married. It was a statement of intent and an expression of hope: a stock for future happiness. We were setting out together and so our young hearts planned that, along the way, previously left reserves of gentle, anticipated, time-softened wine should welcome us and ease our passage through.   And   how   right   that   has   proved   to   be. Cases consumed, memories evoked and memories provoked, times recalled and times created.

To begin with I ventured "maybe 10". Maybe we would build a cellar of 10 cases to be topped up from time to time to keep a neat running total of, well, maybe 10 but then possibly a dozen. That had a nice ring. A dozen dozen. Seven score and four. But then we got to 12 and, well, who's counting?   Not the vintages, not the rolling years. We had a life ahead of us and there was so much (there is so much) to see and to do and to experience and to live. And first there was Bordeaux and then there was Burgundy. But what about the Loire and the Mosel? And the Rhône and the Rhine - rivers of happiness! The world unfurled at our feet and offered its wares. Who were we to refuse? The collection grew. We spread our wings and slowly, inexorably, we learnt of the Douro, of Rioja, of the hills of Chianti and Alba. The learning never ceases. And the years never   cease,   the   subtle   variations   of   vintage   never   tire. Growers come and go, stars wax, reputations fall.   The world flexes ceaselessly and one of the ways I choose to embrace this endless flux is through wine. The thrill of pulling a cork has never left me, not for one moment, not for a single bottle. What story will be told? What scent will fill my nostrils, what new experience will carve a mind map across my conscience for that fresh, single moment? Blessings are multitudinous and everywhere. My idiom is wine.

Wine can be well made, wine can be badly made. Some grapes are riper and richer than others and so some wines will be fruitier or fuller than others. But once the winemaker has stoppered his wine there is nothing objective left about wine. All is subjective. All is in the delivery and its interpretation by the drinker. There is better and worse for sure but it is better or worse in the mind of the drinker alone. The drinker will be the judge and he will not be judged by others. His verdict is paramount and he is answerable to no one. The taster is king. And his opinion will be formed as much by what is in his head and his heart as by what is in the bottle. That is the beauty of wine.

By what is in his head and his heart. Everything to do with wine is ultimately subjective and emotive. It is impossible to divorce memory and emotion from the experience. So what happens if I am not about? What if I am not there to guide you, my love, my little ones, to tell you why we bought them, to remind you of the occasion, to tell you of the past and to express a hope of the future (how will the wine be)? Who will be there to tell you of the head and the heart, of their contribution to the bottle? Memory and place. These cases (these cases: do not worry my love, in many instances down to only a few bottles now) are the receptacles of so many shared experiences and so many hopes.

Whether it is X or Y, I must tell you about the wines. So let us drink them together now, let me fill your heads and your hearts with their histories. And may we drink them again in the future. X or Y, who knows?

This book is imperfect in so many ways. It is not encyclopaedic (there are big gaps: Australia and New Zealand for goodness sake), within countries there are large omissions and there will be errors (I know there will be errors). It is not a text book of facts and figures, of which there are so many good examples nowadays. It is a book of memory, of ignorance, of passion, of opinions, some of them no doubt misguided. But they are opinions born of joy and sharing, of tongues loosened in idle chatter, of a shared interest and a carefree insouciance as to the veracity of the expressed view. They are opinions born of experience and of a little thought and, well, maybe a little less knowledge. So it is a far from perfect record of the world of wine. Instead it is a record of our world, a history in part of our life together and a preview of our life to come.

And so, where to start? Look how little I have written about the rest of the world, how much I have written about France. Perhaps I should start with France but, equally, perhaps I should start where I wish I had been sooner.

"Wine is constant proof that God loves us."

Benjamin Franklin

ITALY

I came to Italy late. No, I must not say that. You always told me not to be so hard on myself and that first sentence suggests blame on my part. No, I came to Italy when I came to Italy.

First memories of Italian wine are of straw-covered fiasci hiding largely undrinkable generic and industrially-produced reds that littered university parties and tables. But what did we care? In that time of gifts, we were only concerned with the exchange of ideas, emotions, glances and experiences. The cheaply-bought light-coloured fruitless acidic mixtures, well, they did just fine.

In the summer of 1990, the bottles became even more idiosyncratic. It was the time of Italia 90 and England's last meaningful effort at the FIFA World Cup. I remember eating in a trattoria at the top of Leith Walk and drinking (largely undrinkable generic and industrially-produced) wine from bottles blown in the shape of the World Cup itself. Again, did we care? Of course not; we were wrapped up in the thrill of the competition and our adolescent minds had not yet learnt to lower our gaze and scrutinise the merits of the detail before us (and I wonder if we were not the happier for it).

It was then Sainsburys in the early 1990's which gave me a first hint of the wealth that Italy might hold. Sainsburys and Jilly Goolden from BBC's Food and Drink. Sainsburys ran a series of own-label cheap regional Italian reds – Valpolicella, Bardolino, Chianti Classico I remember in particular. And gee'd on by Jilly Goolden's frenzied implorings in her weekly slot on Food and Drink, yes I could begin to discern cherries in my Valpolicella, tea in my Chianti and goodness knows what in my Bardolino.

And after that, I am afraid, all went quiet. I caught the wine bug and, with so much to learn and only limited space in my head, concentrated on France, the region all wine lovers lean to when wanting to learn the ropes.

So it was that my first meaningful purchase of Italian wine was not until the autumn of 2009 (full 13 years since I had started buying wine to lay down) and it is worth recording, however banal the words, what I wrote in my cellar book on the acquisition of a case of Palazzino's Chianti Classico La Pieve 2006 (for thoughts on the wine itself, see further on):

A departure for me.   The increasingly fashionable price of Bordeaux, and the strength of the Euro pushing affordability of Burgundy and the Rhône, I must search for pastures new.   So look for conscientious growers, striving to get the best from their sod of earth, as faithfully and naturally as possible.   Price may try and decree otherwise but I don't believe a great Chianti (or Loire or Rioja) is any less great than a great Bordeaux.

Price was one feature of the flight to Italy. But only one. The great appeal to me of Italian wine now is the diversity of what the country has to offer, the lack of hype for all save the best known wines, the food-friendliness of the wines and, as much as anything, the spirit in which Italian wine is produced (maybe) and consumed (absolutely).   Buying and drinking Italian wine is liberating.

Diversity: Italy has over 350 authorised grape varieties. France?   Somewhere around 60.   To the average lay wine consumer like myself, no other country appears to offer quite the array of different wines that Italy does.   This can be daunting, especially, as with me, if you use the world's main grape varieties (the Chardonnays, the Cabernet Sauvignons et al) as the key to unlocking an understanding of wine (much as the mastery of ABC will eventually unlock Shakespeare). So, in a land of 350 grape varieties, where do you begin? I don't properly have an answer to that. Maybe ignore the grapes to begin with. Instead, learn the main regions (a few of which are covered below) and use these as stepping stones to other regions? Conceivably, although I am not sure an in-depth knowledge of the wines of Etna will help you unpick the intricacies of the Alto Adige. Or maybe just drink the wines we have in the cellar, or something like them, and then go where you will. Italy has always carried off chaos and anarchy with so much more panache and charm than any other nation on earth, so embrace this approach and let your haphazard discoveries lead you on from discovery to happy discovery.

Lack of hype: OK, so it is possible to become mired in hyperbole with certain wines (not quite regions, but certainly individual wines) but in Italy these tend to be priced so highly it is easy to avoid them: they stand out like tall poppies. Take the 2010 Brunellos, for example. If the critics' marks are to be believed, then there is little separating a huge range of these wines yet the prices differ wildly. I am not sure other wine regions of the world quite share this disparity. Value can be had, even in the smart regions and most definitely in those less heralded.

Food-friendliness: At the top end of Monmouth Street in Covent Garden is one of the finest restaurants I know, Rossodissera, run by two brothers from Le Marche. The food is simple, peasant simple if you will, utterly honest, utterly delicious and all from Le Marche. I invariably order the same thing – a mixed starter of hams and cheeses with honeys and chutneys designed to go with them (don't ask me if they do; I just tuck in and take the brothers' word for it) followed by truffle pasta. And I always drink the same wine – an Offida Pecorino white, concentrated, filled with peach and other white fruit flavours, soft and beguiling, and then a Lacrima di Morro d'Alba, a wine that tastes unapologetically and incontrovertibly of violets. I was recommended these pairings, both wines I had never heard of before. And I have never deviated Why do I tell you this? Because I can think of no other fusion of food and wine which works so well. Italian regions have not lost the link between their food and their wine and, more importantly, Italian wines have not lost their ability to augment the food they are consumed with. For the most part, they are not overly full-bodied and they retain a healthy balance of acidity, both pre-requisites of a successful food wine.

Culture: if you decide not to embrace the Italian way of learning the ropes of Italian wine by allowing chance and serendipity to divert you, then I am not sure you can do better than read Vino Italiano by Joseph Bastianich, particularly the introductory chapters on each region (details on the individual growers and some of their wines may be, well, too detailed). The author successfully paints portraits of the different regions of Italy and how the main types of wines in those regions fit into the region's cuisine and culture. For Italians, wine is a way of life, simple as that.

So what wines do we have? These follow. We can tick off the best-known regions, Tuscany and Piedmont, and maybe the best-known of those regions' wines, Chianti, Brunello, Barolo and Barbaresco. We can even take in a couple of specialisms, Basilicata and Alto Adige, but there are some fairly big gaps. The Veneto is entirely unrepresented which is not fair; there should be room for the charm of Valpolicella and the surprising depths of Soave. And we have nothing from Sicily, perhaps the most dynamic of all the regions at the moment. But enough of this. Let's not define ourselves by our shortcomings. The following are beauties.

TUSCANY

Chianti Classico, La Pieve, Podere Palazzino 2006
Chianti Classico, La Pieve, Podere Palazzino 2007
Chianti Classico, Vigna del Sorbo, Fontodi 2010
Chianti Classico, Podere Castellinuzza 2013

How do we measure time? In years, months and days obviously but there must be another measure, for how do I explain the surprise of writing down the fact that it is 21 years since we set off on our married life together and honeymooned in Tuscany, just outside Siena, in the heart of Chianti? Maybe we measure time by the intervals between significant events. These come thick and fast in adolescence but ease off as life progresses, as we become more familiar with the world around us and the experiences it has to offer. Why else does our adolescence seem such a long period of time when in reality we are talking about no more than a condensed super-rich period of maybe 10 years? After this, the significant experiences become fewer, even if more life-changing, and time flies faster. Can it really can have been 21 years since we landed at Pisa and headed off in our Fiat Punto onto unknown Italian roads?

We stayed two weeks in a tiny medieval tower, three storeys high, one room per storey, in the middle of an olive grove, somewhere outside the town of Sovicille. Silver-washed Fritillaries patrolled the grounds. Familiar birds from home, Chaffinches and Blue Tits, chattily hopped their way from olive tree to olive tree, confusing my sense of place. It was only the occasional Hoopoe, flashing black and white over peach, and the ambient warmth of the earth that would reassure me of our presence in the South. Our bedroom was on the top floor and from here you could just make out the campanile of Siena's Duomo in the distance. The weather was so-so but we did not care. We ate simply, we travelled the countryside, we tasted the wine. As in so much, we were learning and just setting out. I have a picture of you in the swimming pool (what passed for it anyway), looking over your shoulder at the camera. We look so young! The water was so cold.

Chianti is probably Italy's most famous wine. Brunello was a latecomer and Barolo is a little too refined and expensive for mass appeal. It may be that Chianti's popularity is attributable to the appeal of those fiasci that bedecked many a 70's and 80's table, the straw-covered flagons adding a certain distinction to otherwise pretty indistinctive fare, but I daresay it is as much due to the appeal of Tuscany as a holiday destination for the sun-deprived of Northern Europe.

People's image of Tuscany is typically that of the ink-dark plumes of the cypress trees dotting an otherwise treeless landscape of blowing wheat and winding roads. That is La Crete. Chianti, to the north, is not like that. It is hillier for a start and much more wooded. It lies between Florence and Siena and is (at least for wine-growing purposes) divided into a number of sub-regions, the most important of which is Chianti Classico, followed by Chianti Rufina. The others you are unlikely to come across unless you are in the region. Being English, I always thought Chianti Rufina should be more refined (rufina:refined) than it is, or purportedly is. But to say it is rougher (rufina:rougher) than Classico is unfair, especially in the hands of decent winemakers.

The grape is easy: Sangiovese. Or it should be. In that wonderful way the Italians have of organising things, in the last 40 years or so there have been all sorts of changes in terms of the grapes that are permitted in Chianti. White grape varieties played quite a part until relatively recently and the evergreen bugbear of international varieties, whether they should be allowed at all and if so to what extent, rumbles on. But increasingly, serious producers look little or no further than Sangiovese, perhaps with bit parts only for one or two other local (not international) varieties. And to my untutored mind, that is correct. Sangiovese treads a wonderful balance of lightness and acidity on the one hand (perfect for food) and substance and interest on the other. Typically, Chianti should be medium-bodied at best, with a lovely clarity and with a beguiling sourness of cherries and tea. Full marks if you get all those.

La Pieve: so this was my first foray into Italian wine-buying and I landed with a sure foot. This is not Il Palazzino's top offering but nor is it their entry-level wine. It is serious, sometimes surly, sometimes difficult to fathom (especially if you are not in the mood) and curiously tastes of dust (along with plums). The tannins can appear uncultured, a bit tough, the wine a little unpolished. But in a world of easily accessible, quick to please, easy to forget wines, this can be just the ticket. It is a wine which deserves attention and which grows in the glass. Flavours unfurl, textures develop. It is a wine of dried fruits and herbs which goes magically with food. It does not trump the food or look to compete. We pay little enough attention to wines like these nowadays, we should pay more. There's no need to stand on ceremony with the wine but give it a little love and attention and you will be rewarded. The 2006 is a little more serious than the 2007, the 2007 a little warmer. Neither is a fruit bomb, both are dry. Both are drinking now; neither is in a hurry.

Vigna del Sorbo: I know next to nothing about this wine other than it is often held out as being one of Chianti's finest wines. It must be a trait common to all collectors (or maybe only the sensible ones?) that, once your collection reaches a certain size, you start to wonder if you are ever going to drink all this stuff.

At which point, you can sell some of what you have (anathema, but occasionally necessary), you can drink double-speed (fun, but brings its own complications), you can stop (impossible) or at least slow down (difficult) or you can trade up and buy less. Vigna del Sorbo was an attempt at the latter. We must wait a short while for this wine to come round so I don't know immediately if these six bottles were a wise choice. Suffice to say that the wine's reputation is very high, it is made by Fontodi, a very accomplished outfit, and is, by all accounts, an honest and immaculate reflection of what Chianti is capable of. I hope it is good. Maybe we shall drink it together, maybe we shall not, but either way it comes with my love. The wine deserves respect and will drink for many years.

Castellinuzza: to call this cooking Chianti is unfair. But it is certainly more playful and accessible, and warrantable of less full-on attention, than the other two. Pull a bottle off the shelf when you do not want to think too much and when you have spaghetti bolognese on the go upstairs. If the wine merchant is to believed, he spent a whole day tasting a hundred Chiantis in the Chianti tasting rooms in the middle of Greve and this one was the only one that hit the spot in terms of purity of flavour, a faithful interpretation of Sangiovese and a lightness of touch. I cannot vouch for the 100-wine marathon but I can vouch for these attributes. This is a lovely example of the wine from an area called Lamole about which I know absolutely nothing but which Castellinuzza obviously considers very important given the amount of information about Lamole that is contained on the label. I wouldn't bother reading it though; the wine itself will teach you as much as you need, or want, to know about it. Love it for what it is now.

Brunello di Montalcino, Il Poggione 2010
Brunello di Montalcino, Lambardi 2010
Brunello di Montalcino Luce, Luce della Vita 2010

The sun was shining the day we drove to Montalcino on our honeymoon. We crossed La Crete and its open horizons, the hill towns visible from a distance. We walked around the castle at Montalcino and tried wines way beyond our means. We continued trying them at Fattoria dei Barbi where we stopped for lunch. The wines were way beyond our palate as well, dark and tangled, flavours as intertwined and as knotted as brambles.

We visited the region again this summer, driving up from friendlier Umbria, cluttered with forest and broken landscapes, to the austere expanses of La Crete. We stopped in Pienza, halfway between Montepulciano and Montalcino, the brainchild of Pope Pius II, who was determined to transform his humble birthplace into a model Renaissance town. Pocket beauty, it has stood the test of time - one man's will, still extant after 500 years, order withholding chaos, thought withstanding decay.

Away to the west, squinting against the bright afternoon sun, Montalcino was etched in grey on a false horizon, fainter hills rising beyond. And, all around us, the heat of the Val d'Orcia, penetrating the skin, intensifying the pigment and the depth of the grapes, pitiless and single-minded, degrees warmer than Umbria to the south and Chianti to the north.

But where were all the birds? Near-silent swallows cut through the still air, almost apologising for the silent skies around them. The odd solitary distant bird of prey, beyond shot in all senses, cautiously stayed high and away. Hooded crows, the one constant, flapped worry-free across the shallow open valleys, upholding the corvids' reputation as the great survivors. Only the migrating flocks of bee-eaters broke the tension, long heard before seen, bubbling with joy at the prospect of a winter in Africa, filling the sky with their colours of summer: citrus, terracotta and Mediterranean blue. August in the Mediterranean can be quiet; but this quiet? Seriously, where have all the birds gone?

Brunello di Montalcino. Brunello is the grape, Montalcino the town. Brunello is actually Sangiovese, the same grape as found in Chianti, just a different strain (and so given a different name by the residents of Montalcino). Montalcino lies well to the south of Chianti, across and within the more typical (to Northern eyes) landscape of La Crete. And because of the landscape and the latitude, the region is much warmer and drier than Chianti – indeed the harvest can be up to two weeks earlier than in Chianti. And the grapes, whether as a result of the clone or the climate, are darker and riper, the flesh sweeter, the skins thicker and with more tannin. This means the wine is fuller-bodied, with higher levels of alcohol (the sugar turns to alcohol during fermentation so the riper the grapes, the more the sugar there is and so the more alcohol must be produced if the wine is to be dry) and higher levels of extract and tannin from the skin. So the wine is very different from Chianti, altogether a more serious statement of intent and ambition. And as a rule it is priced accordingly although the campaign for the 2010 release is instructive.

2010 is considered a golden year in Brunello when everything came together perfectly and the critics' scores of the wines, once in bottle, certainly reflect this. Which made the pricing of these wines (barring outliers of course) all the more enlightened when they were released. In the great regions of France, the wines that are released for purchase en primeur are done so before the wine has been bottled and within one or two years of the vintage. The advantage to the winegrower is that he or she is paid early for the wines, long before they are bottled or shipped; the advantage to the consumer is that he or she can buy rare wines before they disappear into private collections and can, or so the theory goes, buy wines at a discount because the winegrower, or so the theory goes, is prepared to offer the wine at a discounted price in reflection of the fact that the buyer is parting with his or her cash long before the wine is physically delivered or even ready to be drunk. The trouble is that in recent years the winegrowers have looked at the prices that these wines eventually collect on the secondary market and have started demanding these sort of prices on release en primeur. This benefits no one and the market has begun to stall badly.

But not, so it seems, in Montalcino. When these wines were released in 2015 (once, incidentally, the wines had been bottled and so could properly be judged and assessed by the critics) there was an audible sigh of relief among wine lovers that here was a region that recognised that these were wines that were not ready to drink now and that, if they were to be purchased now, would need to be sold at a discount. Buyers flocked, including, on a very minor scale, me. These wines will cost a deal more than I paid for them when ready to drink in, say, 10 years' time but the price paid in 2015 was reasonable. What a relief! After all the hand-wringing and gnashing of teeth at the prices now charged by (yes, I will mention them) the Bordelais for the en primeur releases over the last five years or so, what a relief to find a region of world-class wines willing to do a fair deal with the consumer. They will be wines to drink with joy.

Il Poggione: Untouched and I have never tried any of the producer's other wines either. A traditional estate, that is to say wines which will be dry, which will take time to untangle and which will balance flavour and body, neither being dominant.

The estate lies in the southern part of Montalcino, a region which has traditionally produced headier, richer interpretations of Brunello. But, as ever, the wine producer is king. The vineyards lie quite high so benefit from cooler nights and mornings, which allow the grapes to retain sufficient acidity to balance the otherwise rich and sun-baked fruit. Poggione has fashioned, by all accounts, a remarkable wine in 2010. In fact, I read that Wine Spectator, one of America's leading wine magazines, rated it number four in its Top 10 wines of 2015. What do I know. But I like the validation.

Lambardi: Another traditional wine, this time from the cooler north-east of the region. Serious, classic, dry, complex wines, built for the long haul, not too heavily extracted, ruby turning to tawny at the rim, not black turning to blue. And even better, the estate does not make a riserva: its top wine is its straight Brunello.

Luce: So, two wines, Lambardi and Il Poggione, cut from the same cloth – traditional, understated maybe, good value. Luce, on the other hand, is something different, possibly very different.

Do the items with which we surround ourselves define who we are? The books in the shelves, the pictures on the wall, the clothes on our bones, the wines in our cellar? Or do we simply buy in our own image (or perceived image)? And who knows best who we are? Ourselves or others? These thoughts echoed round the caverns of my mind as, quite out of character and quite out of keeping with my usual tastes, I impulsively responded to a wine merchant's email and spent far more than I usually would on a magnum of wine that would never normally appeal to me. It promises to be a bombshell, the product of a joint venture between Robert Mondavi of the United States and Marchesi de Frescobaldi of Florence. Two heavyweights producing, I suspect, a super heavyweight. So why did I react the way I did? The thrill of the impulse to begin with. The prospect of something new, of something different (the older I become, the more my inhibitions subside - why, I might even wear a pair of terracotta trousers one day!). The idea that I might challenge my tastes and my pre-conceptions. And because I have never before experienced or owned a 100-point wine.

Points. Points divide equally. Some love them, some abhor them. It all started really with Robert Parker. He recognised the simple appeal of the system to the uninitiated wine lover. An easy system to calibrate a wine's worth, not lost in words or dependent on pre-existing knowledge. The ultimate objectification of ultimately subjective taste. I neither love nor abhor points. They serve their purpose within limits and, so long as the parameters of those limits are clear (to me, I hasten to add; if points do it for others, so be it and good on them), then they can be of benefit. And what are these limits? Points express a preference and so only work when relative. They cannot be viewed or accurately interpreted in isolation. So if you are tasting a vertical, let's say, of Château Giscours and you award one vintage of the wine 91 points and another 94, then clearly you prefer the latter vintage for reasons ultimately your own but for reasons nevertheless. Or maybe you are tasting a horizontal of the 2015 vintage in Margaux and you rate one château's wine 89 points and another's 87. Clearly you prefer the former to the latter. This is a perfectly valid conclusion that can be derived from and illustrated by the points system.

Where things become more tricky is where like is not compared with like. One day I taste an Assyrtiko from Santorini and I rate it 91 points. I am on the island (I wish!), the sun is shining, I am relaxed and in a good mood. The universe is giving me an almighty nudge and really this wine is delightful and encapsulates the mood perfectly and my wife, my love, you are the most beautiful woman in the world and should we not have another bottle because it seems nonsensical not to? A week later I am in grey London and tasting Château Musar in the company of someone I do not particularly care for and, goodness look at the time, I promised I would be home by 7.30 and I have to do the shopping on the way and this wine, well it is good but it doesn't set my world on fire, but it must be worth 90 points. Which is the better wine? You don't need me to answer that one for you.

Tim Atkin (I think it was Tim Atkin) showed up the nonsense of awarding points by asking his audience to mark Van Gogh's Sunflowers out of 100. Not easily done. Unless of course, Van Gogh's work was just one of a number of paintings of sunflowers that the audience was being asked to mark, in which case the points awarded would highlight where Van Gogh's artistry stood in comparison with the others'. So here is a case where the points awarded might be a useful gauge of the painting's worth, not so much the number awarded (in all honesty, how can you distinguish a 95-point picture from a 96-point picture?) but the number awarded in comparison to the others.

And of course not all points are created equal. One man's points might be harder to earn than another's. Allen Meadows, aka Burghound, who specialises in the wines of Burgundy, is famously parsimonious. If a wine is scored by Burghound in the low 90's, it is a cracker. James Suckling, on the other hand, is a far more generous cove and will scatter high 90's scores about if so moved. Is one more right than the other?

And what about a top score of 100? What if the wine is worth 101? James Suckling's tasting note for none other than this very wine, which he has awarded 100 points, finishes with the question: "could this be better than the legendary 2006?" Excuse me? This wine has 100 points. It is as good as wine can get. It must be better! Oh, but hang on, the 2006 got 100 points as well. What if the 2010 is better? Does that mean the 2006 must be downgraded? Because as sure as eggs is eggs, the 2010 cannot go any higher.

The truth of the matter is that the points system unravels if subjected to any form of scrutiny. But it does serve a purpose and is a consumer-friendly way of quickly and easily articulating a critic's general feelings about a wine. Nothing wrong with that.

And what about this wine? For the simple reason, I suppose, that it is easier to measure things that are capable of being measured, critics have awarded higher points to those wines which have greater mass and accumulation, be it in terms of body, fruit, alcohol, tannin, extraction, first impressions maybe. So it is invariably big wines which get big marks. Not subtle wines; they get subtle marks. Not wines where the pleasure is in the consumption rather than the constitution. And Luce is no different. The Wine Advocate even goes so far as to say that this Brunello maybe the most extracted Brunello of the 2010 vintage. It is a big dark beast of wine that will probably hit you between the eyes at 50 paces.

Which brings me back to my musings on what defines us. I was once asked by the sommelier at Chez Bruce what my favourite wines were. I answered in terms of style rather than specific wines. I said that my favourite wines were those on the edge. Not edgy (I am too easily exhausted to find wines of unusual flavour or character hugely appealing) but on the edge – wines that slip under the radar, that are underappreciated, that are beautifully made, that are full of character but that, for whatever reason, hide their light under a bushel. Is that me?

Certainly not the beautifully made or full of character. But is there a link between the wines I like and who I am? I have no idea but others I suspect (again, who knows me best?) will be in a better position to say. All I can say is that wines like Luce do not appeal to me at all. Ambitious, made for the modern palate, heavy wines, expensive, all (forgive me) tits and arse, all deep and weighty fruit, soft tannins hiding a heavy structure. Or am I wrong? If I do not try these wines from time to time, what chance do I ever have to challenge my prejudice and to give the wine its proper due? This wine may well turn into a stunning swan in 10 or so years' time and I will be proved wrong. But what fun to have a 100-point wine in the house. And my goodness, the packaging. A smart wooden presentation box and a quite horrible label, like a Christmas decoration gone spectacularly wrong. Not of course that I should judge a book by its cover, a wine by its label…

Incidentally, the other main wine of Tuscany (I will leave to one side the wines of Bolgheri, on the Maremma coast, which are a relatively recent development, centred around the international grape varieties of Cabernet Sauvignon and Merlot – great (expensive!) wines which do not necessarily conform to our preferred stereotype of time-honoured wines from ancient vines in an ancient landscape) – as I was saying, the other main wine of Tuscany is Vino Nobile di Montepulciano. It is made, like Chianti and Brunello, from Sangiovese. I am not sure why it is called Vino Nobile, I am not sure there is anything particularly noble about it, but it comes from Montepulciano, another hilltop town of La Crete.

We visited Montepulciano in 2001, when Emily was barely three. We made the steep climb up the main drag to the square at the top of the hill. Like countless thousands across the years before us, we sat on the bench skirting the Palazzo Contucci on the east side of Piazza Grande, to recover ourselves and take in our surroundings. Unlike countless thousands before us, we left Emily's old, rare Ladybird edition of Cinderella there when we stood up to leave. And more surprisingly, perhaps, it was you and me who were more upset than Emily by the loss, knowing what a collector's item that book was. Emily was simply happy to carry on in her merry little way, shortsighted by the blissfulness of childhood.

Vino Nobile de Montepulciano – I am afraid there is none in the cellar.

PIEDMONT

I would never have thought of buying Barolo, if I am honest, were it not for John Arnold of A&B Vintners who, having displayed such success unearthing the most beautiful bottles from Burgundy and Southern France, branched out into Piemonte. If you find a good wine merchant, stick with him or her and don't be afraid to try his or her recommendations. Really, I mean it. Find a good merchant, stick with them.

You know this so really I do not need to tell you but Piemonte is in north-eastern Italy, rolling hills backdropped by the Alps. Turin is the major town but the main winegrowing regions congregate around the town of Alba to the south. The grape here is Nebbiolo, derived from the Italian (maybe even the Roman) for fog, which blankets the area in autumn and which I am sure (though it will take you a winemaker to tell you) contributes to the nature of the wine. This is also white truffle country. In fact, to understand the region and to develop a thirst and hunger for the wines and food of the area, read Michael Dibdin's "A Long Finish", one of his Zen mysteries. Such a good book, spoilt only by the tritest afterword I have ever read in a book. But that comes right at the very end and spoils nothing of what comes before. It will have you reaching for a bottle.

I would never have thought of buying Barolo for the simple reason that I thought it was beyond my means and so I never properly investigated the possibility until John implored me to. When I started out on this wine adventure Barolo sat at the top of the tree with the other great wines of the world and with a price to deter casual investigation. It is a measure, I suppose, of how wildly out of kilter the prices of Bordeaux and top Burgundy have become that, with a few notable and easily avoidable exceptions, Barolo no longer (thankfully!) has to be considered in the same breath. Everyone wins by that, even the wine producers who can rely on a ready market of enthusiasts and consumers, not speculators and equity-chasers.

Barolo is a difficult wine to know. I have tried in the past to get to know it by entry-level introductions at relatively small prices from relatively large supermarkets. But these wines show little, usually displaying plenty of Nebbiolo's firm tannins but little of the grape's fruit and wraparound love. It took a wine from the washout vintage of 2002 to show me something of what the wine had to offer. The deluge of rain delivered that year watered down both the tannins and the winegrower's ambitions sufficiently not to chase a wine of structure but instead to produce something that could be drunk on its faint fruit. From this pretty example I could detect a distant echo of what Barolo is meant to be about.

And what is it about? My limited experience teaches me it is a wine of contrasts. Nebbiolo is a thin-skinned grape and so really has no right to be as tannic as it is (tannins reside in the pips and the skin). On the other hand, the grape is predictable in that its thin skin imparts only a modest amount of colour. So your first taste of a pale-coloured red can knock you off balance by the strength of its tannins. Winegrowers have learnt to tame these tannins now and so a 10-year wait is no longer obligatory before broaching a bottle. And you are further knocked off kilter by the punch of flavour that such a pale wine delivers. I have always detected roses, violets and tar in a broad sweep of a taste that, as I said, wraps around your mouth. And it is not weak! Again, a notable contrast between such a light-looking wine and the 14%, sometimes 15%, alcohol that is always found in these wines. So not a wine for the faint-hearted but undoubtedly one of the world's greats – distinctive, worshipped for centuries, inimitable. A wine for big dishes and long lunches when there is nothing to make you leave the table.

Barolo, Vigna Santa Caterina, Guido Porro 2009
Barolo, Vigna Lazzaraisco, Guido Porro 2009
Barolo, Vigna Lazzaraisco, Guido Porro 2010
Barolo, Ascheri, Ellena Giuseppe 2009
Barolo, Ascheri, Ellena Giuseppe 2010

Porro: the two Porros are very different from each other. I recall that the Santa Caterina is grown on sandier soil than the Lazzaraisco. It is certainly a lighter wine (which is not to say better or worse in this instance), less tar, more citrus, less violet, more floral. The Lazzaraisco is the quieter, more serious, older brother – deeper, wider, tar and malt to the fore. You will be surprised when you pour these wines, both of them tawny towards the rim (and only 7 years old) and so surprisingly pale, almost onion skin! Barolo (and Barbaresco) have made a good job of mapping their vineyards and, whether official or not, have sought to grade them as they have done in Burgundy. Lazzaraisco forms part of the bigger Lazzarito vineyard which is given, in effect, grand cru status. Santa Caterina is from a slightly less exalted vineyard. They are honest wines, with minimal manipulation, the tannins still retaining a pleasing edge to promise steady progress in the cellar and a decent life to come. I wish I could recall the ultra-fashionable and expensive Barolo that I was given to try alongside the Porro as I sat in Medlar on the Kings Road enjoying one of those sunlit wine-fuelled carefree long lunches that I so took for granted at the time – the wine was delicious but so polished and layered in velvet. It lacked the honesty and the bite of the Porro. Winemakers around the world are so accomplished nowadays it is difficult sometimes to retain full honesty in the finished wine. These Porros succeed. 2009? 2010? Differences between the wines? I am afraid I have no idea but there is no rush to find out and it will be a pleasure one day to do so. With age, the tannins will soften, the wines will deepen and you will lose yourself more and more in a deep dark core.

Ellena: this wine, from a vineyard called Ascheri, is a softer rendition of Barolo, not as demanding as the Porro maybe, an utter pleasure though. Almond, steeped cherries, coffee, marzipan, smoke. Powerful. A wine without pretension. You can drink them now if you must but similarly leave them a while, perhaps not quite so long as the Porros but allow them time to say all they are capable of saying.

Barbaresco, Produttori del Barbaresco 2010
Barbaresco Montaribaldi, Fiorenzo Nada 2013

Throughout I have been talking about Barolo. I am sure that the Produttori di Barbaresco, if they were reading this (luckily they won't be), would be tearing their hair out, gesticulating wildly at the printed page and uttering unrepeatable Italian oaths. "But what about Barbaresco?" they would be demanding. And they would be right. Barbaresco lies just to the north-east of Barolo and produces, traditionally, a slightly lighter earlier-maturing (but just as "equal" if that is important) style of wine, some magnificently expensive.

What this wine shows is the power of a good co-operative. People are quick to dismiss the efforts of a wine co-operative, sometimes for good reason. In parts of the world, small growers with little eye on the quality of what they produce will sell their grapes, based on nothing other than weight, to the local co-op which will then chuck everything together, ferment it and then pay back the growers with the finished product. Good for subsequent distillation into ethanol, maybe, or for washing down the farm machinery but less so for internal consumption. But things (as they ever are) are changing. Co-ops now pay closer attention to the quality of what the farmers bring in, paying on quality rather than quantity, producing several different crus and all round just paying much closer attention to the finished product, to the extent there is now an established market for the successful co-operatives' wines (La Chablisienne in Chablis we know well, Roquemare in the Languedoc we briefly, and happily, crossed swords with and here, the Produttori di Barbaresco). Indeed, the esteemed Produttori may be the finest of them all; they certainly have a reputation.

Normally, the Produttori produce different bottlings of the smart crus in Barbaresco (the named vineyards) but in 2010, although it was a very good vintage, rain spoiled one or two of the wines destined for the individual cru bottlings. Such are the rules of the Produttori, one for all and all for one, that unless all the crus can be bottled separately none of them will be and so, in 2010, they all made their way into the generic Barbaresco. Their loss, our gain. Incidentally, I have tried the wine only once – it is darker than the Porros and still young. No rush.

As for the Nada, this is a wine for the long haul and this is how it was sold to me. In the words of Antonio Galloni, a well-respected reviewer, particularly of Italian wines: *"Dark spices, lavender, sage, menthol and dark cherries are front and center. Large-scaled, ample and super-expressive, the Montaribaldi captures the power and intensity of this site. Sweet mentholated notes round out the finish. What a gorgeous wine this is."* How could I possibly resist? I have an image, 20 years hence, of a gathering round a kitchen table, deep into autumn, the windows misted, the cold and dark outside kept at bay by the warmth and laughter of the family gathering within. You, or one of the children, will produce this wine to go with the casserole. Although nearing 25 years of age, the wine will envelop all with an overwhelming sense of richness and beneficence, the world will close in even tighter around you and life will appear very nearly perfect. For me, that vision is worth the price of the wine alone.

Roero, Val dei Prati, Matteo Correggia 2011

And then an even fainter voice I hear – "what about us?" cry the producers of Roero "what about us?". Roero lies to the north of Alba (the other two to the south). It is a lighter interpretation of Nebbiolo (though, again, so much depends on the individual winegrower's hand) and can be broached much earlier. The wine is lovely. Sandalwood, nutmeg, roses and violets. Sappy, balanced, persistent. It was a great hit with your father who kept up the early pace on subsequent glasses and offered no resistance to successive refills when silently offered. I think there is only one bottle left: drink it with your father.

BASILICATA

Aglianico del Vulture, 400 Some, Carbone 2008

Those in the know, or possibly those with nothing better to say, will declare that the third great grape variety of Italy, after Sangiovese and Nebbiolo, is Aglianico. This is a grape of the south, a grape which produces well-balanced wines, ripened in volcanic soil under the Campanian and Basilicatan sun, which .retain a freshness and balance and structure to support long ageing. There is fruit in there, undoubtedly there is, but wine made from Aglianico is as notable for its minerality as anything else. Berry Brothers put me on to it. I was principally drawn by its promise of something new, of something different and noteworthy, and the reasonable price at which the wine was offered but, I have to admit, I was also attracted by the name of Carbone's top offering, Stupor Mundi, named after Frederick II, an idol of mine. And that brought connotations entirely unrelated to the wine, of the Normans of the South, the romance of their adventure, the breathtaking success and the speed at which they established their kingdom, the cosmopolitan nature of their rule, allowing access to all, be they Moslem, Byzantine or Christian, the climate of the area, the exoticism of their legacy, the simultaneous regard and contempt with which they held all others. I could go on. "So why, after all this," I hear you say "did you not buy the Stupor Mundi?"

This is a good question. Stupor Mundi is a big wine, by all accounts a very big wine. As well as bringing up images of Frederick II in his pomp, the name also brings up images of catatonic stupefaction caused by intemperate consumption. I have always told Gus second is the place to be – ahead of the pack but tucked in behind the leader – and I think the analogy holds good for wine as well. Less, as everyone knows, is as often as not more. I am not talking here about the "second wines" of Bordeaux – I will have a pop at them later – but I have often thought the second-placed wine of a producer, in his mind as much as anyone else's (like La Pieve above, maybe), benefits from all the care and attention of the winemaker but is untroubled by the pressing ambition of the grower to show off as best he possibly can. In this case 400 Some might suffer in comparison to Stupor Mundi if tasted next to each other but, if so, I bet not by much. How often have I seen critics score top wines a single measly point or two better than the producer's next wine but at considerably more than one or two price points' difference.

And the wine? We tried the wine the night we flew back from Italy this summer, the pervasive heat of Rome still warming our bones. I anticipated what would greet us even before I had pulled the cork. The stillness, the dust on the tracks and the dust in the fields, the tired chirrup of the quietening sparrows, the heat, the monotony of the cicadas, the false shadows of the cypresses, the stooped welcome of the umbrella pines. All was there. The wine was savoury with pruney depths not yet fully fathomed. A twist of bitter, a scent of the sun. Very dry, so very dry, and no hint of tawny, it has a while to go yet.

The name, by the way, refers to Charles of Anjou. He was so enamoured of the wines of Aglianico del Vulture he ordered 400 barrels (400 Some) a year for his own cellar. Charles of Anjou – a significant king and, like Frederick II, something of a headache for the Papacy - but not a patch on Stupor Mundi.

ALTO ADIGE

Voglar, Alto Adige, Peter Dipoli 2012

So if you are after an example of just how mixed up and confusing (and so how wonderfully rich and intriguing) the Italian wine scene is, how about a wine produced with a French grape in a predominantly German-speaking part of Italy that is trying to emulate one of France's great wines?

The Alto Adige is Italy's most northerly wine region, dropping down from the Austrian Tyrol. Steep Alpine vineyards, a cold climate, which produces beautifully fresh and well-crafted whites.

You have always expressed a dislike of Sauvignon Blanc but this is only of badly-made Sauvignon or high-octane examples from New Zealand. I have seen you pursue enough bottles of Sancerre and Pouilly-Fumé to know that your beef is not with the grape but rather the wine. So you might like this one. It is a wine that still requires two or three more years ageing as it creeps towards the Loire profile of flint, understated elderflower and blackcurrant leaves. Judged on the bottles consumed to date, I think it will get there.

GERMANY

It seems wholly wrong that, in the 49 years of our existence, we have only ever once visited the land of Charlemagne, the Reformation, Beethoven and Goethe, and even then only for one day, either of us! We were staying in Riquewihr, across the border in Alsace, and thought it would be fun for the kids to pick up a new country on their travels. So we crossed the border and spent a day in Freiburg. Emily was the only one among us with any smidgen of German so she ordered our coffees in one of the city's squares. Almost as an afterthought, we asked her to order glasses of water for us as well. Quite why the waitress then thought it fit to bring out five enormous bottles of mineral water I do not know. I suspect Emily's German less than I do the grumpy waitress who was keen to make a point, for whatever reason.

We walked around the town happy to take ourselves where whimsy directed. Many of the streets are lined with open drains (I see they are called bächles, little streams) and we frequently warned the kids not to trip into them. But given how Gus will inevitably, and wilfully, step into a puddle if one lies in his path, especially if we have warned him about it, it was only a matter of time before he took the plunge and planted his feet firmly into one. This means, according to legend, that just as inevitably he will marry a girl from Freiburg. I daresay she will have to be more impressive than Freiburg's football team. Gus followed the team for a short while (he has the woolly hat somewhere) until he realised quite how forlorn the life of a Freiburg supporter must be as the team continually battled to avoid relegation.

After lunch we took a ride on the Schauinsland cable car, Germany's longest (I read). From the top the Black Forest stretches away to the east. To the south, so they say, you can see the Eiger and other of the great peaks of the Alps. We had *half a mind, once we had finished at the top, to walk back down. When we bought our tickets we asked about this. The ticketmaster peered over the edge of his booth and down at our footwear, particularly Claudia's. "Your footwear is not appropriate" he said, bluntly. Whether this meant that we were not permitted to walk down I could not work out but it reminded me how funny they can be about rules in this part of the world.*

We drove back to Alsace through a lowering western sun. We passed through Kaiserstuhl, an area given over to wine production, the low hills containing precisely sculpted, gently terraced vineyards. These are given over to Pinot Noir, Spätburgunder in German. They carry a good reputation, if expensive.

It is inevitable, when you catch the wine bug, that you will voraciously read all you can on the subject. In the days before the internet, this largely comprised Decanter magazine, Wine magazine (now defunct), weekend columns in the papers and remaindered or second-hand tomes, some charmingly old-fashioned but written beautifully and no less relevant for the wisdom they sometimes impart. After all, wine has been with us for such a very long time, much of the pleasure we derive from the liquid now will be exactly the same as it was for our forebears 10,000 years ago.

And just as inevitably, if you have the wine bug, you will soon enough read of the almost universal esteem in which the Riesling grape is held by the world's critics and wine writers. And you may even have read Hugh Johnson's pithy hyperbole that, tasting Mosel, "all Chardonnay tastes gross after this".

So it is maybe not surprising that I came to Germany relatively early in my journey. My first experiences were a series of dry, or at least off-dry, Rieslings that the German producer Deinhard ran in the early 1990's, each one named after a famous wine village, so not vineyard-specific but certainly village-specific and designed to show the differences between them. They were an attempt (a delicious attempt) to introduce consumers to a drier style of Riesling and to move away from the Liebfraumilch stain which has done so much to destroy the German wine industry. The wines were sold as bin-ends in a corner store nearby, £2.99 each I recall against a retail price of £8.99, and were, ridiculous as it might sound, sublime. Each label carried a different colour – lime, violet, yellow I remember – and were simply labelled Hochheim, Johannisberg, Piesport, Nierstein and others I cannot remember. It might sound silly but the wines displayed an authority and a breeding which were startling. They made a strong statement of their origin and of their identity and they convinced me that all this needed further investigation.

This was subsequently reinforced at a wine fair we went to. Can you remember it, my love? I had far too much to drink, far too much. Towards the end of the afternoon we came to a German wine stall and were offered a taste of a Trockenbeerenauslese. Now much has been written about the idiosyncracy of the German wine laws and, even more so, their wine labelling. Until recently, when in an attempt to simplify things I think they have just complicated things further, I have found a certain Teutonic logic in their labelling and have never had any difficulty deciphering them. You start with two levels of wine – QBA and QMP. QBA is basic stuff and need not bother the wine enthusiast. QMP is where the quality is. I won't even try to elaborate on what QMP means (something to do with quality) because the acronym hides an alphabet's worth of letters, absurdly long words of course being a German pastime. So take Oberemmeler Hütte Riesling Kabinett as an example. On first sight this doesn't look too promising. But follow logic and you shall find. The village is Oberemmel, the vineyard within Oberemmel is Hütte, the grape is Riesling and the ripeness of the grape is Kabinett. And the grades of ripeness are easy to master – Kabinett is the driest (off-dry really) followed, in order of increasing ripeness, by Spätlese, Auslese, Beerenauslese, Trockenbeerenauslese and, finally, Eiswein (grapes picked in mid-winter when frozen).

So, back to the wine fair, yes I was offered a glass of Trockenbeerenauslese (wine produced from grapes shrivelled by botrytis, a friendly rot, to little more than raisins – so think utterly sweet, super-concentrated). What the grape was I do not know (I doubt Riesling because Riesling TBAs are truly sought-after and expensive) and, I am ashamed to say, I do not know what the region was either. As I said, it was the end of a long afternoon. But I will never forget the wine. It literally exploded in my mouth, layer after layer after layer of fireworks sending my senses to the ends of the earth. Simply put, even in my diminished state, it was extraordinary.

"My goodness" I must have said "this is phenomenal".

The girl behind the counter nodded her approbation. "Yes, it is grown on the steep slaty slopes of [this remains a mystery]".

"The steep slaty slopes, eh?" At least this is what I tried to say. But the day's efforts were now beginning to take their toll and, try as I might, the combination of these three words was more than my lingual co-ordination could muster.

The girl behind the counter looked at me, disappointed. In fact worse than disappointed. I fell in her estimation quicker than if I had been rolled down those very same steep slaty slopes. "There are a lot of drunk people here today" is all she could muster.

I left with my tail very firmly between my legs. But I also left with a fierce resolve to come to grips with those steep slaty slopes. There lay magic.

And so it was, not long afterwards, that I bought my first case of German wine. I remember clearly the flimsy, pale green offer from the Wine Society that fell through the letterbox. It extolled the virtues of the 1997 vintage in Germany (France did not have much to shout about that year) and I thought "why not?". Steep slaty slopes were my target and so this naturally drew me to the Mosel and its tributaries, the Ruwer (no more than a stream) and the Saar. 1997, if I recall the offer correctly, was a warm vintage and the Saar, traditionally the coolest of these three, had outperformed. Which led me, happily, to the wines of von Hövel and, yes, the Oberemmeler Hütte Riesling Kabinett. And I have bought this wine ever since. I will bore you about it below.

You will see that I have never strayed from the Mosel (it used to be known as the Mosel-Saar-Ruwer but, in order to simplify things, the three are now simply referred to collectively as the Mosel – here, though, I retain the distinction). The wine world is such a rich and many-varied place of treasures that I have never felt the need to explore Germany beyond the Mosel. It provides all the Riesling fix I need, all the fruit-bursting mineral-laden life-affirming sparkling rush of energy that I know it will deliver (and, a rare beast this, I have not been disappointed by a single glass of the wines I have had below or their previous incarnations). I am now joining Hugh Johnson in his hyperbole. For me, granted not for everyone (not least you, my love!), it really is that thrill-givingly lovely. The world is undoubtedly a better place for it.

Yet everyone's taste is different. The traditional style of the

Mosel, and to a lesser extent, the Rheingau and the Pfalz, wines with residual sweetness, now finds less favour on the modern palate and so more and more Riesling in Germany (and pretty much exclusively elsewhere in the world) is vinified much drier. In Germany they have learnt to tame the rapier acidity that dry vinification can bring (aided by a long run of warmer summers), in Alsace, the wines have traditionally been vinified dry anyway and in Australia the turning of the sugar into alcohol gives full rein to the full-throttle kerosene nose that hits you firmly between the eyes. To each their own. For me, I am not sure that white wine reaches any greater apogee than along the banks of the Mosel. As Farmer Hoggett said to his sheep-pig in marvellous understatement, "that will do, pig, that will do."

MOSEL

Brauneberger Juffer Sonnenuhr Riesling Spätlese, Fritz Haag 2001
Brauneberger Juffer Sonnenuhr Riesling Spätlese, Fritz Haag 2006

So the village is Brauneberg and the vineyard is Juffer. In fact the vineyard is better than that, it is that part of Juffer surrounding the Sonnenuhr, the sundial. As logic dictates, that part of the vineyard with the sundial is the part of the vineyard with the most sunshine, important in this cold and northern clime where every last opportunity must be taken if the grapes are to ripen. So the Sonnenuhr will produce the ripest grapes. Nothing but logic in this part of the world.

I have not tried the 2001. Cellartracker.com tells me that it is still full of youthful vigour, becoming of a great vintage and

2001's reputation maybe. Cellartracker is one of the great developments for wine lovers in the last 10 years or so. It is an enormous collective cellar book in which anyone who wants to can record their impressions of wines they have tasted. Clearly not everyone is going to be a Robert Parker, Jancis Robinson or Hugh Johnson but, using your own judgement and reading all the reviews (which do often even themselves out into something approaching a sensible middle-ground tasting note), it is a remarkably effective tool for assessing the maturity of wines you are interested in opening. Use it.

I have tried the 2006. It was a warm year and so the wines are rich. This Spätlese, although sweeter than some, still treads the perfect tightrope of sweetness, acidity and minerality. It is a gem. A ball of complexity, threading a yarn and spinning a tale as it gently unravels. It has body but ballerina feet. Gentle scents of petrol come through on the nose. And did I mention the alcohol? 7.5%. Last week we came late from a stressful afternoon at the hospital. "Cup of tea?" you asked. No. I sat in the garden with a glass of this. The joy of Mosel is that it is perfect for the witching hours, just before noon, just around 5, just when something sometimes needs a little fix. There is a God and there is redemption, even if it must sometimes take the form of a glass of chilled Mosel. Balm for a troubled soul, nectar for a damaged palate.

Wehlener Sonnenuhr Riesling Spätlese, JJ Prum 2001
Wehlener Sonnenuhr Riesling Kabinett, JJ Prum 2015

Pull down a copy of Hugh Johnson's and Jancis Robinson's World Atlas of Wine and look at the (extraordinarily good) maps of the Middle Mosel. The vineyard areas are coloured mauve, the "first class" vineyards purple and the "great first class" vineyards a deeper purple. I think these are classifications of the authors, not official, but it is easy to see what makes the great first class vineyards great. The river turns this way and that and it is where the steep slopes face due south that they catch the full force of the sun and produce grapes worthy of the vineyards' reputations.

Wehlener Sonnenuhr – a great first class vineyard, indeed one of the most famous vineyards in Germany. And another sundial, of course. What the Atlas does not show, however, is the sheer awe-inspiring spectacle that this wall of vines, which has Wehlener Sonnenuhr at its heart, presents. Five miles in length, 700 feet high, vast, precipitous, a straight line following the Mosel in a north-westerly direction, this is one of the most dramatic sights the wine world has to offer.

And were there to be a classification of the country's winegrowers then Joh Jos Prum would undoubtedly be coloured deep purple too. Which makes the pricing of German wines almost as extraordinary as the wines themselves. This case, one of the best vineyards in the hands of one of the best growers in one of the best years of recent times, cost no more than £150. £150! In the 19th Century, and for much of the 20th, Germany's wines were valued more highly than those of Burgundy and Bordeaux. I have in front of me the Wine Society's list from Winter 1967, the time of my birth (and the time of yours, my love). Bonnes Mares 1959 (Bonnes Mares! One of Burgundy's top Grand Cru vineyards that you will struggle to find for less than £150 a bottle in today's market) is priced at 19 shillings and 9 pence a bottle. Conversely, a bottle of Ayler Herrenberger Riesling Spätlese 1964 from the Saar would have set you back 25 shillings and 9 pence. Ayler Herrenberg – not even coloured deep purple in the Wine Atlas…

And now look. A travesty. Why this should be the case I am

not sure. Fashion of course. And the general dumbing down of German wine (see below) undoubtedly has a part to play, as does the current aversion to sweet wine or what is perceived to be sweet wine. Mosel is sweet in the same way as a Cox's Orange Pippin is sweet; in other words, it has the acidity to balance out the sweetness and to produce a flavour profile that is not so obviously sweet (if that makes sense). And the irony is that, not as common perception would have it, these wines go very well with food, not least the fusion foods of the world that are now so popular.

That said, my love, I see this wine is now trading at £700 a case. It breaks my heart but this style of wine is not to your taste. Sell it. There is no rush. Tasting notes on cellartracker suggest the wine is still an infant and, the longer you leave it, the less there will be, the better the price (maybe). But, in the end, sell it if you want to and don't feel guilty doing so.

And the 2015? Seriously, in my state and condition, investing in that? Seriously, yes. So that, if the 2001 does go the way of the hammer, you are not denied the beauty of the place. And so that in time, late on a midsummer morning, with peace in the garden and silence in your heart, you might sit quietly, stare through the green-glinted gold of the wine in the glass and experience one of the greatest expressions of Riesling in the history of the world. Seriously, yes, and quite literally.

Piesporter Goldtröpfchen Riesling Spätlese, Reinhold Haart 2001

Another great first class vineyard, from the same glorious year as the Brauneberger and Wehlener. I once had ambitions that I would try the three side by side and pick apart the differences between the sites (Riesling, like all the noble grapes, is partly judged noble on account of its ability to pick up the identity of the site on which it is grown). Unlike the other two, however, I have tried this wine, indeed almost all of the case. It started out sparkling, unctuous maybe (as "the golden drop" name of the vineyard would suggest) but filled with fireworks. With age it has settled down. It now offers a mature statement, reflective even, of its origins and, yes, as is often noted, has lost some of its sweetness and lain back into a gentler mellowness. Quite quite wonderful.

Piesporter Michelsberg must not be confused with this Piesporter or other of the individual named vineyards of Piesport. Piesporter Michelsberg is an abomination, a blend of less than noble grapes from less than noble sites (the flat lands on the other side of the river), that looks to play on the reputation of the great wines of Piesport. Piesporter Michelsberg, Hock (running on the coat-tails of Hochheim, one of the great villages of the Rheingau), Niersteiner, Liebfraumilch – these wines have unfairly destroyed the reputation of one of the greatest wines of the world. I hope one day people properly recognise what these wines have to offer.

Graacher Himmelreich Riesling Kabinett, JJ Prum 2011

Back to Joh Jos Prum and back to the wall of vines with Wehlener Sonnenuhr at its centre. Graach the village, Himmelreich the vineyard. "Himmelreich" – the Kingdom of Heaven. It gives some idea of the height of this vineyard, indeed the height and majesty of this whole wall of vines.

The wine is too young. Indeed, I think it is a mistake to drink any of these wines too young. Drink them in the first flush of youth, the first year or two maybe, but otherwise leave well alone, for at least five or six years, longer for those above

Kabinett. Until then the wines have not meshed, they have not developed the panoply of flavours that this particular style of Riesling offers. I read somewhere that young (too young) Mosel is "sweet and sour" and that description works. The nose might be sweet and beguiling but the palate is sour and the acid of the young wine still dominant. It is almost as if they are two different wines.

So when the time comes (these wines last forever, there is no rush) you will find this case of 11 bottles at the back of the cellar, behind the Christmas decorations, behind the old LPs, behind the years of children's clutter that has washed up in the dust and the dark.

RUWER

Maximin Grunhauser Abtsberg Riesling Spätlese, von Schubert 2004
Maximin Grunhauser Abtsberg Riesling Spätlese, von Schubert 2007
Maximin Grunhauser Abtsberg Riesling Spätlese, von Schubert 2012

When I was starting out on this great adventure, I discovered a wine shop behind Goodge Street, off the Tottenham Court Road, that was a proper bin-end shop, selling the most wonderful wines at some quite ridiculous prices. The shop owner was fairly open about it. "Oh, I will take wine from anywhere – liquidations, shop closures, even off the back of a lorry." This way I was introduced to the wines of Maximin Grunhauser, one of the twin pillars of the Ruwer. There was clearly something fishy with the wines I tried because, in one or two instances, the vintage on the cork was different to the vintage on the label but who was I to care? Stolen or not, fiddled or not, the wines were sublime. I have followed them ever since.

I must also admit that, apart from being beguiled by the flavours, I am also tickled by the nomenclature of the vineyards of this estate which used to belong to a monastery. There are three vineyards, the Herrenberg, the Bruderberg and the Abtsberg. The Herrenberg wines were destined for the gentry, the Bruderberg for the brothers and the very best wines, from the Abtsberg, were the preserve of the abbot. Wholly unacceptable nowadays, of course but there is something shamelessly honest about the grading which makes me smile.

As to the wines themselves, well the 2004 is quite simply one of the best wines in the cellar. 2004 was a good vintage but not one people raved about. On the cool side. But cool brings acidity and this wine absolutely crackles, it is a living force that will not cease to sparkle, it is blistering. I have not tried the 2007 or the 2012. The future is theirs, ticking timebombs waiting to burst into flame.

SAAR

Great wine is grown on the margins. The Romans knew this. Plant vines where nothing else grows. If vines have it too easy, the grapes are no good. The vine will overproduce, the grapes will be dilute. Make the vine struggle. Make it dig deep to pick up nutrients from far within the earth, only allow the vine to produce a few bunches of grapes, grapes which will have all the effort and flavour of the vine's labours concentrated within them. The soil must be poor, the climate marginal. When Baron Pierre Le Roy de Boiseaudemarié (a magnificent name and no doubt a magnificent man) agreed to help delimit the extent of Châteauneuf-du-Pape (creating, in the process, the first controlled appellation area) he insisted that only land suitable for growing lavender and thyme (both of which thrive on arid, infertile soils) should be marked as land suitable for growing grapes destined for Châteauneuf-du-Pape. Make life as difficult as possible.

Which brings us to the Saar. The Saar actually lies to the south of the Mosel and so should be warmer. But it is not. In a region where grapes struggle to ripen at the best of times (hence the suntraps on the Mosel that contain the best vineyards) the Saar is dealt an even more challenging hand. A look at the map shows how few the great sites are in the Saar. In a cold year, the acidity is too much without the sugar to balance it and the pickings from the Saar are lean indeed. In the great years, however, when maybe it is too warm in the Mosel and the grapes there lose the thrilling acidity in the heat of the year, the Saar flourishes like a desert bloom. The wines have a knife-edge thrill, teetering the right side of extraordinary, the fruit and acidity taken to levels not really seen elsewhere in the wine world. And all with alcohol levels lower than some of the stronger beers.

Saarburger Rausch Riesling Spätlese, von Zilliken 2007

2007 was not the warm vintage of 1997 (or 2009 below). It has a reputation instead of being a typical racy Mosel vintage with plenty of acidity to lift the wines out of the ordinary and transform them into the bracing refreshing wines so loved by followers of this region. Which makes me wonder why I bought this case. Undoubtedly it will have been because early reviews suggested Zilliken had produced a fine range of wines that year. It is an odd feature (well, maybe not that odd, we are all human) that winegrowers will have good years and less good years. Obviously the better the grower, the fewer and less noticeable these discrepancies. I have sometimes been puzzled why the perfect mix of good winegrower and good vintage has produced a less enjoyable wine than the same wine from the same winegrower from a less propitious vintage. Puzzling, maybe, but part of the unpredictable beauty of wine.

Oberemmeler Hütte Riesling Kabinett, von Hövel 2009
Oberemmeler Hütte Riesling Kabinett, von Hövel 2011
Oberemmeler Hütte Riesling Kabinett, von Hövel 2013

Last, but certainly not least. In fact, the wine closest to my heart, the wine that introduced me to the glorious pleasures of Riesling from the Mosel. It is quite possible that, were I to compare this wine to the Spätleses that have come before, yes the wine would be shorter and perhaps without quite the depth of the others. But comparisons like this are invidious and strip all the wines of their identity and their qualities. Suffice to say that I have never had a bottle of this wine from 2009 or any of the previous vintages that I have had (I have not tried the 2011 or 2013 which rest quietly in the cellar) which have been other than glorious, life-affirming, smile-producing, revelatory. A shiver of acidity balances the generous fruit. There is a freshness in them that puts Helmut Dönhoff, master of the Nahe, in mind of a mountain stream or, better put, rock water.

SPAIN

It should have been so much more fun that it was. The office cricket team, perhaps a little fey and certainly Corinthian (well, in spirit if not in ability which, come to think of it, is probably a pre-requisite of being properly Corinthian), bunking off at lunchtime one weekday to head down to Windsor and take on the Royal Household Cricket Club. A gentle 20 overs here, 20 overs there in beautiful surroundings, all very relaxed and civilised.

Except it wasn't quite like that. On account of securing lottery funding (or so the old man told me after the event) the Royal Household CC had been forced to open its membership to the public and, well, it had attracted (and why wouldn't it?) very talented and competitive members of the local community, many, come to think of it, Antipodean.

To say we were mugged would suggest that we would normally have had an opportunity or the ability to defend ourselves but the fact of the matter was that the gulf in quality rendered a competitive fixture impossible. So we were put to the slaughter. What irked, though, was the nature of the slaughter, the call for blood and the determination of our opponents to hammer home every last opportunity to humiliate us and, in the process, to boost their own personal figures. Contested appeals which did not go their way were met with aggressive incredulity, wickets (our wickets) with needless posturing of their superiority. Not what us softies were used to or expecting.

But there were two saving graces (three if you include the anger and frustration that one of their batsmen petulantly displayed when giving his wicket away cheaply late in proceedings which, poor petal, meant his average for the season fell just short of some magical figure – a small but enjoyable victory): the Royal loo and the wine.

The clubhouse was an Edwardian structure with wonderful oak panelling and looked as if it had hardly been touched in the intervening 100 years, with no finer part than the loo with its own oak panelling and fashioned oak seat (and was there even vitrified tiling?): glorious! And, as was pointed out to me, the loo will undoubtedly have been graced by the seat of more than one monarch as and when obliged to attend staff cricket matches down the years. Truly a memorable structure which I very much hope is listed.

And the wine. In our pursuit of knowledge about wine, and desire to taste ever more highly thought-of bottles, we risk losing the pleasure of well-made everyday wines that can remind us just what a hugely enjoyable thing wine is and how there is blessing and grace in the humblest bottles.

I forget the detail of my innings but it is quite possible that I was out first ball. In any event, I found myself helping an old-timer set out the cricket tea. Wickets were falling with such charming regularity that the host had to get his skates on and so it was that I found my help enlisted.

"Here, try this." He handed me a glass of wine.

Maybe, battered as I was after the afternoon's drubbing, the thinnest, most acidic glass of wine would have hit the spot but even now I can recall the richness, balance, softness, generosity and warmth in the glass of red wine that I was given.

"That is lovely."

"Ain't it just."

"Where's it from?"

"Cariñena."

"Oh yes" I replied, nodding vigorously. I had never heard of it. The old-timer looked at me askance. "Oh yes? You know of it?"

"Oh no" I thought. He was reading me like a book. I let my silence admit my ignorance.

The old man answered his own question. "I had to look it up myself. Somewhere south of Valladolid. But I'm pleased with it. Very popular at the club. Tried it out of a dozen or so and it was a clear winner. Cheap too."

Neither of us cared about the cricket at that moment. He was clearly proud of the wine and I was equally pleased, for I had safely arrived into the bosom of a caring matriarch to protect me from the day's ravages at the crease.

For me, this is a recurring theme of Spanish red wine, the warmth, generosity and softness of the tannins that together create such a welcome. It is rare to come across a Spanish red that is challenging, that presents a wall of tannin or a mouthful of youthful acid. The wines are mellow and, dare I say it, easy. Is this why I have never properly explored the wines of Spain? Because they are too "easy" and unchallenging? If so, then this is grossly unfair to the quality of the wine that is on offer and greatly to my loss and detriment. The wines of Spain are absurdly undervalued and, late as I may have tried to rectify my mistake, I have been wrong to ignore them for as long as I have. I feel sure that Spain is a country on the move, filled with a dynamism and ambition that it would not pay to neglect. And this applies as much to the country's cheap wines as to their high-end ones. We might laugh about the preponderant reliance we placed, in younger days, on the likes of Don Darias and Don Hugo (I am not sure where they came from – Valdepeñas?) but they fulfil their purpose beautifully, with great pleasure and, without wanting to become too sentimental, in many cases with great honesty. Just like that Cariñena. Pleasures come in all sizes.

<u>RIOJA</u>

That holiday. That holiday! We will not forget it in a hurry. Dad's 70th birthday and the kindness he showed in transporting us all (by ferry, except for lucky you and Claire who pleaded little ones and took the bairns by plane) to the Basque country for a fortnight. We all stayed together, all 17 of us, in a house high up a wooded hillside. It should have been a sylvian paradise except that the dirt track, by which the house stood, was the main thoroughfare for the local timberlogging industry. Peace was hard to come by.

The Basque country (I am told) is called El Urinale by other parts of Spain on account of the constant rainfall. It did not rain constantly but it was certainly not absent. It is a landscape of tight wooded valleys with few expansive views, a steady stream of traffic jams and plenty of light industrial ribbon development.

We felt hemmed in. Until one day it was touted that we should break out and head to Rioja for the day. Why we chose not to go I cannot recall. Maybe Claudia was just too little, maybe, all of us living on top of each other, we thought a break from the collected family's company might be beneficial to all. As the party left, I remember thinking how I wished we were going. How I wished we had gone!

Hugh, always partial to a glass of Rioja, came back in the evening filled with fervour at his sight of the promised land. He recounted how they had driven over a pass and laid out before them was all of Spain, or the beginning of Spain, plains of wheat and expansive horizons, probably a castle or two, space. And, at lunch (a lunch at which Dad lost it until put in his place by a waitress who had the measure of his temper), wine, gentle mouth-filling red wine, sun-soaked.

We have never been to Rioja but, since that holiday, I have always associated Rioja with escape, with wide horizons, the plains of Spain spread out like a welcoming carpet. Hugh's image has haunted me. Yes, like Don Quixote and Sancho Panza, we might have looked out ourselves across the rumpled tableau of Spain, the sun over our shoulders, our shadows falling before us and beckoning us on. Nonsense, I admit, but every wine paints a picture, whether you have been there or not.

Rioja Gran Reserva 904, La Rioja Alta 2001
Rioja Gran Reserva 904, La Rioja Alta 2005

Rioja. Such a simple word. Like Chablis, perhaps, a victim of its pronounceability. Familiar to the point of its own detriment. Unjust.

These two examples are, supposedly, some of the finest Riojas on the market and, given their reputation, remarkably reasonably priced. Another disconnect with the wine world which is a happy hunting ground for those who choose to look. They are old-school Rioja, that is to say released when well on their way to tertiary aromas and flavours (think a touch of sourness, a lightness, leather but with a strong undertow of gentle red fruits). And the wine will be the work of different vineyards. Whereas the rest of the wine world pays ever-increasing attention to terroir (the concept of place, of the uniqueness of flavour that is created by the soil and microclimate of a particular vineyard that must be captured and bottled separately – I prattle on about this later) the Riojanos have been happy to continue to produce wine the way they have since the middle of the 19th century when the area came to the fore on the back of the phylloxera epidemic which wiped out so many of France's vineyards. That is to say by blending and by long ageing in large barrels. The grades of wine are easy – Joven (or plain Rioja) for new wine, Crianza for wines aged for one year in barrel and one in bottle, Reserva for one year in barrel and two in bottle, Gran Reserva for two years in barrel and three in bottle. Strictly speaking, only the better wines, those able to withstand barrel-ageing, should be allocated to Crianza, Reserva and Gran Reserva but (Spanish practices!) that is only strictly speaking and the world is not like that. So Gran Reserva is not a guarantee of quality, unless of course you are dealing only with a reputable bodega.

Things are now beginning to change. Growers are focussing more on individual vineyards, fermenting the grapes differently (to create fresher, more concentrated wines), ageing the wine less and bottling much sooner. This creates a very different profile, for better or worse depending on your taste. But these Gran Reservas will be good wines of the old style. Raise a toast to El Urinale and all our memories there.

I have not tried the 2005 but the 2001 is reassuringly its own thing. Dry, light to medium-bodied, resolved tannins, Flavours unravel the length of the long finish. High-toned and developed, the gentle balance brings the taster inexorably on and delivers you safely at the far end. Remarkable wine that will last a very long while yet.

RIBERA DEL DUERO

Alion, Bodegas y Vinedos, Ribera del Duero 2004

There is but one bottle of this, kindly given to me by a trainee on qualification at work at a time when I was the partner in charge of the trainees during their two-year training contract. It is a smart bottle made by the same team as Vega Sicilia, Spain's most famous wine. It will be rich and hit you between the eyes and probably worthy of a decant. It will be wonderful.

More than anything, however, this bottle reminds me of an important lesson I wish I had learned sooner. We were at a drinks party hosted by some inordinately wealthy parents from Emily's school. It was a champagne reception. I had come on there from the pub after work. Whether it was on the back of pints of bitter, or whether the champagne really was mediocre, I cannot say but the fizz tasted mean.

I approached the host.

"Sorry, would it be possible to have a glass of wine instead of champagne?"

"Of course. Would you prefer red or white?"

A generous glass of red duly appeared. I took one sniff and the wine stopped my heart.

"Goodness gracious me," I thought "what on earth is this?"

My host had moved on by this stage so I resolved to find out only once my glass was empty. The wine was complete, though, a strong statement of intent and purpose at the beginning, in the middle and at the end. A big wine but well-balanced and full, so it seemed, of the universe.

Like Oliver, I meekly approached the host with my empty glass.

"Hi, I wonder if I could have another glass."

"Of course."

This time he came back with the bottle. The wine was a Ribera del Duero and was none other than Vega Sicilia's second wine, Valbuena.   Ribera del Duero is a richer expression of Tempranillo than Rioja (it's the same grape), more modern and glossy perhaps but in the right hands truly inspiring. Valbuena – maybe £80 a bottle and certainly in a different league to the champagne on offer that night. May the Alion be likewise.

So that is the lesson. If somewhere (for want of a better word) "posh", and the champagne isn't up to much, then ask discreetly for a glass of white or red, especially if it is not on offer. Chances are you will be trading up and, quite possibly, spectacularly. It has worked elsewhere for me too – at Hoares Bank (I do hope I am not giving away trade secrets here) I have upgraded from Laytons champagne to Pape Clement once, La Conseillante another time. That's not too bad.

Keep it in mind. It might work.

JEREZ

La Ina Muy Especial Fino

We sat with our backs to the restaurant, overlooking the Guadalquivir estuary, our feet almost on the beach. It was just the two of us, down at Sanlucar de Barrameda for the day from our parador in Carmona. Even though it was only springtime, the sun was hot and bright. We ordered a bottle of Manzanilla and it tasted of the sea. Ozone and salt and a strong lick of yeast. The menu was simple: fish. I ordered prawns, you ordered sardines. I ate bread (always too much bread) waiting for the marisco to arrive and we sat in semi-silence, watching the walkers along the beach, the odd brightly-coloured boat and, on the other side of the river, the birds over the Coto Doñana. The fusion of the sea, the prawns, the sherry and you, my love, took me to the heart of silence and the single finest meal I have ever eaten. Nothing has ever matched that simplicity and that beauty. After lunch we walked down the shore a while. We toyed with the idea of getting a boat across the river to the reserve but the sun, the heat, the sherry, they all advocated a gentle afternoon on this side of the river. We sat on the sand and shielded our eyes against the sun.

And I could just as easily add the second finest meal I have ever had, on a later visit to Andalucia but again involving a bottle of Manzanilla, Dover sole and just you, this time in a ramshackle restaurant on a station platform.

You might gauge from this that the common theme, the secret, to a memorable lunch is a bottle of Manzanilla. You cannot be blamed for thinking so. Sherry is one of the great wines of the world and one of the most underappreciated. It might sound an odd thing to say but if you are a sherry drinker, you know about it. You know about the panoply of flavours on offer in its various guises (Manzanilla, Fino, Amontillado, Palo Cortado, Oloroso et al), the appetite-inducing nature of the wine (salty as it is), the versatility of the wine (different wines for different moods), its food friendliness, its general tonic qualities for a long and healthy life. Those who drink it cannot do without it.

But the true secret is not the Manzanilla, it is the company in which the wine is drunk (and the meal shared). If I have learnt one thing from a life of loving and collecting wine, it is this: the pleasure of the wine is in direct proportion to the affability of the company in which it is drunk. I read an article, a number of years ago, in Decanter magazine in which an Indian brain surgeon was interviewed about his life in wine. He divided the pleasure that a bottle of wine can bring into the following proportions: one third the history of the wine (in other words, the connotations, the expectations, the memories that the particular bottle carries), one third the company in which it is drunk and one third the innate quality of the wine. I would go further than this: maybe one quarter the history, one quarter only the quality and one half the company. How often have I drunk some of the great wines of the world which for me present little more than an academic exercise because I am not sharing the bottle with soulmates? How often have I drunk execrable bottles of plonk that I swear could give Romanée-Conti a run for its money because I have been sharing them with those I love and with whom I laugh? And company can just mean yourself. One of life's great pleasures (as an exception rather than the rule and never when it is a chore) is cooking supper for yourself with only a bottle to keep you company. A third of the bottle while cooking, a third of the bottle with supper and then the rest between the cork and your conscience. Never lose sight of this. The enjoyment of wine is universal; it is not restricted to better bottles.

And this wine? It is a fino, so not as dry or salty as Manzanilla maybe, but nevertheless it is a dry wine that works incomparably well as an aperitif or with seafood. That said, La Ina is renowned as being one of the most yeasty of the finos so don't expect a shrinking violet. Drink it fresh; bottle age does nothing for it.

PORTUGAL

I must have been nine. I am walking down the stairs of the cellar in Lisbon, my father in front of me laden with bottles of cheap red that cost little more than one or two escudos. This was the late 70's. Unless you were a rock star, or conceivably a member of OPEC, times were hard. We had just arrived in Lisbon for a two-year posting and my father was ecstatic that wine could be purchased so cheaply. He would stock up in the local supermarket and cart his hoard downstairs to lie in the darkened cellar. The wine was called Mesa d'Ouro, or some such, and had a plastic peel-off cap instead of a cork. I never tried the wine but my parents became committed followers.

My first true experience of Portuguese wine came at the hands of the bin-end shop behind Goodge Street. In the early 90's, it used to sell garrafeira bottlings by José Maria da Fonseca, bottles which had plenty of age and which carried cryptic codes as to their origin (TE was a favourite: apparently a bottling from Quinta da Camarate). Garrafeiras are reserve bottlings, highly thought-of, containing some of the best wine an estate has to offer. And the wines were heavenly. Age had wearied them to a sublime level of ease and harmony and age had brought all the unique flavours that Portugal's indigenous grapes can bring to the fore. The fruit teetered on savoury and the wines leaned to tawny. I have long looked to find wines like them again but, once the bin-end shop had been closed (who knows, maybe by the police), I have never found them.

Portugal is enjoying a renaissance now, especially for its table wines. I have tried a few of them. Portugal's trump card is the array of grape varieties peculiar to the country and, by extension, the flavours of these wines. I particularly like the sound of the grape variety called dog strangler though cannot promise I would recognise it in a blind tasting. But I have to profess a concern that, in this renaissance, the country risks losing the uniqueness of its offering. Modern winemaking has a lot to commend it – a focus on riper grapes, hygiene in the cellar, temperature-controlled fermentation – but it can lead to a certain standardisation of flavour and texture. The taste of Red Burgundy has changed over the years, undoubtedly for the better because of better techniques, but gone is an element of idiosyncracy, gone is the strong taste of the farmyard that used to accompany so many memorable bottles. If this is the price to be paid then it is a price worth paying but it cannot prevent me wistfully longing for a little more identity in some of the wines I drink.

Is Portugal going the same way? Maybe, maybe not. Others, with greater experience than me, will be better placed to opine. But show me another of those garrafeiras, with their leather, umami and mellow uniqueness and, for me at least, I will be looking at the true identity of Portuguese wine.

If I had my time again, I would investigate the wines of Mouchão in the Alentejo. I think this may be where the secret is still held.

<u>ALENTEJO</u>

Mouchão, Herdade do Mouchão, Alentejo DOC 2010

But wait. I have. This very moment. Not half an hour ago, an e-mail arrived from the Wine Society extolling the virtues of Portuguese reds, citing the very same tasting in Decanter magazine on Alentejano reds that I had read and extracting, from all the wines and all the tasting notes, the very same wine and reasons for the wine that I would have picked had I had free run: Mouchão. So it took less than 30 minutes, 30 minutes of unforeseen guilty pleasure at the unanticipated prospect (how wine lovers adore these moments), to persuade myself, as if I needed persuading, that this was a sign and that my life really would be richer if I bought six bottles. Six bottles to peruse over time as its hefty statement and solid tannins fade from midday heat into late afternoon warmth, its blood red into tawny, its fruit into earth. Give the wine time, allow this to happen.

Time has almost forgotten the Alentejo, caught midway between Lisbon and the Algarve, between the Atlantic and Spain, a land of sparsely scattered settlements, lonely winds, cork forests, spring irises, open plains and roads to other places. The wine will remind me (and can inform you) of the old country and the new world my nine-year old frame discovered and fell in love with all those years ago, the open expanses of billowing wheat, the white-washed villages, the cerulean skies, the linger of time, the perspective of loss, the echo of fate.

Saudade, the Portuguese call it. A sadness and desire for what has gone, inextricably tied to a love and happiness for what it brought. Maybe, in time, this wine will speak of saudade.

DOURO

Altano Reserva, Quinta do Ataide, Douro 2011

The previous incarnation that we had of this wine, the 2008, was lovely. Dark, a hint of tobacco, more than a hint of coconut. It was polished and modern. 2011 (a supposedly "great" year) should promise at least that. But I am interested to see what it might develop into and so have planned to leave it a good while to see what the wine has to say for itself. You might do likewise and, together or otherwise, we'll play brinkmanship with drinking dates which as often as not are conservative. After all, name me a wine merchant who would recommend drinking dates that might fall after a wine has started its decline? Not one. The Wine Society, for one, gives absurdly early drinking dates for its Red Burgundies – I will not normally broach a case until after the end date recommended by them. OK, maybe an element of hyperbole there but wine does last longer than many give it credit for, especially if well kept, and it is often only at the secondary or tertiary stage that a wine starts to reveal its true character. So be patient with this one and see where it takes you.

PORT

Dow Vintage Port 1985
Quinta de la Rosa, Vintage Port 1994
Tesco Vintage Port 1994

We have visited the Douro twice, both times staying with Miri and her family, once at Miri's house on the left bank of the river, once at Quinta da Malvedos on the right bank. Being guests of the Symington family is, as some would say, "the way to go".

The first time we visited you were pregnant with Claudia and Gus was only two. It is difficult to believe he was that little. We found a video of Jurassic Park in Miri's house and this was how he would relax at the end of each day. The T-Rex didn't bother him so much as the velociraptors but over time familiarity with the film took the fear away.

We flew into Porto and then took the train upriver,

disembarking at Pinhão, to be picked up and taken cross-river to Quinta da Vila Velha (the home of Miri's parents). Distances are small but journey times are long. We worried all the way whether Emily's car-sickness would hold (I am not sure it did). But is there any more beautiful spot in the wine world than the Upper Douro valley? Terraced vineyards ripple down to the river which twists this way and that, new vistas and horizons constantly opening up. Miri's house sits high on a promontory, the river far below, the wakes left by boats visible in the water long after they have disappeared around the bend. Vines fall away all about and Montagu's Harriers quarter over the vineyards. We ate pork and beans most nights and drank absurd amounts of port (except poor you - that must have been tedious).

And one day we got a boat across the river to Malvedos for a lunch party. It was a large group. As we were leaving Gus stumbled and, to steady himself, he put his hand against the wood-burning stove. He was brave! On the way back across the river, he sat on your knee, gently keening at the pain his blistered hand was causing. And when we got back to Miri's house he sat on your knee again, this time in front of the television, distracted now by the velociraptors and the T-Rex.

We revisited again in 2009, this time the full complement of five. We drove up to the Douro from the Algarve where we had had a week of quite surprising sun given it was only April. This time we stayed at Malvedos to begin with before crossing the river to Miri's house. Spring was more advanced than on the last visit. The bee-eaters had arrived and a higher sun imparted a degree more warmth. We continued the habit of drinking absurd amounts of port (including you this time) almost to the exclusion of anything else. Occasionally we would start with a white port spritzer but there was little space for table wine. It was a very easy habit to slip into and, on our *return to England, I found myself, certainly for a week or so, wistfully dreaming of a glass of chilled port come midday.*

One day we drove to a castle way to the east (Emily was most certainly sick on that journey). It felt like the end of the earth and it felt like the roof of the world. Turning full circle, I could see no sign of man, no sign of the 21st century, no sign of any human involvement since the 13th century battlements on which I stood. Distant hills circled us – we could be in Spain for all I knew. I lined up the children for a typical family shot and took endless pictures of them. For all my efforts, I am not sure a single one of those pictures really captured the looks I wanted though, looking at them now, if they are not picture-frame perfect they are at least an honest reflection of who those little people were that year.

Why do we no longer drink port? The health police I suppose (heavy-handed and misguided), the drink-driving rules (essential and a necessary evil), fashion? Maybe. Port has become as unfashionable as all the other post-prandial drinks, maybe with the exception of whisky (serving equally as well as a pre-prandial has probably saved it). I have always loved port, that mix of weight, sweetness, complexity, warmth, maturity, length – a long kiss goodnight.

Dow: these last two bottles were Dad's. Now 32 (32!) years old, there is no rush to drink them but they should be à point.

There is a great deal of ceremony around the serving of port, most of which should probably be ignored. First, you need to get the cork out. The corks on bottles of vintage port are invariably tricky to extract, sometimes crumbling when you no more than look at them, so take care when you pull it. Use a good corkscrew with a long thread and pull it out straight. If it crumbles and creates a mess, don't worry too much, the contents will still be delicious.

Next, decanting. Decanting vintage port is difficult, not only because there is normally a considerable amount of fine sediment but also because the bottles themselves are unusually dark. Standard procedure is to shine a light underneath the neck of a bottle so that, as you decant, you can see when the sediment reaches the neck of the bottle, at which point of course you stop pouring. Except that with the near-black necks of bottles of port, well, it just requires a little more guess work, that's all.

Dad used to enjoy the ceremony of decanting as, I suppose, do I. Quite apart from the perennial excitement of pulling the cork on a worthy bottle and the anticipation of what the wine will offer, it prolongs the pleasure the bottle gives as decanting may be done a good while ahead of the wine's consumption (allowing you an early taste of the wine, often at an inappropriate time of the day, well at least inappropriate in the eyes of others). That said, and I am with Miri's father, James Symington, on this one, don't take decanting too seriously. Decant the wine but do not worry if sediment gets into the decanter or glass. Don't let its presence deny you (or more importantly delay you) the pleasure of the glass's contents. Life is short: keep moving.

And then of course comes the question of always passing the port to your left. "Do you know the Bishop of Norwich?" is the question politely asked of a neighbour who has allowed the decanter's passage round the table to stall with him. To the left, to the left? I will comply if it is important to the host, unless I am bored in which case I will not. If it is not important to the host, or if I am the host, I will let the bottle go where it will.

Quinta de la Rosa: a single bottle given to me by our

ambassador in Brasilia, a school friendship rekindled after 30 years' interval. Too long, a shame. The act of giving. Wine collectors, or even enthusiasts, become very generous at giving bottles to others of a like mind. It is not a question of having so much wine in the cellar that there are not enough days under the sun to drink the contents dry. It is rather the pleasure that one enthusiast knows another enthusiast will experience that drives the gift. And, as we have all been taught, the pleasure lies as much in the giving as in the receiving. It is true. I honestly believe that my father, in his (too young) dotage, having scrimped and saved for the cases he laid down for his retirement (a public service salary only goes so far), derived as much pleasure from handing these cases on to his children as he would have had he kept them and drunk them himself. In any event, this wine is from the 1994 vintage. It still has years ahead of it.

Tesco: the supermarkets, the bane of producers' lives, the unscrupulous ones driving prices down to such an extent it sometimes feels as if there is no economic sense in the producers selling to the supermarkets in the first instance. But they do and they complain bitterly and, really, if we consumers had to pay only a few pence more for each product, would we really notice? The producers would certainly notice. There is something awry here.

Someone told me this is Smith Wodehouse by any other name. It is certainly a Symington wine and I have certainly heard Symingtons complaining about the supermarkets. It is from 1994 and so, again, there is no rush. In 2011 we went to the Isle of Wight for a long weekend and I took a bottle with me, inspired by the father of a colleague at work who always opened a bottle of port at the beginning of the Open Golf Championship and made sure he finished the bottle simultaneously with the final putt of the new champion four days later. Except I wasn't feeling too hot that July (only three months before I was first diagnosed) and I struggled to keep up (or, particularly, to enjoy it). But I suspect it is good and will remain good for a long while. If ever you have the interest, you could buy a bottle of Smith Wodehouse 1994 and open the two side by side. This will reveal Tesco's hand.

Incidentally, the colleague's father had it right. It's a myth that, once decanted, vintage port can keep a long time without spoiling. That is not true. It should be knocked on the head within the week, maybe two if you keep it chilled or in a cool place. And as we learnt at Malvedos, chilled port, vintage or not, really is very good indeed.

MADEIRA

Blandys 10 Year Old Malmsey

Madeira, on the other hand, well that really does keep. Open a bottle and, as it is already oxidised, it will not deteriorate for as long as you care to keep it. It does beg the question why you should want to sit on it for too long as it is such a wonderful drink, a tangier lighter version of port.

It was in 1993 that I had my first meaningful experience with Madeira. The wine bug had properly got hold and that year the Sunday Telegraph ran an amateur winetasting competition. Round 1 involved answering 20 questions and submitting a short essay on the Syrah grape. Some of the questions were tricky, especially in the days before the internet. And an essay? On the Syrah grape? This was serious. But I was studying for my law finals and so was happy of the distraction.

Round 2. A letter dropped through the door inviting me to the London heat, 20 of us lined up against each other in a blind tasting, chief officiator Oz Clarke. This was fun. Spouses/girlfriends were invited so you and I trotted along one evening to the old Whitbread brewery in Chiswell Street. I was going no further in this competition so, whereas some of the competitors, old timers on this circuit (the spouses knew each other; you were a fish out of water), kept their powder and palates dry, we tucked into the champagne and canapés on offer before the commencement of hostilities.

I forget all the questions but I remember there was a round on fortified wines, three wines I think. I recognised the sherry and guessed, because it was all I knew, that it was a fino. I recognised the port but plumped for ruby instead of vintage (the sediment was the giveaway that it was vintage) and the third wine, well I really had no idea at all.

I sat there in silence. But silence was bringing me no nearer the answer.

"Aah, I think I recognise this one."

I looked to the competitor on my right. A smug smile spread across his face. "Yes," he continued, sotto voce, "I think this third one is from where I went on holiday only a couple of months ago."

"Oh yes," I whispered "where was that?"

"Now that would be telling" he replied, with a self-congratulatory grin.

You can guess what I thought of that. But I looked at the man and sized him up. Middle-aged, greying and slightly thinning on top. I didn't have him as a regular at Magaluf. Reid's Hotel in Madeira I guessed. And I had heard of Madeira as a fortified wine, not something I could say for Magaluf. So Madeira it was. But then the question sheet asked of me what type of my chosen wine was it? What type? Did Madeira have types? I racked my brain. It was only three years since I had done my finals, one of which was the Crusades. And hadn't the town of Monemvasia, perilously perched on the edge of the Aegean, hanging on for dear life to the eastern rim of the Peloponnese, which had played some role in the Crusades which I had long forgotten, hadn't this town given its name to a type of fortified wine? Malmsey? Was Malmsey a type of Madeira? Who knew but I was a beggar at the table. When the answers were revealed, one competitor looked surprised the wine was not a Sercial, a couple genuinely puzzled it was not a Verdelho and the vast majority almost scandalised it was not a Bual. And only one competitor looked bemused that it was indeed a Malmsey, the sweetest of the types of Madeira.

Before the final scores were revealed I was relieving myself of the champagne that I had so gleefully consumed beforehand and Oz Clarke walked up to the adjoining urinal. I was enjoying myself too much to comply with standard urinal etiquette of eyes averted and silence. Oz Clarke was a celebrity.

"I am sorry we all got the Riesling question so wrong" I proffered, all of us having guessed the wines were Sauvignon Blanc.

"Yes, I am not sure how that happened" Oz replied.

"Just one example among many misses on my part, I fear."

Oz leaned over and peered at my name badge. "Oh well," he

said "not as many misses as some".

Kind man, I thought, reassuring me like that, until of course he announced my second place and qualification, by one point, for the grand final.

I could make many excuses for my failure to be crowned Sunday Telegraph Chief Champion Winetaster of All Time at the grand final – possibly the fact that my Law Society finals had finished the day before so I was off the leash with a mighty thirst, possibly that I must have been close because I achieved more correct answers than in the previous round – but all of these would be misguiding because frankly there were better tasters than me in the final. But what fun it was, and all because my knowledge of the Crusades led me to Malmsey. I think of it every time I drink it.

Incidentally, I met Oz Clarke once again, years later at a tasting of Burgundies. Once again it was in the urinals and once again I could not resist the urge to engage him in conversation. Next time I shall have to tell him that we must stop meeting like this.

LEBANON

On her 10th birthday you and I took Claudia and Gus (Emily was at school) to a smart Lebanese restaurant in Knightsbridge. We drank Massaya. The wine may have been "cleaner" than Musar but it still had a distinct savoury Lebanese character. I remember the wine well but I suspect the three of you remember the evening for other reasons.

Towards the end of supper, an old gentleman, sitting on his own at the next door table and enjoying a cigar and a brandy, leaned over and asked me if I minded if he spoke directly to my wife.

"Not at all" I replied, slightly puzzled.

The gentleman then spoke to you and remarked on what charming children we had and, with a sailful of wind behind him, began to tell us how he was travelling home to Amman the following day and how he would be greeted by his wife, children and grandchildren and how his grandchildren were only ever interested in the presents he had brought them, not his company, but how delightful they were and forgivable their actions.

We spoke along such lines for a good 10 minutes or so and then he asked about the occasion and we told him that it was Claudia's birthday.

"Then the birthday girl requires a birthday present."

With this, he pulled a roll of notes out of his pocket and ever so slowly unfurled a £50 note and handed it over to Claudia, her eyes at this point as wide and round as the plate holding her cake.

"And you," the old man turned to Gus "when is your birthday?"

"Not until November" Gus replied, slightly downhearted that he was missing a present by a good five months.

"Well, I do not know if I shall see you then so I better give you your present now."

And with that he ever so slowly unfurled another £50 note and handed it to Gus.

"God bless you all" he said and with that left the table.

The kids laughed, we all laughed, astonished by the man's kindness and generosity. The only one who did not laugh was Emily who no doubt felt she had missed out on a rare bonanza.

As we left the restaurant, Claudia exclaimed how it was so unusual to leave a restaurant richer than you went in. I started to agree with her and then wondered, actually, when had Claudia last left a restaurant poorer than she went in?

We bought some of that Massaya on the back of that evening but the bottles are long gone now.

Château Musar, Bekaa Valley 2000

If there is a risk of Portugal losing some of its identity as it embraces modern winemaking practices, I do not think the same accusation can be levelled at Château Musar, for so long the flagbearer of Lebanese wine (and now, I suspect, happy to share some of the burden with other growers whose wines are finding an ever more prominent place on the international market). To say Musar is idiosyncratic is probably something of an understatement. There is no guarantee when you pull the cork what you are going to get - is it going to be spoilt by excessive brett or volatile acidity? Conceivably, for such unreliabilities are in the nature of the beast, but probably not and you will be presented with a remarkable panoply of flavours unlike anything you have experienced before, a mixture of savoury, warm baked fruits, elements of dirt and dust, a real sense of place. Serge Hochar, the winemaker for so many years, died last year. Maybe the next generation will tidy up the production and the wine will lose some of its soul but these bottles are firmly of the old school.

I picked up these bottles in Sainsburys years ago when they were selling the last few bottles at a knock-down price. I swiped all five and then felt guilty in case any other wine lover should stumble on the empty shelf seeing the discounted price for the now-gone Musar. I put one bottle back for such a person. A couple of days later I had a change of heart and thought I might as well take all of what was on offer. But the last bottle had gone, I hope to a good home.

The one thing I would say, despite James Symington's possible protestations, is that it makes sense to decant the wine. From memory it throws quite a sediment and you will lose a fair amount of the bottle to murkiness and powder if you don't. The other reason for decanting of course is to allow the wine to breathe (particularly useful for young wines). I am not sure that is necessary here but be careful decanting if the wine is old. It will deteriorate quickly and in such cases I would lean towards serving the wine straight from the bottle and hang any sediment that creeps into the glass. Besides, for an old bottle, the pleasure may as much be in the bottle and its label as in its contents.

<u>CHILE</u>

Years ago I went to see the late Lord Anglesey at his ancestral home, Plas Newydd, on the banks of the Menai Straits overlooking Snowdonia on the mainland. A magical spot. For lunch he served the Wine Society's Argentine Malbec. Although he had smarter tastes and smarter bottles (that evening he served a Hermitage) he professed that his heart lay with the Malbec and that this bottling was the mainstay of his cellar. His son mentioned it again at his memorial service and it struck a chord with me. And for me it is as follows: thank God for Chile, thank God for Chilean Cabernet Sauvignon and thank God for the Wine Society's Chilean Cabernet Sauvignon. I am surprised there is not a single bottle of it in the cellar at the moment but it has been such a faithful servant over the years that I cannot pass without citing its honourable service. For every cellar must contain a workhorse, a faithful stalwart that requires no thought, no special attention, a wine that can be reached for safe in the knowledge of what it will deliver, something easy that will do the trick without effort. And for me that wine has always been the Wine Society's Chilean Cabernet Sauvignon. There is something about Chilean Cabernet that I find irresistible – a generosity of blackcurrant, full deep flavours, a warmth, a toothsome crunchy texture. This extends to other Chilean wines too, their Merlots, their Chardonnays, even their Sauvignons. A brave world of refreshing flavours.

I might just as well have added "and thank God for the Wine Society". If my golden rule is that wine is only as good as the company in which it is drunk, a second rule would be to join the Wine Society. Being a mutual it is run on very different lines to other companies which means not only that prices are always competitive (this is particularly noticeable and effective in the £5-£15 range where most happy drinking occurs) but it is only obliged to sell wines it wants to. This might sound strange but, without the need to satisfy shareholders' demands for fat dividends, it does provide the Wine Society with a liberty only to stock wines that it rates and which it thinks its members will like. Be a member of the Wine Society for as long as you possibly can. Grandpa was a member, Dad was a member, I am a member and you, my love, and you, my little ones, you must become members too. Seriously.

TH Cabernet Sauvignon, Pirque, Undurraga 2012

One risk that every Chilean wine runs is tipping over into a lack of balance. There is such a wealth of potential in the raw material that it takes a sure hand to balance the fruit, the acidity, the tannin and the alcohol. My beloved Society's Chilean Cabernet Sauvignon manages it but many don't. This one does. It is more grown-up than the Society wine but is nevertheless restrained enough to encourage you back for subsequent glasses. Lovely stuff.

Carmenère Reserva, Falernia 2012

Carmenère. Long considered to be Merlot until the ampelographists (there's a word) crawled over Chile's grape heritage and discovered that much of their Merlot was Carmenère, once a key grape variety of Bordeaux. Chocolate is the tasting note most often associated with Carmenère. Maybe. I have not tried this and, in fact, am slightly intimidated by it. It is made in the ripasso style (the wine, once vinified, being run over semi-dried grapes to extract further flavour and texture) and the alcohol content looks punchy. I do not suppose it is a wine of subtlety but perhaps it is not a wine of surfeit either. Mum swears by it though: courage, mon brave.

SOUTH AFRICA

During my days at university, I mostly drank 80 shilling, Scotland's malty dark answer to England's bitter. Wine-wise, my mainstays were Bulgarian Cabernet Sauvignon (quite delicious), Muscadet (one of the world's great wines but, in those days and at that price point, paint stripper), a rare bottle of Rioja, slightly more frequently Chianti and a great deal of KWV.

KWV was not very good. It was the state-run South African wine co-operative and, in those apartheid days, the only South African wine readily available on the UK market (Victoria Wine used to peddle it). There was an insipid Sauvignon Blanc, a tasteless Steen (the local name for Chenin Blanc) and a largely undrinkable Pinotage. Why, you might ask, did I persevere with KWV? That is not a question I can easily answer. Maybe I thought there was an element of sophistication in drinking wine from such an outcast country. There certainly wasn't much pleasure.

And for many years afterwards my knowledge of South African wine progressed no further. I gave up KWV as quickly as I could but the few examples of South African wine I experienced were normally of badly-made Pinotage with an overwhelming smell of burnt rubber. In fact, I still haven't had the courage to go back to Pinotage which I know, from all I read in the wine press, is wrong and my loss. For the fact of the matter is that things have changed. There is a surging renaissance in South Africa (I can hear some Boers complaining that there has been a surging renaissance for some considerable time) and the wines can be of the highest quality, red and white. Many talk about how South Africa has one foot in the Old World and one in the New and I can see that – the generosity of the fruit is restrained (in a beguiling way). Consider them.

Red, Meerlust 2011

For the last few years at work I have run a series of wine talks exploring the four V's – vineyard, vigneron, vintage, vogue. They are all different but which is the best pointer to the quality of the wine in the bottle (for vogue, read price)? I must be honest and say that I did not know when I started out but it soon became obvious.

For vineyard, I would select three wines from one vintage and one winegrower (easily done in Burgundy with a generic, village and premier cru wine), for vigneron three wines from three different growers of the same vintage and origin and for vintage, three identical wines from the same grower but from three different vintages. For vogue, I am afraid, I would simply show the audience a picture of a bottle of Romanée-Conti, ask them to guess the price (no one ever got near the £12,000 a bottle answer – absurd) and then remind them of the golden rule that most pleasure is derived from the company in which wine is drunk.

In any event, on each occasion I have conducted this talk, the clear winner was vigneron. Whatever critics (or even the vigneron himself!) might say about the site-specifity of the vineyard or the vagaries of the weather, the single biggest influence on the quality of what lies within is the winegrower and his skills, his judgement, his conscientiousness, his philosophy, the list can go on.

And so we have a perfect example here. Meerlust's flagship wine is Rubicon, a Bordeaux blend of Merlot, Cabernet Sauvignon, Cabernet Franc and Petit Verdot. Except in 2011 the winegrower did not think the grapes were up to scratch and so declassified all the Rubicon into a wine simply labelled "Red". And sold it for a song. The wine is glorious. I cannot tell you if the wine is any worse than a Rubicon or if the wine really suffers the dilution of the wet year but I can't taste it. And the producer says it can age for 10 or more years – even in declassifying the wine the grower wanted the best for his wine. It is a wonderful wine. We are onto our second case of it and not a single bottle has disappointed. Indeed it even held its own when pitched into the deep end and compared with a declassified Latour 2005.

Follow the grower, nothing else.

UNITED STATES

One of the great wine tragedies of recent years, and I mean this (at least I do for UK consumers), was the sale of Oddbins to Castel Frères, a French conglomerate. The new owner saw this acquisition as an opportunity to inundate all the numerous well-sited shops with worthless generic French plonk at the expense of all the trailblazing idiosyncratic astonishing wines from around the world that Oddbins had first introduced us to in the late 1980's. Needless to say, the wine-buying public soon cottoned onto the change in emphasis and quality and moved on. The brand plummeted, the shops closed and Castel Frères, having wreaked its worst, sold the company and the shops, it seems, separately, almost exclusively to estate agents. The company is beginning to make a comeback, a few shops here and there, and Oddbins once again is becoming synonymous with quality. But it will be a long and arduous climb back to the heights of the late 80's and early 90's.

It is difficult to overestimate the effect that Oddbins had on the UK wine industry and the tastes of its consumers. I remember the first occasion I tried a bottle of Seaview Chardonnay from Australia, bought for £3.99 in the Stockbridge branch of Oddbins in Edinburgh. Used to a diet of mouth-puckering Muscadet and indigestion-inducing KWV Steen, the wine (such a golden colour!) was a revelation. Layers of ripe fruit, butter, oak, glycerol. Not a sharp edge, generous to a fault. This style of wine has fallen out of favour in Australia now, all producers keen to promote cool-climate credentials and wines majoring on minerality and tension but I do still sometimes hanker after this early, sometimes blowsy and certainly over the top, style. It was a hefty dose of golden sunshine dropped into the anaemic life of a Northern European wine drinker. This is what Oddbins specialised in: bursts of flavour and faraway wines.

I had drunk a fair share of American wines growing up, as I

did, in New York but, until the arrival of Oddbins at least, they were difficult to find on the UK high street and expensive when you did. And, apart from the Gallo jug wines and their like, they remain relatively expensive to this day on account of the strong domestic market. So I have never bought many which, to some extent, is a surprise given how dear one Oddbins Californian offering was to my heart. Franciscan Pinnacles Pinot Noir – from Monterey and £6.99 a bottle. Gone now, swallowed up in some enormous conglomerate, but what a wine it was – smoky, an undertow of earth, soft red fruits. Stephen put me on to it and it was not everywhere. So where I saw it I bought it. And once it had gone, well, California, like so much else, slipped from my mind.

Mas Cavalls Pinot Noir, Dona Margarita Vineyard, Marimar Estates 2010

I read a tasting note of the 2006 vintage of this wine a few years ago, penned by Michael Broadbent, who is no slouch when it comes to tasting wines. It was a remarkable tasting note, a paean to the wine's virtues and likening it in its growing complexity to a first-growth claret. This is not usual Broadbent-speak who is generally given over to the reserve and understatement of your archetypal English gent.

So when an offer of this 2010 bottling landed in my inbox last year, and maybe reflecting on my need to commune once more with West Coast pinots, I jumped (as did everyone: the wine sold out in moments). And the wine has not disappointed. Now six years old, it shows a tawny rim, a relaxed nose of strawberries and peaches and a palate reminiscent of malt. Interesting and delicious.

Maybe on account of the Franciscan, I have always "rated"

West Coast Pinot as the most successful example of Pinot Noir outside Burgundy. Now there is much wrong with that sentence, to begin with the equally absurd concepts that I might with any authority rate a wine and that one expression of a grape is more or less successful than another. But Pinot Noirs from California and, increasingly, Oregon have an ease and an expression and a depth that I have not found in New Zealand (good wine, just a little too earnest for me whereas New Zealand Chardonnay, well that does set my heart on fire), Australia (lovely wines, sometimes a little warm) or South Africa (a bit thin?). Maybe Germany, curiously, gives the West Coast the closest run for its money. Another equally absurd notion is that wines grown in one location must seek to emulate wines from another. A wine must speak of its origin and its roots. There is nothing to be gained by chasing shadows and it does the wine a disservice to be compared with something grown in an entirely different climate, in different soils, quite possibly a different hemisphere. We must celebrate the diversity of the wine world, not look to create a monoculture where all wines must aspire to some standardised example, however elevated.

Freedom Hill Vineyard Pinot Noir, Willamette Valley, Patricia Green Cellars 2013

The Willamette Valley in Oregon is very fashionable nowadays. Pinot Noir thrives best in a marginal cool climate and so, on the West Coast, the vineyards planted to Pinot have retreated up the hillsides or nearer the coast where the cool air of the Pacific creeps in during the late afternoon. Or, of course, further north, as is the case here. The wine is a lighter interpretation of Pinot Noir than the Mas Cavalls – slight and shy, charming and kind. I would suggest drinking these bottles in the next few years.

FRANCE

And so to France. My spiritual homeland. And isn't it obvious? Compare the wines past with the wines to come. If I have some 260 bottles of wine from outside France, the number of French wines I have must be three or four times that. I suspect France is the spiritual homeland of most Northern Europeans. Not having our own wine industries to support (or if so, minimal) we have no conflicting allegiance to draw us away from the country on our doorstep which is, it is difficult to dispute, the greatest winegrowing nation on earth. If I say this, it is not to detract from others nor is it an excuse not to explore and enjoy other nations' wines and nor is it a reason not to criticise much about the French wine industry. If we do criticise it, though, it is out of love and respect for what the country has to offer and how much pleasure it has given us over our lives. Curious to say this as an Englishman but culturally I feel as closely allied to the wines of France as I do to aspects of British culture. We are that closely linked.

Of course, it will have all started earlier than my own interest in wine. Previous generations will only have known French wines, and maybe German, with a smattering of Spanish and Italian, but predominanty French. The New World was unknown and our fathers and grandfathers will have honed their palates on the French classics. So it is natural that this will have been the first education that we received. Our children, though, they will have a broader introduction and maybe the tie to France will become weaker. That is for them.

Where to start? The four most substantial wine regions in France must be the Rhône Valley, the Loire Valley, Burgundy and Bordeaux. For no real reason, I will start with the Rhône.

RHONE

It's easy to be daunted by the Rhône Valley. It produces the most spectacular amount of wine (second only to Bordeaux) and covers a vast area. If you are starting out with stepping stones of individual wines, it would be easy to categorise the Rhône in the "too big to understand" category. This is not necessary. It can quite easily be broken down into component parts and, even if this is not going to bring you universal knowledge of the region, it will at least enable you to navigate the area with some understanding and perhaps a little ease.

To begin with, divide the region into two (as I have done below): the Northern Rhône and the Southern Rhône. The Northern Rhône (as a winegrowing region) occupies a tiny strip of land following the river south from Lyon for 60 miles or so. For the most part, the vineyards cling to the right bank of the river. We are quite far north here and the vines must garner every last lumen of sunlight if the grapes are to ripen. So think steep, terraced vineyards, small production and expensive wines.

Once past Montelimar, the Rhône fans out into an enormous river basin that becomes an even larger delta and here we are into the land of the Southern Rhône. The landscape is completely different. The river, previously hemmed in by the granite of the Massif Central, can now spread out. The climate is warmer. The land is flatter. The area is vast. Here is the engine room of the Rhône Valley – 95% of all Rhône wine is produced in the Southern Rhône (so only 5%, for those of you good at your maths, produced in the Northern Rhône).

So think of two different regions and also consider this: the Northern Rhône is homogenous, the Southern Rhône heterogeneous. The Northern Rhône has a single identity, borne of a single landscape, that of steep terraced vineyards close to the river, and of single grape varieties, Syrah for its reds and Viognier for its whites (OK, with accompanying roles for Marsanne and Roussanne in some of its whites). In the South, however, the landscape differs hugely from place to place (how can it fail to in such a large area?), It is a land of many different grape varieties (up to 18 different types are allowed in Châteauneuf-du-Pape), led by Grenache, the mainstay of the region, Mourvèdre and Syrah among the reds and goodness knows how many obscure varieties among the whites.

If you can start with these distinctions in mind, then it all becomes much easier.

NORTHERN RHONE

Viognier, Vin de Pays des Collines Rhodaniennes, Julien Pilon 2014

I have heard it said by many collectors that they have always bought too many reds at the expense of whites. This is easily done. One of the appeals of putting together a cellar is the concept of longevity, not only on account that you are setting aside something for your dotage (!) but also, I suspect, because it somehow justifies the outlay and expenditure you are making now: if the wine lasts a long time, it will inevitably become scarcer over the years, and hence more expensive, and so it is in effect a saving to be buying the wine now. So works the mind of a wine collector. Added to this, most white wine is made for consumption in the short, or at best medium, term and so there is less of a need to cellar a white wine to uncover, in due course, its true expression.

Whatever the reason, it is a common observation that wine lovers concentrate more on red than on white. I suspect it is equally common, however, that over time wine lovers look to redress this and adjust their wine-buying habits accordingly. It is certainly something I have looked to do (too late, of course). I also wonder if my tastes are changing and if I now find white wine as rewarding, and maybe more refreshing, maybe less demanding on my constitution, than red wine. In any event, watch out for this and always keep an eye out for interesting whites.

I only make this point because I see this wine is only one of two white Rhônes that we have. We should have more, at least we should certainly have more Viognier. If I am honest, I am unmoved by the great whites of Hermitage (Marsanne and Roussanne) and Châteauneuf-du-Pape (Grenache, Bourboulenc, goodness knows what else). I have tried some terribly smart bottles of white Chave Hermitage and Clos des Papes in my time but to me they have always tasted neutral, a little flat and of old nuts. Not for me. Viognier, on the other hand, well that is remarkable and utterly delicious, a wine redolent of apricots and crème fraiche, a wine that walks the line between unctuous and mineral.

Viognier's heartland is in Condrieu. Condrieu very nearly disappeared entirely as a wine-producing region. In the early 1960's there were no more than 12 hectares left in production. The history of Condrieu follows a similar pattern to that of many other wine regions in France. Wiped out by phylloxera in the late 19th Century, the industry barely had time to get on its feet again before being floored by two world wars interrupted only by a depression. After the Second World War there was then a large migration from the countryside into the towns where all the best paid jobs were to be found. So really for the best part of one hundred years, Condrieu and other regions like it suffered a downward spiral almost into extinction. And then slowly in the 1970's and gathering pace in the 1980's, as peace and prosperity properly took a foothold, disposable income could once again be spent on wine and demand for Condrieu and others like it returned. Thank goodness it did. The vines need all the warmth they can get (remember the steep terraces), the grape variety is finickity in the extreme (difficult to ripen and then, as soon as ripe, with a propensity to spill over into overripeness) and the resultant wine is expensive but there is no wine lover in the world who is not grateful for the revival of Condrieu.

You can taste some of the glory of Condrieu by going for a good grower's entry-level wine which, as here, comes from vines that fall just outside the Condrieu appellation (hence only entitled to "vin de pays" status). The wine lacks the full generosity of the Viognier fruit that you will find in a good Condrieu but not by much and it has that wonderful mineral spine to keep the baroque fruit in check. The wine is actually called "mon grand-père était limonadier". I did ask the winegrower once why he named the wine so and the answer he gave was wholly unconvincing. But then, I thought, why does he need to convince me of anything? The wine does that quite well enough on its own.

Drink it young. Drink it fresh on its fruit.

Côte-Rôtie, Domaine Ogier 1999
L'Ame Soeur, Vin de Pays de Seyssuel, Domaine Ogier 2010
Côte-Rôtie, La Péroline, Vignobles Levet 2009
Côte-Rôtie, Maestria, Vignobles Levet 2012

Our weekends with Rachel and Hugh in Dorset have, for so long as I can remember, followed a similar pattern. We arrive on a Friday evening, having run the gauntlet of the A303 and frazzled from a week in London, kids hungry and tired. They are quickly fed and into bed and the evening is then ours. We may drink the wine we bring or we may just as well drink something Hugh has dragged from his cellar. The only certainties are that we will drink well and we will drink too much. Whenever we reach the end of a bottle, filled with chat and a following wind, Hugh will get a glint in his eye and hurry to the bottom of the garden to pull another bottle from the rack. Why is this so? Why is it so every time? Because it is a law of nature that when away with friends or family, the brakes are never applied on the first evening. If you wake up with remorse or guilt the following morning, do not. Celebrate the power of wine to bring you together and the love and friendship that flows. It is a blessing, one to be embraced.

The following morning, as often is not, we will go into Mere and visit Yapp Brothers, a Rhône and Loire specialist. I will end up buying something, possibly to take home to London (they do a very good Brézème, a strong Syrah from the last outback of the Northern Rhône) or possibly for lunch that day (maybe Vernay's vin de pays Viognier). We will walk it off in the afternoon anyway.

That evening we will try and work as hard as we did the night before but inevitably will fall one bottle short. As often as not it will be a Burgundy that we have brought down (Hugh forever scornful of Red Burgundy's ability to perform, I forever looking to persuade him otherwise).

On Sunday we will leave after lunch. You, my love, will always offer to drive us back to London so that I can drink more than I should and Hugh will produce a claret for Rachel's roast, a gentle coda to a full weekend. I will fall asleep on the way back, having promised myself some days off, and that very evening I shall inevitably break my resolution.

There is nothing magic in what I say here. It may well sound banal and everyday but the simple truths and pleasures are so often ignored and overlooked.

And what does any of this have to do with Côte-Rôtie? For the simple reason that I always associate our trips to Dorset with the wine. It is not a wine you often come across and, whether because of my sister's proximity to Yapp or her husband's predilection for the wine, it is something we have often had there. Côte-Rôtie is a wine that requires like minds. It can be a demanding wine if you are not in the right mood for it, or among fellow enthusiasts, and so requires planning, effort and attention which, to be fair, is exactly what one of the finest wines in France deserves.

Look at images of the Côte-Rôtie vineyards on the internet. The Romans were the first to plant grapes here, indeed some of their terracing still remains. Is it any wonder that such an intense landscape of vertiginous terracing and of such intense labour to grow and harvest the grapes should produce such an intense wine? Côte-Rôtie is not a monster of a wine, even if it is baked on these roasted slopes of a good summer. I have always thought it more akin to Burgundy to the north. Made from Syrah (in fact, up to 20% Viognier is allowed in the final blend, probably an accident of mixed vineyards rather than any perceived benefit from the addition of a few white grapes), it is only a medium-bodied wine with strong scents of leaf mould on the nose and a beautiful mix of raspberry and malt on the palate, all the time run through with mineral streaks of granite lending structure: it really is a wonderful wine. The key tasting note, however, unmistakeable in all the examples I have had is this: smoked bacon crisps. You will always find it and it is tell-tale.

Buy, or at least enjoy, Côte-Rôtie while you can; it is hugely underpriced for what it is. Quantities are small, it is difficult and expensive to produce, it is unique and complex and yet its pricing has stood still for the best part of 20 years. I have in front of me the Wine Society offer from the 1995 vintage, the first year I bought any wine to lay down. Pierre Gaillard's Côte-Rôtie, a stylish wine, was on offer at £145 in bond. By comparison, Faurie's Hermitage was £175 and Vieux Télégraphe's Châteauneuf-du-Pape was £112. So a clear hierarchy and order, Hermitage slightly ahead of Côte-Rôtie as would be expected, and Vieux Télégraphe, again as would be expected in terms of volume produced and production costs, lagging slightly behind. Leap forward to the 2014 vintage. Faurie's wine is now £420 a case and Vieux Télégraphe £350 but the Gaillard is only £240. Eh? What has happened? Fashion is what has happened. It has left Côte-Rôtie behind. Benefit while you can. I repeat: this is one of the great wines of the world.

Ogier: two examples here, one fully mature and the other the product of a more ambitious age.

In 1999 Ogier was still relatively new and only produced two cuvées, this Estate bottling and a super-rare limited bottling called La Belle Hélène (nothing to do with Offenbach: Michel Ogier's wife). I have always been distrustful of estates that render too many bottlings because I cannot get away from the feeling that the bottle I am drinking has had something stolen from it to put in another bottle. Keep it simple, I say, keep it faithful. Nowadays Michel's son, Stéphane, is in charge and he has gone wild on the number of different bottlings. Maybe this is to satiate the modern desire for wine to be ever more identifiable and attributable to individual plots. I would counter, as I am wont to do, with a hackneyed cliché that the whole can often be greater than the sum of the parts and the wine world is full of successful examples of blends.

Anyway, 1999 was a great vintage for the Northern Rhône (sticking with the analogy of Red Burgundy, the two often share propitious vintages) and this wine will be at its peak now. Drink the last bottles soon. A lady in her prime, the edges only now beginning to lose their shape.

As for L'Ame Soeur, this is a new venture for Ogier. Côte-Rôtie's "soul sister". A number of growers have started planting vineyards on the left bank of the river instead, at Seyssuel. The Romans grew grapes here and so there must be something in it. The grapes catch the evening sun rather than the morning sun and this creates a beefier profile. We tried a couple of bottles one lunchtime down at Rachel and Hugh's last year. It was a bigger party than usual. I was not in the mood for it that day. The wine was rich, polished and ambitious. It left me behind. As I said, Côte-Rôtie can be a demanding wine and sometimes you must pick your moment. Maybe the first evening of a weekend away. But no great rush.

Levet: a great grower, as underrated as Côte-Rôtie itself. Wines filled with character and structure, a perfect balance of fruit and savoury and, yes, with bacon crisps to boot. Péroline is Levet's top bottling but is it really any better than the Maestria? I have touched on this before. I am not sure I believe in comparisons, other than by way of education. I have tried the two next to each other and maybe the Péroline shows a more mineral profile, maybe it is a little stronger in the glass but this is to do the Maestria a disservice as the Maestria is a perfect wine in its own right. True wines. Hugh would enjoy them, at least in due course. The Péroline is good to go (there may only be one bottle), the Maestria needs a few years yet (and the pleasure of a whole case to look forward to).

Crozes-Hermitage, Domaine de Raymond Roure, Paul Jaboulet et Aîné 1996

The *primum inter pares* of growers of Hermitage, which is considered by most to be the Rhône Valley's finest wine, is Jean-Louis Chave, the 16th successive generation of Chaves who have produced wine from the Hermitage hill since 1481 – now there is pressure to produce an heir for you. I met him at a dinner showcasing his wines. An intense thoughtful man with whom I had an intense thoughtful conversation, not so much about his wines (I cannot remember too much about them, having drunk too much of them, other than to say they were impeccably balanced and filled with breeding), more about what is the ideal drink to finish off an evening such as this when you have had a surfeit of fine wine. Some, misguided I say, suggest a digestif but that is too strong and too short. No sooner have you finished than you will need a refill, something you will only fully appreciate the following morning. No, you need something longer, something that will slake your thirst, something like lager. Jean-Louis fully agreed. And so, armed with Kronenbourg 1664, we carried on a while, talking nonsense thankfully since forgotten. I also like the man because, by all accounts, he swears like a trooper. It is a widely-held and universally acknowledged truth that you should never trust a man who does not drink or who sports facial hair. I would add that a man with too clean a tongue is to be treated with caution. In any event, I digress.

If Côte-Rôtie's calling card is bacon crisps, if Saint-Joseph's is olives and that of Cornas (the other noble wine of the Northern Rhône) something altogether darker, then Hermitage is far more polished and betrays none of these characteristics other than in perfect balance with everything else. It is more reminiscent of claret than any of its neighbours, betraying cooler red fruits. This was not lost on the Bordelais. In the 19th century Hermitage was often shipped over to Bordeaux to bolster and beef up the Medoc's finest growths, including Château Lafite and Château Palmer. This used to be openly acknowledged – "Hermitagé" was the adjective used – and so presumably was something to be admired as a quality rather than simply being an early example of honest trade description. The comparison between Hermitage and claret is not that fanciful.

I only once bought a case of Hermitage and there is a lesson there. The year must have been 2000 and the vintage on offer was 1999, the best in the Northern Rhône for a long while. I bought a case of Jaboulet's flagship wine, Hermitage La Chapelle, with no intention of drinking it but instead of treating it as an investment. Great year, legendary wine – what could go wrong? Perhaps not much, I subsequently learned, other than a rapid tail-off in the fortunes of the Jaboulet family, whose inspirational father figure, Gerard had died suddenly in 1997, leaving an extended family to pick up the pieces and tiptoe through the subsequent vintages as best they could. It is not a bad wine by any stretch of the imagination – I tried it only last year and, although quiet, it showed understated balance (that word again) and gentle fruit – but it is not in the league of La Chapelles past. Worse than this, the great guru of the wine critic world, Robert Parker, expressed his displeasure at the wine and this, more than anything, did for the investment value of the wine. Over the years I eagerly looked for new reviews as evidence that the wine might have turned a corner and blossomed into a masterpiece but such reviews never materialised. In the end I sold the case and rued the rashness of my decision to buy the case in the first place. I have never subsequently bought wine as an investment, not because I didn't learn my lesson here (which is blatantly simple: do your research on the particular wine before you buy, do not just wing it on combination of vintage and producer) but rather because wine owes me nothing other than the beauty in the bottle and the company and love that it will uncork.

Anyway, enough. What about this wine? Away from the hill of Hermitage which stands like a colossus on the left bank of the Rhône, facing due south to the sun, lies Crozes-Hermitage, a region which spreads out to the north and the east. Crozes can be one of two things: a light, gluggable Syrah that requires little in the way of attention (not in a bad way; there is a wine for every occasion and a well-made Crozes in this mould can be delightful) and a darker, more ambitious wine made from tried and tested vineyards, occasionally on steep slopes that echo those of Hermitage itself. This wine is one such, from terraces in Gervans, and is the product of the Jaboulet family when all was still in order (the family eventually sold its business to the Frey family of Bordeaux in the early 2000's).

This Crozes is, quite possibly, the single wine which has given me the greatest pleasure in my entire wine collection. I picked up six or so bottles of it as bin-ends in Fortnum & Mason. Once (like all junior office workers, I suppose) I had lunchtimes to myself and often I would venture afield to see what I could find in well-known wine shops across the West End. These bottles were just such an example and I remember making two or three visits to pick up one or two bottles more until I had exhausted the shop of its stock. "Think of it as a baby Cornas" Robert Parker wrote. I think of it is as more than that, as a grown-up Hermitage in fact. The wine has been phenomenal. Reading my tasting notes, indeed, I see I have become quite carried away at times, likening (forgive me) the wine to Beethoven, as assured and powerful in its quieter moments as in its fortissimo moments. The wine shows breeding and purpose. So much have I enjoyed the wine I have been nervous to broach the last two bottles for a number of years now. You should.

So Crozes can in some cases approach the heights of Hermitage and even, sometimes, scale them. I recall once trying Jaboulet's 1990 Crozes-Hermitage Domaine de Thalabert, a legendary wine (second that year only to La Chapelle). Thalabert has for as long as anyone can remember been the yardstick by which serious Crozes has been measured. I cannot say whether it has regained that position following the wane in Jaboulet's fortunes, it quite possibly has, but I remember puzzling how any wine could extract the intensity and body from a bunch of grapes the way that wine did in 1990. Which goes to show: great wine abounds, regardless of the appellation.

Saint-Joseph, Domaine de la Côte de l'Epine 2005
Saint-Joseph, L'Olivaie, Domaine Coursodon 2006
Saint-Joseph, L'Olivaie, Domaine Coursodon 2009
Saint-Joseph, L'Olivaie, Domaine Coursodon 2012
Saint-Joseph, Pierre Gonon 2006
Saint-Joseph, Pierre Gonon 2009
Saint-Joseph, Pierre Gonon 2014
Saint-Joseph, Lieu Dit Saint-Joseph, Ferraton Père et Fils 2009
Saint-Joseph, Clos de Cuminaille, Pierre Gaillard 2009

Saint-Joseph. Even the name is seductive, gently rolling off the tongue, softly sybaritic.

When the wine bug bit, for a long while I was rudderless. Although I might look to concentrate on France, I would still drift between nations and appellations which I could not place or understand. I would lurch from wine to wine, not knowing how each interrelated with the next, not knowing sometimes where the wines even came from. Such was the case with Saint-Joseph. I eyed it in an off-licence in Pimlico. The label was so simple, the name so straightforward. What was this wine? What grape was it? Where was Saint-Joseph? And the wine was not cheap - £10 or so I recall. What made it worth that? In the end, there was nothing for it, I had to buy the wine and find out. I was smitten and I have been ever since.

If the big three of the Northern Rhône are Hermitage, Côte-Rôtie and Cornas, I like to think that Saint-Joseph is next in the pecking order. Traditionally made from grapes grown on steep terraces on the right bank of the Rhône opposite Hermitage, the wine suffered a setback in the 1970's when the appellation was expanded hugely to incorporate softer land (above the terraces, on the plains) which produced concomitantly softer and less interesting wines. You need to learn to ignore these and to stick with the growers from the original sites because the products are remarkable. There is something beguiling and velvet-textured about a good Saint-Joseph, not the bold statement of Côte-Rôtie, the classicism of Hermitage or the saturnine intensity of good Cornas, a mix perhaps of all three, always with a hint of black olives in the background (in my mind at least).

L'Epine: there is one bottle lurking somewhere in the cellar. I have not tried it in a long while, both because it is one of Dad's (I am reluctant to see the last of his bottles go) and also because, when I did try it, maybe in 2010, it was tough as old boot. 2005 was, and continues to be, hailed as a legendary vintage all across France. But until it has softened and yielded up its pleasures, it is hard work. How many bottles of 2005 have I uncorked anticipating the pleasures of the great year, only to be confronted with a discordant jangle of unknitted parts? Come to think of it, Jean-Louis Chave, between draughts of Kronenbourg 1664, warned me of such. So, it may have turned into a swan or it may only be fit for the casserole by now. It will not improve any further. A punt.

Coursodon: faithful to my first love (it was exactly this wine, the L'Olivaie from Coursodon, that introduced me, all those years ago in Pimilico, to the joys of Saint-Joseph), you will see I have not deserted it. I read that Coursodon is quite a modern interpretation of Saint-Joseph. It has wonderful texture, well-managed tannins and supple fruit. Whatever it is, it is an honest interpretation and, to me at least, indicative of its place. Pierre-Yves Colin-Morey (see below) is a great fan and, if such a talented winemaker as he rates it, then that will do for me. Allied with black olive (is this just because it is called L'Olivaie?), there is autumn smoke, raspberries and a small lick of tell-tale Northern Rhône sourness.

Gonon: a purist's wine maybe. Purity is so often damned in the modern age. We have lost the ability to treasure measure. Everything must be full-throttle and, in the wine world, this is particularly the case. Unless the tasting notes (which are now so readily accessible on the internet) talk in terms of absolutes, wines will wrongfully be dismissed as having been damned with faint praise. To be properly appreciated, the wine must be associated with "gobs" of fruit, "massive" extract, "years" of ageing potential and plenty of points. There is little space left for the still small voice of calm. So this wine: it plays a higher register than the Coursodon, focussing more on brighter flavours. Seamless and authoritative, deep and clear. It is a wine to fall in love with.

Ferraton and Gaillard: I have coupled these two together (a) because I have not tried them and (b) because something tells me that the hand of the winegrower may be more visible, that they may be less typical than the Saint-Josephs of the other two. Do I have any justification for saying this? Absolutely none other than to say Ferraton, for long an idiosyncratic traditional grower was taken over by Chapoutier, one of the big players of the Rhône Valley, and that reviews of Gaillard's Saint-Josephs tend towards this opinion. Still, I was delighted to get them when I did and, besides, I may well be proved wrong.

Saint-Joseph, Saint-Joseph. And still it whispers, from my hospital bed it whispers across the breeze and seduces my battered bones. When to drink them? The 2006's now, the rest can wait. 2009 has produced big wines that time will not soon tire. 2012 and 2014 are less full-throttle: balance and harmony will be their trademark. Try them when they are 10 maybe (or sooner if circumstances so require). But there is no great rush. Be beguiled for a good long while.

SOUTHERN RHÔNE

And so we come to the south, the Méridionale as opposed to the Septentrionale of the North. The valley widens out, the stone warms up, granite gives way to sand (in colour as much as texture), cypress trees populate the landscape, lavender creeps in, the sun flexes and the cicadas, "Summer's second god", strike up.

Syrah leaves centre stage to Grenache in the South. Although Syrah might struggle to ripen in the Northern Rhône, the grape will easily overripen if it is too hot and so now must play second fiddle to Grenache (even third fiddle to Mourvèdre) on the valley floor. Grenache – there are no sides to Grenache. Thin-skinned and sweet, it packs a punch. It is all up-front, heady, broad, light in tannin, strong.   Whereas the Bordelais would seek out Hermitage in the 19th Century to strengthen their Pauillacs and Margaux, the Burgundians would look to Gigondas and other Grenache-rich regions to bolster their weedy Pinots Noirs.   And why not?   The grapes share a sweetness, delicacy of tannin and clarity of colour. Mourvèdre, on the other hand, is dark, leathery, tannic.   It softens beautifully with age but lends structure to the loose-knit Grenache, the Syrah adding further body and flavour. So the South is the land of blends (GSM they like to call it in Australia – Grenache, Shiraz, Mourvèdre), the flavours become more expansive and less cerebral, heat infuses the wine, intellect cedes to pleasure, reserve to largesse.   The wines of the Southern Rhône are about love and comfort, democracy and bounty.

Beaumes-de-Venise, Cotes-du-Rhône-Villages, Paul Jaboulet et Aîné 2003

Again (like the Saint-Joseph from Domaine de l'Epine) one bottle left from Dad's cellar and a son reluctant to see it go. A red wine, not the more famous Muscat de Beaumes de Venise, a popular dessert wine.

2003 was the year of the heatwave when people struggled as much as the grapes. Grapes need an even growing season to show of their best – tannins must ripen slowly so they are not harsh, the sugars must develop in tandem with the acids (which require cool nights) to retain balance between the two and there must be rain at even times to replenish the vines and hydrate the grapes. The sun must ripen but not burn. Goldilocks: too much of anything is bad. Make the vines work on a restricted diet of even amounts.

2003 provided none of this. Too little rain, ridiculous day and night-time temperatures, the grapes were already bursting with sugar by August, even if the tannins were not yet ripe. Little wonder that much of France witnessed one of the earliest harvests on record. To begin with (especially after the sun-starved, rain-drenched harvest of 2002) the growers and the wine merchants hyped the vintage to the heavens – look at the ripeness and the concentration! – but in time questions were raised. Look, instead, at the alcohol (all that sugar needed to be fermented into alcohol if the wine was to be dry), look at the hard tannins, look at the lack of balance, look at the lack of structure: blowsy. "Dolly Parton wines" some critics called them.

And yet, and yet…life will find a way. Some wines have fallen off a cliff but others, well it is as if the wine has taken charge of its own destiny and sorted out its problems in the bottle. I have drunk bottles of Meursault Charmes from 2003 (Pierre-Yves Colin Morey) that have retained freshness and typicity (or maybe, even, discovered them in the bottle). And I recall Daniel Ravier, the winemaker at Domaine Tempier, imploring me, during an England-France rugby match at Twickenham, to drink and be done with his 2003 Bandol – it had fallen apart, he said, and was not worthy of the label. I knew the wine well and when he told me to do so the wine was certainly in an unhappy place. But I persevered and ignored Daniel's advice and the wine knitted together and ended its days, with me at least, in a far happier place. As with everything in life, I suppose, things are never as good or as bad as people predict. 2003 is not the write-off that some have decreed and, in many cases, appears to be finding a balance previously considered unthinkable. I wonder where this bottle lies. Maybe it is over the hill. But maybe, as it is a wine of the South and so used to heat anyway, and as it is red (white wines, which rely on cooler temperatures than reds to shine, had a difficult time in 2003), maybe it will have survived well. Try it one midweek evening, with sausages.

A quick word about hierarchy in the South: it is easy (if easily misleading). Imagine a pyramid with three tiers. At the bottom is straight Cotes-du- Rhône, a familiar moniker if ever there was one. Next up is Cotes-du-Rhône-Villages, as with this Beaumes-de-Venise, where the wine must come from a specified village and meet tighter production controls than generic Cotes-du- Rhône. At the top of the pyramid are the wines from specified villages that can simply trade under the name of the village. Since 2003 Beaumes-de-Venise has been promoted to this status and so would now simply be labelled Beaumes-de-Venise, losing the Cotes-du-Rhône-Villages description. Again, there are tighter controls on production, designed to protect the reputation of the village and of the other villages entitled to their own appellation. The most famous village entitled to its own appellation is of course Châteauneuf-du-Pape, closely followed by Gigondas and a host of others now, including Lirac and Vacqueyras, all producing wines worthy of attention, so long as they never lose sight of course of the need for love.

Lirac Blanc, Reine des Bois, Domaine de la Mordorée 2014

This wine has got me thinking about the nature of immortality, well this wine and Raphael. Which is curious.

This summer we went on a tour of the Vatican Museum, a quite horrendous tour, the crowds even outnumbering the exhaustive exhibits on show. There was barely room to move in some places, perhaps no more so than in the Raphael Rooms, rooms commissioned by Pope Julius II and which hold some of the artist's best-known work. These rooms, along with the Sistine

Chapel, are what most of the visitors will have come along to see. Undoubtedly one of Raphael's most famous paintings is the School of Athens, a montage of great thinkers from history, all involved in debate or expostulation. Tucked into the corner of this fresco is a self-portrait of the artist as one of the crowd listening to Ptolemy's discussions with Zoroaster. Not only did Raphael want others to see his work, it turns out, he wanted them to know what he looked like as well. Was Raphael unsure of this inclusion? The look on his face suggests so, as he peers out slightly sheepishly and follows the viewer around the room with a surreptitious look.

Why did he do this? Was it to secure immortality? In a moment of uncertainty, was he not confident that the skill of his hand and the artistry of his vision would achieve this? And what is immortality? Is it simply being remembered or is it to live beyond death by influencing or determining the thoughts and actions of the living? Raphael may have wanted us to know what he looked like but, even without this, he is still, through his painting, directing us to look at what he wants us to see and to consider what he wants us to think. From beyond the grave, the writer with his book, the artist with his painting, the architect with his building, the composer with his music is as influential and listened to as if alive. One day even Raphael will pass from human consciousness, and his rooms and frescoes will turn to dust, but the ability to fix human expression (which is what I assume art is) allows the artist an audience beyond his years.

Might a winemaker feel the same way? Is he an artist who will leave a legacy that will affect how we the consumers think or view things? Might he, the winemaker, manipulate our own thoughts the way a poet or a painter might? It is the winemaker, after all, who determines the nature of the wine and who will, for better or for worse, determine our reaction and influence our thoughts (even our outlook) when we drink his wine.

These idle thoughts have crossed my idle mind this summer as we have embarked on this case. And the reason for this is because this is the last vintage that Christophe Delorme produced before he died of a heart attack, aged 52, in June 2015. Not that he will have had a chance to reflect on this but it is, I hope, a thought that gives comfort to other winemakers as they confront the final question, that they might leave a legacy and that others might know their character without actually knowing them, in itself a form of immortality. Their gift to the world will outlive them, perhaps for many decades, not for as long as Raphael maybe but, in certain cases, for generations. Their gift is unfixable in words or pigment but no less valid for that.

And so each time we open a bottle, I offer a nod of gratitude to all the Christophe Delormes, Denis Dubourdieus, Serge Hochars and others of the world who have peddled this particular happiness for our benefit. I did not know Christophe Delorme, I never met him but through this wine, through his art, I am connected to him, however briefly.

As for the wine, this Lirac Blanc is a cornucopia of Southern white varieties, including meaningful amounts of Viognier (more commonly found in the North) and Marsanne (likewise). Chemotherapy means I cannot discern the more subtle flavours on offer but in the past this wine has been positively bursting in flavour – "smokin' white!" one reviewer has it down as so it should perform well. I am always astonished how much freshness can be preserved in these Southern Rhône whites. As I said, I am not their biggest fan but, drunk in youth, there can be a vibrancy and vigour which is quite disarming.

Two other points:

1. Whites from the Southern Rhône have a curious habit of going into a sulk for a few years if not drunk young. If this happens with the Lirac, put it away at the back of the cellar and revisit in a few years. The wine might have recovered its emotional joy, in which case good, or it might not have, in which case risotto.

2. Don't ask me why but Southern Rhône whites seem to go particularly well with tomatoes. In fact, you might say that tomatoes are the best reason for Southern Rhône whites. Given that tomatoes bring out the worst in most wines, this is worth remembering.

Lirac, Reine des Bois, Domaine de la Mordorée 2007
Lirac, Reine des Bois, Domaine de la Mordorée 2010

Twice we stayed here, or was it three times? We would take the morning train from London, direct through to Avignon. Across the deep green of Picardy, we would whistle through the Western Front, pocket cemeteries of Portland stone silently remonstrating remembrance, and on past Paris in the distance. The only vines we would see were those sheltering beneath Solutré and Vergisson just shy of Mâcon. We would then shadow the Rhône off to the west until emerging into the valley. Grey would give way to ochre, rolling fields to scrub, oak to cypress, mute to bright.

We stayed in an old mill house outside St-Laurent-des-Arbres, our room lying directly above the channelled, tamed stream, its sole purpose now a mirror to the sky. In the dead of day, the heat lay heavy, a proper Southern warmth. We would lie by the pool, cold-blooded refugees, recharging on rest and silence.

Except, if I cared to listen, the silence was none such. Cicadas relentlessly drilled holes in the air and Golden Orioles occasionally dropped their liquid call from the poplars. Leaves rattled gently, distant tambourines persistently worried by the insistent warm breeze. Not much else stirred. Even the deep blue of the morning sky was exhausted by the sun, washed pale with a high skein of transparent cirrus.

Why I chose to put down my book and scan the empty sky I do not know. Maybe I was too hemmed in by the claustrophobia of the castaways in Jamrach's Menagerie, maybe I had been subliminally distracted by movement off the page. I lifted my binoculars and high above me, impossibly high above me, a constant stream of Honey Buzzards glided south, carried on a current of beneficent air, the birds motionless, the high wind carrying them at breathtaking speed on their migratory journey to Africa. These birds kept the metronome of the season just as the cicadas did likewise of the day below. Life goes on everywhere and we never realise, each of us engaged in our own private narrative.

Some days we would bicycle to Lirac and then to Tavel to the south, the sun on our faces on the way, on the napes of our neck on our return. Scarce Swallowtails would shepherd us the length of the roadside vineyards before veering off and disappearing into flower-choked ditches where the vines gave way to trees. We would sit in empty bars, drinking citron pressé, quietly planning how to fill the rest of those silent days.

I have always had a soft spot for Domaine de la Mordorée, if only on account of the fact that all their labels sport woodcock and the names of their cuvées are all different words for woodcock – Mordorée, then La Dame Rousse and, for their top wines, La Reine des Bois, the Queen of the Woods. Even La Plume du Peintre, their ultra-rare accomplished Châteauneuf-du-Pape references the woodcock (a small delicate feather taken from the woodcock's wing, perfect by all accounts for watercolourists). So I was just a little disappointed, when we visited, to catch one of the Delorme brothers who run the domaine (at least until Christophe's tragically early death in 2015) on an obviously bad day. He was rushed, arrogant, pleased with himself, uninterested, all of which made his ambition, at other times no doubt laudable, naked and hard-edged. Lack of humility was verging on hubris.

I have said before there is little objective about a love of wine. Did this visit colour my subsequent enjoyment of the Domaine's wines? Weak as it sounds to say so, I suspect it has. The 2007 should be a lovely wine, born of a soft generous vintage which delivered pleasure from the start. But I have always found the 2007 tough going. I have imputed it with too much ambition, the hand of the winemaker forcing the wine to go faster and further than it wanted to. Despite its modern polished sheen, it has a hard edge, maybe the result of the alcohol being out of kilter with the fruit which is not as warm as it should be – a cool reticence fully to engage and share of itself. I like to think I have been patient with the wine and have waited for it to unravel but, well, maybe we were just never bound to be happy bedfellows.

2010 is a legendary vintage in the Southern Rhône. I suspect this will be a legendary bottle one day but no rush – like all so-called legendary vintages, you need time on your hands if you are to benefit from it. Wait a good while.

Vacqueyras, Cuvée Floureto, Sang des Cailloux 2007
Vacqueyras, Cuvée Floureto, Sang des Cailloux 2010

By contrast, and although I have never met the man, I imagine that Serge Ferigoule, the owner of Sang des Cailloux, must be one of the warmest people on Planet Earth. I make this ridiculous claim on three grounds – his moustache, which is absurdly life-enhancing and smile-inducing, the fact that he names his wine after his three daughters (Floureto, Doucinello, Azalaïs), rotating the name each year, and thirdly, the fact that his wine is quite so brilliant and filled with love. I recall serving the wine at a dinner party once and one of the guests, Marcus, interrupting the conversation to exclaim how wonderful the wine was. Of course, that made me proud as a host but even more than that it pleased me that someone else had discovered the magic that lies in these bottles. Often enough you will receive approving murmurings about how lovely the wine is but rarely if ever has a wine stopped a conversation like this. I am constantly reminded of this when I think of this wine and I constantly smile at the memory. This is the gift that wine can bring.

Vacqueyras lies high up on the eastern side of the Rhône Valley. In my experience it has been a constant source of pleasure, the wines not as baked as some you find on the valley floor. 2007 was a great success here. Not that it has bothered me, but our case has had a lot of trapped carbon dioxide in the bottles. Not enough to make it exciting (unanticipated explosions from the cellar past midnight) but enough to need to do something before drinking the wine. Decant it and, if you are in a hurry, bash it about a bit, with a wooden spoon or even a thumb over the top of the decanter (or bottle if you have double-decanted it) and a shake. You will then be rewarded with something lighter and brighter than Châteauneuf-du-Pape, less malt, more raspberry, more song.

I have not tried the 2010 but I suspect it will come round sooner than the Lirac Mordorée (and quite possibly deliver more love). Give it another couple of years.

Gigondas, Domaine du Cayron 2007
Gigondas, Domaine Santa Roc 2012

As with most things, I suppose, you can make as much or as little as you want of wine. At one end of the spectrum you might have no more interest in the subject than to be sure that you like the taste of what you are drinking and, if you do, going no further than repeatedly buying the same wine to ensure you repeatedly enjoy the same pleasure. Nothing wrong with that. At the other end of the spectrum, each cork pulled promises a new world, a new landscape, a new experience to add those that have gone before, a new memory to add to the bank for that particular wine, style, grape, vintage, whatever. And that leads you on. You then want to know why this wine is different to the one tasted before and you are sucked in, on an endless fascinating journey.

Take Gigondas as an example. You might just be happy to know, as with Vacqueyras, that the village lies high up on the eastern side of the valley (you might not even be interested to know that) and that because of the altitude the grapes ripen a full 3 or 4 weeks later than in Châteauneuf-du-Pape down on the plain. Or you may want to know more than that, that the village boundaries take in any number of different terrains, low-lying garrigue with marl and clay to the west, up through the limestone and marl surrounding the village to the steep parts of pure limestone beneath the Dentelles de Montmirail (we walked here once across slopes of rosemary, holm oaks and Aleppo pines) and even beyond these jagged peaks to the sandy soil of the hinterland beyond. And you may then want to know what effect all these different climates and terrains have on the wine (they do make a big difference), who produces what, are the wines best blended or bottled separately? Whole books have been written on the subject. You can take it as far as you want, or not at all. The only restraint is the time on your hands (and conceivably the depth of your wallet if your interest is particularly piqued by Vosne-Romanée).

This to me is one of the great pleasures of wine. Drinking wine is, for many of us, an everyday occurrence but one which can provide endless intellectual and physical stimulation (for the sheer pleasure of it). Many years ago, a work colleague and I were musing on the endless cups of tea that we were unthinkingly drinking each day. Is this all we could do? Unthinkingly drink endless cups of the same unidentifiable anonymous tea day in day out? Why did we not know more about what we were drinking? Why did we not know more about what we were putting into our bodies? Were our minds really that unenquiring? We resolved to change. We learnt our Darjeeling, our Yunnan, Assam, Ceylon Orange Pekoe, our Kenyan, our Russian Caravan and our Lapsang Souchong and would test each other each day. It brought an interest that previously wasn't there, an interest that I have not lost and which informs each cup of tea that I am offered. Admittedly, I have not taken this interest in tea any further but I know that for many this is only the beginning of the journey and that tea, like wine, is a source of endless fascination.

Which maybe has little to do with Gigondas.

Cayron: Summer pudding. The wine bursts with such fresh flavours. Whenever I drink this wine I do wonder if the world would not be a better place if it was not run by women. This domaine is now run by the Faraud sisters and they have such a sure accomplished hand in what they produce that I immediately feel reassured and safe in their hands. The wine has typicity and such honesty and, being 2007, such welcome. I fear there is only one bottle left; drink it now.

Santa Roc: this is one of the most exciting wines I bought last year. It is the product of a joint venture between Santa Duc, one of Gigondas' leading players, producing powerful, substantial wines filled with intent and statement, and Roc d'Anglade, a new domaine from the Languedoc run by Rémy Pedreno, a computer analyst in a former life. Two things you need to know: first, Gigondas is, or should be, all about freshness. Because the grapes are grown at altitude, they escape the relentless attention of the Midi sun and, ripening late in the season, retain an element of acidity that keeps the wine on its toes. Secondly, Rémy Pedreno's passion (and he means it: I once spoke to him about it and I have never heard a man articulate the word "passion", well, with such passion – the sibilant "ss" positively fizzed out of his mouth) is for a lightness of touch in his wines, a digestibility so that the wines can be drunk and enjoyed rather than ploughed through. So this joint venture was an intriguing experiment – the powerhouse of one allied with the legerdemain of the other. And it works. It works brilliantly. The wine is (as I said on my own cellartracker note) bright and sappy, almost translucent. It is a companion, not a competition. A sure-fire winner.

There are only a few bottles of these wines left. Enjoy them now.

Domaine du Vieux Télégraphe, Châteauneuf-du-Pape 1995
Domaine du Vieux Télégraphe, Châteauneuf-du-Pape 1998
Domaine du Vieux Télégraphe, Châteauneuf-du-Pape 2000
Domaine du Vieux Télégraphe, Châteauneuf-du-Pape 2001
Domaine du Vieux Télégraphe, Châteauneuf-du-Pape 2003
Domaine du Vieux Télégraphe, Châteauneuf-du-Pape 2004
Domaine du Vieux Télégraphe, Châteauneuf-du-Pape 2005
Domaine du Vieux Télégraphe, Châteauneuf-du-Pape 2006

Domaine du Vieux Télégraphe, Châteauneuf-du-Pape 2010
Clos des Papes, Châteauneuf-du-Pape 1998
Clos du Mont Olivet, Châteauneuf-du-Pape 2010
Piedlong, Châteauneuf-du-Pape 2012

Galets roulés. The archetypal image to emanate from Châteauneuf-du-Pape, well that and the ruined "new castle" that Pope John XXII commissioned in 1317 which remained largely intact until the Germans, in their wisdom, decided to blow it up on their retreat in August 1944. Galets roulés, the large, sometimes very large, rounded stones washed down from the Alps in an altogether more violent age millions of years ago. These stones cover large parts of the appellation (and others, such as Lirac) – it is said that in high summer they reach such a heat that you can fry an egg on them. And at night-time, like storage heaters, they return the heat from the day.

We walked by the castle and across the galets roulés of the neighbouring vineyard. I was keen to take a stone home with me and we weighed up a number before settling on one, wondering how much I would regret it as we dragged our suitcase back north to London the following day.

That evening we stayed in Châteauneuf for supper, in a restaurant recommended by John, outside, among trees and under the stars. A travelling flamenco band was installed for the evening and we sat in happy silence listening to the band blister out their frenetic tunes. In silence or in nonsense chatter – "who think the same thoughts without need of speech / who babble the same thoughts without need of meaning".

I brought the stone home. Reassuringly dense, the curve of the stone rests neatly, perfectly, in the cradle of my hand, one side a little straighter as if to perfect the grip of my fingers around its girth. Feeling its weight lends me a certainty, David's certainty against Goliath. Apart from one or two minor snicks and blemishes, it is perfectly smooth, washed and weathered by the elements of millennia. It sits on top of the cellar books in the bookshelf; it even makes a small imprint on the cover of the top one. Washed up on a new foreign shore in its travel through time.

I am in two minds about Châteauneuf-du-Pape. In its pursuit for perfection (laudable), is it losing its way (regrettable)? Is it trying too hard and losing its identity and purpose in the process? Luckily there are enough growers in the appellation to ensure that this never does happen but there have been enough trophy bottlings and price hikes in the last 15 years to make it a concern, at least for uninformed amateurs like myself who ultimately judge what they drink by what is in the bottle and the price they pay.

What should Châteauneuf-du-Pape be about? For me, it should be about the bottle of Clos du Mont Olivet 1989 that we had down at Rachel and Hugh's (again) all those years ago, about an unbridled gift of warmth and texture, an abundance of poached fruit, soft sides, generous alcohol in balance, the heat of the sun and the texture of evening. It should not be too cerebral, it should not be unbalanced by alcohol, it should not be ambitious beyond the bounty that nature has bestowed on it (which is quite ambitious enough). It should not be rare, it should not be (overly) expensive. It should be about giving. That for me is what Châteauneuf-du-Pape should be about. That is the DNA of the wine. There are plenty of other wine styles around France and the world to satisfy all the other criteria but I am not sure anywhere else does Châteauneuf quite like Châteauneuf can.

The upsurge in global wealth which has been so welcome in

resurrecting the world's wine industries also has its downside as producers seek to push the envelope ever further, producing ever more exclusive cuvées and adopting ever more stringent practices in the vineyard and cellar. It is the law of diminishing returns – do these cuvées and practices really make all the difference the prices demanded for the wines look to justify? Beyond a certain degree, I would say not. Heavy bottles, heavy wines, thumping alcohol, thumping prices. Modesty and, among some, honesty have their place and it is to the growers who exercise both that we should all be turning.

Vieux Télégraphe: despite my wide-ranging ignorance, I had actually heard of Vieux Télégraphe when, in 1997, I made my first venture into the Rhône and bought a case to lay down. And look at the plans I have had for it since then! Ah well, of mice and men. I had heard of it, yes, and I also liked the label: heavy gothic script showing permanence and purpose. To show my hand completely, I am a sucker for a pretty label – you may laugh, but it is all part of the aesthetic experience that wine delivers. And, what is more, the wine was cheap (£112 a case).

And now? And now I have stopped buying it. It has simply become too expensive and (really, this is probably heresy) having tasted several vintages, I am not sure it is Châteauneuf in the mould I like. It is a beautifully structured wine, almost like a claret sometimes, it is demanding, it is cerebral, it requires concentration and it has a strong flavour of malt and licorice (for so long I did not know what "réglisse" meant – I do now). But it is never an easy wine. It is not the Mont Olivet 1989 that wrapped itself around me and told me all would be alright. It is asking as much what you can do for it as what it can do for you. And the price now – north of £350 a case. I am not sure that is right.

But look at all the vintages we have! This is another feature common to wine collectors: once you have started collecting a particular wine, when do you stop? There is an unnatural fear at work that if you get off the bike you will miss quite possibly the best vintage of all for that wine. And what if, in future years, the wine you have started collecting becomes your very best wine or the world wakes up to what you have known all along, prices sky-rocket and there is suddenly a gaping hole where should have been the 2007? Insecurities such as these drive the wine collector just as much as they do anyone else in any other sphere of life. But in the end, I did stop. What of the ones we do have?

1995 – the year we were married. I have been reluctant to finish the case. The wine was tough to begin with, malt and iodine laced with fire. Even seaweed (Robert Parker is right about this). It has now settled down beautifully, softer fruits presenting a gentler profile.

1998 – a great vintage for Vieux Télégraphe, so much so that I have been hesitant in drinking it too quickly (more fool me). I first tried it in 2002, at the hands of Daniel Brunier himself. "At the beginning of its long life" he absent-mindedly mused as he poured. The last bottle we had, I see, was in March 2012 would you believe it, pulled out of the cellar without fanfare or forethought to accompany a Saturday lunchtime Spaghetti Bolognese. And wonderful it was. And will remain. A strong Grenache vintage. There is another lesson here: management of expectations. Don't always stand on ceremony with a good bottle. Catch it unawares. Act on the spur of the moment and pull the cork on a fine bottle without preparation or anticipation. Live in the moment with it and chances are that the wine will be at least as enjoyable as if you had planned the evening carefully around the bottle. The less expectation...

2000 – easy to love all along. As is often the case, the slightly less than stellar vintage has produced wines less hefty and extracted than normal and so all the more delicious for it.

2001 – a lighter vintage, very classical, balanced, measured. Some would damn it for this (in this age of absolutes and accumulation) but I do not. In fact, I have discovered the wine benefits from decanting. Give it an hour to breath, to stretch its legs and the wine fills out beautifully.

2003 – the heatwave vintage. Châteauneuf-du-Pape is used to heat so, as is to be expected, coped better than other regions. You can still taste it though – the fruit is a little heavier, sweeter (overripe?), the alcohol a little heavier, the tannins a little tougher (they did not have time to ripen properly if the grapes were to be picked before they had turned into raisins). But I am not complaining. It is still very good wine.

And the rest? Untried. 2004 I suspect will play in a minor key, maybe in the mould of 2001. 2005 promises to be a very strong vintage but, like most 2005s, will be slow to yield its charms. 2006 is probably a richer 2001, I am not sure, but you will find it at the back of the cellar, behind the Christmas decorations, in the wooden Vieux Télégraphe 1995 case (the 2006 arrived in an assortment of cardboard so I decanted the bottles into a case prepared earlier). And the 2010, purchased after I had resolved to give up on Vieux Télégraphe? Well, you know, because 2010 is meant to be such a strong vintage in the Rhône (1978 again, according to Jonathan Livingston-Learmonth) and Vieux Télégraphe nailed it, absolutely nailed it, that year and, well, Vieux Télégraphe is after all such a lovely wine, despite what I have said and sometimes think, and I have been following it for so long it feels part of me and yes, it is such a lovely label and, well, really I should know better but…

Clos des Papes: only the one vintage here, 1998. Purchased before the price of Clos des Papes catapaulted to such ridiculous heights. A similar appeal to Vieux Télégraphe, in fact, in that the Avrils do not produce a premium cuvée, heavy on extract, ambition and price, and so the flagship wine is the estate wine. And what a beauty it is. I read one tasting note which suggested that it was Pomerol-esque. Maybe. It is soft and round, beguiling and becoming. Gentle but with a hidden punch. Pure, with a consistent thread of truth running from beginning to end. Glorious wine. A lovely wine to follow if you have deep pockets. A wine to drink now.

On one occasion when we visited Châteauneuf-du-Pape, we sat out and ate lunch in the central square. It was hot. The sun cast only small, pitiless shadows. But that did not stop me ordering a glass of red Châteauneuf with my lunch and I was delivered of a very private epiphany. The miracle that is wine (and it is a miracle, born of starlight, water and rock through the medium of the vine) found its most natural expression that day in the glass of blood-dark wine in front of me. The wine gathered within itself the brightness of the light and the intensity of the heat that surrounded me. It expressed in a more forceful way than I have otherwise encountered its origins and its roots in the bedrock beneath me and, by extension, the elemental forces that shape us all. Serge Férigoule's Vacqueyras is called the blood of stones — it is precisely that. And every once in a while it pays to drink these deep reds in the height of the noonday sun, to be reminded of their origin and, more than this, to reconnect, to recreate that atavistic link with Mother Earth. Trust me, it does.

Clos du Mont Olivet: so apart from that wobble with the 2010 Vieux Télégraphe, I resolved to spread my wings and consider other wines from Châteauneuf-du-Pape. And the obvious solution was Clos du Mont Olivet. And I have not been disappointed. The wine is still young (thick, liquorous and sweet) but even now I can detect common traits with the 1989 in terms of flavour, texture, warmth and love. You may even call it jam. Critics will be cruel and damn it with such a description. I don't. I like a bit of jam in my Châteauneuf. Not much, but a little is just fine. Leave the wine a while. It will deliver in spades. It is beautiful.

Piedlong: the important thing to do is keep your head down and keep going. Come 2012 and come a new wine in the Brunier stable. If I was going to desert Vieux Télégraphe, I could at least retain some sense of loyalty and belonging by buying from the same producer at, needless to say, slightly less of a cost.

The topography of Châteauneuf-du-Pape is complicated. Vieux Télégraphe comes from a large plateau, to the east of the town, called La Crau. The surface is covered by galets roulés and, a couple of metres down, a large bed of clay which retains moisture during the dry summer months. It is, by all accounts, almost the perfect terroir. But not all the finest wines in the appellation come from it. To the north and west of the town the soil is a mix of sand and limestone which lends its own flavour profile (Château Rayas, perhaps the most famous of all the Châteauneufs, is grown almost exclusively on sandy soil). And this wine is the product of two sites, Piedlong and Pignan, situated on this sandier soil. It promises a softer wine than Vieux Télégraphe, more gentle fruits than malt and licorice. Maybe this is the answer? Perhaps we will find out together or perhaps you will have to tell me one day. No rush though.

PROVENCE

Bandol Rosé, Domaine Tempier 2014

When God created Perfect, he created the Luberon. I think this has to be right. I cannot think of another place on God's earth where the good (the great) things in life are so aligned. Natural wonder, a gentle climate, culture, peace and beauty, an environment utterly beneficent and beneficial to man – really, can anywhere else match it?

We spent four days there in that wonderful villa in the lee of the Grand Luberon, with John and Sally and their family. We drank like royalty – Tempier, Clos des Papes, Ramonet, maybe even my beloved Mugneret. We swam, the sun shone relentlessly, we walked through kind meadows of thyme and fritillaries, bee-eaters hawked overhead, days were filled with the devotion to pleasure. We visited nearby villages, sometimes on foot, and rested beneath ancient plane trees with demi-pressions. In the evening the land breathed back the fire of the day and we ate outside, wrapped in the warmth of friendship and rosé, endless glorious rosé, the essence of summer's sanctuary. Those four days, we were running with the very grain of the universe.

More than anything, rosé is a mirror. It reflects the mood of its drinker more faithfully than any other wine. It does not impose itself but instead let's you, the drinker, impute the wine with flavour and purpose. So sometimes you will get nothing, or little, from a glass of rosé (if you are down, the weather is poor, the company is poorer); at other times, in fact most of the time given people tend to drink rosé only when the mood takes them, you will get a fix of sunshine, of love and laughter, of carefree attitudes and an overwhelming feeling of all being right in the world. What a wonderfully beautiful wine it is.

And none better, many would argue, than Tempier's rosé from Bandol. Before you have even pulled the cork, the clear bottle, the ever-so-slightly crushed strawberry tinge of the wine and the iconic naïve label of a round-bottomed caravel with two masts and billowing sails (and fleur-de-lys in place of stars to steer her by) draws you in. And the wine itself delivers in spades – the freshness of snapped celery, a sparkle, a crunch delivered by the Mourvèdre – well then, all really is well with the world. The wine does not lose that freshness, either. In fact, you could argue that the wine is better for an extra year in bottle, to allow the fruit to mellow and establish itself over the sheer brightness of the wine. But then the next year's allocation arrives and you think it properly is time to be cracking on. A breath of life, a breath of sheer unadulterated life. A whole happy case is there; enjoy it this year, even next if needs be.

Bandol, Cuvée Classique, Domaine Tempier 2004
Bandol, Cuvée Classique, Domaine Tempier 2006
Bandol, Cuvée Classique, Domaine Tempier 2010
Bandol, Cuvée Classique, Domaine Tempier 2011
Bandol, La Tourtine, Domaine Tempier 2012
Bandol, La Tourtine, Domaine Tempier 2013
Bandol, La Tourtine, Domaine Tempier 2014

I have such a soft spot for Domaine Tempier. The label, the memories that its rosé has given me, the fact that I was first put on to the domaine by what is undoubtedly the finest book that has ever been written about wine, Kermit Lynch's Adventures on the Wine Route. If you have not read it, you must. The book is filled with passion, with a search for authenticity in a France increasingly drawn (at the time of writing, in the 1980's) towards mass production and uniformity in its wines. The author is tireless in his pursuit of capturing (or rather capturing the winemakers who capture) as much of the natural grape in the bottle as possible. He rails against pesticides, against excessive interference in the cellar, against filtration before bottling, against other than domaine bottling, against unrefrigerated transport. He is on a crusade and, in his travels, meets the greats of the French wine world, the Clapes, the Chaves, the Bruniers, the Jobards, the Raveneaus, the Joguets and, at Tempier, the Peyrauds. It is the most remarkable book (with beautifully atmospheric photographs taken by his wife) and, of course, much of what Kermit Lynch was fighting for in the 1980's is now considered to be best and often standard practice.

Some would say that Lucien Peyraud single-handedly saved the appellation of Bandol from the property developers of the mid-century who were covering the Azur coast with holiday homes. Whether it was single-handedly or not, we have all benefited from his efforts for Bandol is one of the noblest crus in the south of France. Its chief component, its DNA, is Mourvèdre, a wine that, in its youth, is difficult, tannic and structured, but that mellows in age into gentle overtones of tobacco, leather and soft fruits. It is a grape, it is said, that must have its head in the sun and its feet in the water, a hot climate with water-retentive soils, so not the easiest combination. And what I have always loved about Bandol is that I have never been able to pinpoint its flavour, I have never been able properly to remember what it tastes like so each time I pull a cork it is almost like the first time. This is almost unique. For most wines I have a very good memory and, for whatever reason I do not know (a gift? Unlikely; most likely, an interest), for most wines I can recall their flavour, even many years after having drunk them. Bandol eludes me every time. It is complicated, a tangle of competing tastes which nevertheless seam easily into a gorgeous whole, dark, with many corners and different facets.

Needless to say, it speaks of the sun.

The current winemaker is Daniel Ravier, an utterly accomplished vigneron and an utterly dangerous driver. When we were staying in the Luberon, we visited the domaine (well, not you; you sensibly decided to remain by the pool for the day). The four men of the party, John, his future son-in-law, a friend of his and me, drove down to the coast early one morning after a big night. At this stage of the day, I think it is fair to say none of us were relishing the prospect of the visit. There remained in our systems enough unprocessed wine to carry us through at least until lunchtime. But things soon changed, of course they always do. We were soon out of the indecently bright light and down into the cellar, Daniel pulling samples of what must have been the 2011 vintage out of the vast foudres lining the walls. The young wine, full of vigour and bursting with growth, restored our humour and our faith, the cool of the cellars calming our troubled constitutions.

For whatever reason the conversation turned to Kermit Lynch and here Daniel Ravier was reminded of something Kermit had shown him on his last visit to the domaine. Daniel disappeared into the recesses of the cellar and emerged with a venerable bottle that had clearly served its time in the dark. He brought it out carefully, upright, ensuring the sediment that had gathered at the bottom of the bottle did not mix with the wine. Hiding the label, he pulled the cork and asked us to hazard the year and the cuvée. The year? The wine had that lovely soft wood varnish flavour of old wine, delicate, precious. I forget what year and cuvée combination I suggested but clearly both will have been wrong. From recollection, it was a Migoua 1990. In any event, however, what Daniel then did was fascinating. He put his thumb over the neck of the bottle and tipped the bottle up and down a couple of times to mix the sediment with the wine. He then waited a short moment to allow the worst of the sediment to sink and then repoured. The wine was transformed. Gone was the fragile dame of a 25-year old wine. In our glasses was an entirely different beast, a wine of vigour and of body, mature for certain but with a life to it that I would never have guessed. How absolutely fascinating. Maybe James Symington is right after all. Maybe sediment hides some of the life of a wine and should not be so quickly discarded. That is where our bones lie, and maybe our stories too. It is certainly a lesson worth remembering.

The driving comment. Ah yes, after the cellar visit, Daniel said he would treat us to lunch in Sanary-sur-Mer. We bundled into his car and he set off like a demon. I say "set off"; the fact of the matter is he kept going like a demon. It was lucky this was not a journey undertaken a couple of hours earlier but our constitutions had now been fortified by all we had consumed (the human body really is a remarkable thing). We lunched by the sea, in a room framed by expansive windows. We ate sea bass cooked in salt and drank others' rosé, not the domaine's, Daniel obviously keen to keep an eye on the opposition while appreciating the gifts others can bring. In the bay, large aeroplanes practised flying low and picking up sea water. They flew in long, lazy circles, jettisoning the water that would normally be dropped over forest fires, before coming in again on a low run to practise the procedure once more. We returned to the domaine. Daniel's mean cruising speed was not tempered by the sea bass or the rosé and we made the journey back in even, or quite possibly quicker, time.

The wines? Bandol ages superbly so there is no rush with any of these. I have not tried other than the 2004 which is a joy and, in the best sense, a mystery on account of my goldfish-like inability to recall what it tasted like last time. The Cuvée Classique is largely Mourvèdre and so age favours it, dissipating the surliness, mellowing its taciturn outlook, draping its structure in cloths of gold. Vintage matters less this far south and so I am sure 2006, 2010 and 2011 will all be equally good.

Beyond the Classique, Tempier makes three other cuvées of red – Migoua, Tourtine and Cabassou. We emerged from the cellar and, looking out across the Plan de Castellet, Daniel pointed out, in the distance, the vineyards which produce these three wines. Migoua has a greater degree of Cinsault in the blend so is rounder and less austere than the Tourtine which can have an even higher proportion of Mourvèdre than the Classique. Cabassou, which comes from a small area of vines within the Tourtine vineyards (Daniel pointed out the shallow terraces in the distance), is so exclusive that Daniel says he rarely gets to try it either. So it is irrelevant for our purposes. La Tourtine – three six-packs, 18 green bottles sitting on the wall. I love La Tourtine, its straight lines and academic poise, but these three vintages are young. Time will need to temper them and then the heat will fade and maybe smoke and leather will wrap around a pastille core. Look at the drinking dates in the cellar book! You may wonder what on earth I was doing buying these wines. To chase life is the answer, because every now and then you can catch it.

FAUGERES

Western Orphean Warbler. Maybe something of a specialist subject. Our paths have only crossed once, when its white eye set in its black executioner's hood surprised me, not more than 10 feet away, when I opened the morning blinds in our villa in Ronda some 20 years ago. Until I heard one, as we walked back down the hill into Faugères in May last year, on the outskirts of the village, deep in a garden behind a thick hedge.

I tried to call it out, playing its song back to it, but it would not budge. It shrank deeper into the dark garden, its call determined and protective. Unlike all the other birds that day. Life was at work and creation was in full flow. We had climbed the hill above the village to a windmill which gave a view away to the south towards Béziers and the sea. Subalpine Warblers chattered indignantly in the short oaks, Common Whitethroats joined the chorus from the scrub below, Chiffchaffs and Willow Warblers sprinkled song randomly over the cacophony. Rain threatened but it could not suppress our spirits or, manifestly, the spirits of those around us.

We had come to Faugères to visit Domaine Alquier, unannounced and without an appointment because, if I am honest, I am not sure what I would say to him. We continued our walk down into the village. We stopped at a wine shop which showcased the wines of the village but Jean-Michel's wines were not on offer, only those of his brother Frédéric. We continued through the village and I knocked on the door of Domaine Alquier. No response. I knocked again, half-heartedly. No answer. We left. Sans visite, sans dégustation, sans vins.

What would I have asked, what could I have asked, Jean-Michel Alquier if he had answered the door? I felt all the answers lay in the bottle and that I would have been no more than an impostor wasting this magician's time. I was secretly quite relieved at the tomb-like silence behind the domaine door that met my repeated knockings.

Les Bastides, Faugères, Domaine Alquier 2000
Les Bastides, Faugères, Domaine Alquier 2001
Les Bastides, Faugères, Domaine Alquier 2004
Les Bastides, Faugères, Domaine Alquier 2005

Les Bastides, Faugères, Domaine Alquier 2007

Not for all the tea in China would I be a winegrower in the Languedoc. This is not to do a disservice to the likes of Alquier or Rémy Pedreno or Gérard Gauby (OK, technically in the Rousillon) or all the other giants of the wine world who fashion exquisite, characterful, ageworthy wines down there. It is, on the contrary, precisely because of that. Without a famous region to back up your (hoped to be) famous wine, it must be the devil's own job to make a name and a market for your produce. And if you are not an Alquier, a Pedreno or a Gauby? We drove through seas of vines last May, all on flat featureless plains, all I assume destined for the local co-operatives (some good, some less so). If Bordeaux remains the largest wine region in France in terms of area, I am not sure that the Languedoc is not the largest in terms of production, much of it mediocre and so much of it hiding the genuine efforts of the minority who strive to produce the best they possibly can. Which means the secret (so as much for the producer in this case as it is for the consumer) is to find a good importer or wine merchant who can raise your wine above the parapet and help it to fly.

Or maybe this is just a snapshot of the times in which we live. Maybe, just as other wine regions of France have benefited from peace and increased global prosperity, the Languedoc will also flourish. There is certainly greater attention paid to the region now than, say, 50 years ago, not only on account of the steeply rising prices of the traditional fine wine regions, which have forced exploration elsewhere, but also because of a dawning awareness that conscientious growers can produce noteworthy wines in the Languedoc; the region is no longer the preserve of the mass producer of plonk for supermarkets and bars that in the past it has been. And coupled with this attention comes the increased understanding that, yes, certain areas of the Languedoc stand out as producing particularly good wines, often high up, away from the sun-baked plains, on the hard-to-work hillsides where vines struggle to dig deep enough through the rock to survive, where night-time temperatures temper the vine's growth and nurture the grapes' measured development. Jean-Michel Alquier remembers his father forcing him, as a child and as a young man, to smash rocks by hand so that he could plant vines in propitious soil.

These appellations are slowly emerging. Some have been around a long time, some are only now being delineated. Maybe in 50 years' time all the hard work will have paid off and the Languedoc appellations on the label will be as marketable as those, say, from the Southern Rhône. Until then, there is hard work to be done.

Faugères is maybe luckier than some. It is an established appellation, well since 1982 at least, and it is a small and compact area with a clear identity, based as much as anything on its schistous soil (good for grapes: it adds a degree of definition). It is also an appellation blessed with good and ambitious winegrowers, a number of whom have found a ready market in the rest of Europe. I was first put on to Alquier by the Wine Society, backed up by a glowing report on the domaine in Norman Remington's Rhône Renaissance, a great book if you can still find it. The wines appealed to me – they were relatively inexpensive, they were unsung and they were the product of hard labour, passion and belief. It was long after I had bought the first few vintages of these wines that I even first tried them.

Jean-Michel Alquier produces two principal cuvées of red, one Grenache dominant (La Maison Jaune) and one comprised of 80% Syrah, Les Bastides. I am sorry not to have followed the domaine since the 2007 vintage. Why not? Head turned by other more glamorous appellations? Shame on me. The wines are remarkable in their intensity, their polish, the finery of their tannins. Being predominantly Syrah, Norman Remington likens Les Bastides to Côte-Rôtie. I don't see that. Instead, silly as this might sound, I am reminded of a grand cru from the Côte de Nuits. There is no wildness there, rather a broad, sweeping statement of breeding and confidence, smooth and assured. Maybe new oak adds to this impression but the results are sometimes breathtaking. The early vintages of this wine, well we are down to our last few bottles now, stragglers washed up high against the tide line in the right-hand corner of the cellar, their tissue-wrapping betraying Monsieur Alquier's deep care and love for his product. There is no need to dawdle with these wines but do decant them. They improve greatly for a yawn, a stretch, a flex. We have a few more bottles of the 2005, a deep, rich, powerful wine of almost lupine potential and intensity. The tannins are so fine, and so ripe, however, that the wine's birthright is carried with consummate ease. Decanting this wine, for at least a couple of hours, is essential, as I suspect will be the case with the 2007, as of yet untried. Both of these wines hold many years ahead of them.

One final word about Alquier and, poor man, this is nothing of his doing. The sad fact of the matter is that I have always associated Alquier's wines with Paris goblets. Paris goblets – the scourge of the wine world, responsible, I am sure, for more disappointing bottles than any cork spoilage. One regular host, who shall remain nameless, forever served wine from Paris goblets and it was on one occasion when I had taken around a bottle of the Bastides that the destructive ability of these innocuous-looking vessels struck home. They are small, they have thick rims, they gather the scent of dust more effectively than neglect ever could and, conversely, the roundness of the glass dissipates the scent of the wine more effectively than the Aeolian winds. They kill wine and, on that occasion, they murdered the Alquier. Dust. Dust was all I got. I tried to swirl the wine to release the flavour but the glass was so small there was no room for the wine to stretch. The broad rim scattered the wine across my palate and it disappeared down my throat with hardly a taste to remind me of its presence.

Wine collectors become exercised by this kind of thing and some wine collectors will go overboard on their glassware. Not long after I became properly interested in wine, Riedel hit our shores and their glasses became all the rage, different shapes for different types of wine, enormous tulips for Red Burgundy, impossibly tall stems for Syrah, straight sides for Chianti, curious rolled lips for Rieslings from the Rheingau, the list goes on. As with everything, it is possible to get carried away. I remember trying out the glasses in a wine shop in the Fulham Road. The sales assistant was showing me the difference between the Vinum range and the much more expensive Sommelier range.

"Go on, hold one in each hand, just feel the difference. The Sommelier is so much better balanced. Hand-blown you see. And the stem – so delicate, so subtle."

"Oh yes, I see what you mean," I replied, "the difference is remarkable. The quality. Really, you can tell. So how much is this Sommelier?" I asked as I proffered him the clearly superior glass.

"Um, that is the Vinum. The other one is the Sommelier."

"Oh" I replied, both of us clearly embarrassed at my inability to appreciate the difference.

As I said, you can take things too far but, for any self-respecting wine lover, you have to start with a decent glass and that will never be a Paris goblet.

RIVESALTES

Domaine de Rancy Rivesaltes Ambré 1990

I am looking again at The World Atlas of Wine. A measure of
my ignorance can be gauged by drawing a straight line south-
east from Sauternes to Béziers and beyond to the sea. How
many hundreds of thousands of wine-producing hectares lie to
the south and west of that line? The Atlas suggests something
well over 500,000. Who knows. And what do I know of any
of the wines produced beneath that line? Apart from a brief
smattering of familiarity with the wines of Cahors and Gaillac
(actually they probably lie just to the north of that line),
precisely nothing. For a Francophile who proclaims France as
his vinous spiritual homeland, that is chilling and galling in
equal measure.

There is a whole world of wine there, in Gascony, the Western
Languedoc and Roussillon, producing the full gamut of wine
styles. Fronton, Marcillac, Madiran, Jurançon, Irouléguy (what
a name), Maury, Banyuls, Collioure – they are all familiar
names to a wine lover such as myself but they remain a
mystery. I cannot tell you if they are red, white, dry, sweet,
fortified, sparkling. My ignorance shames me.

And take this Rivesaltes. I had to look in the Atlas to see where
it came from. From down by the Spanish border, it turns out.
It is sublime. I had to read in the Atlas that it is predominantly
Grenache, that the grapes are left to wizen on the vine to
concentrate the sugar, that the fermentation is subsequently
halted by the addition of grape spirit before all the sugar has

turned to alcohol and that the wines can last forever.

1990 – the year we met, the year we left university, the year Chris Waddle tanked the penalty over the crossbar and sent England crashing out of the FIFA World Cup semi-final. A seminal year and a wine to match it. Think Madeira – a beautifully sweet, oxidised, complex wine, layers unfurling and new landscapes opening. The last bottle I drank when really I should have known better and after far too much Rioja. I say this only because it is probably best treated as a contemplative wine, to be approached slowly and preferably soberly. Magical. Uncommon. And very much a mystery.

BEAUJOLAIS

"When from a long-distant past nothing subsists, after the people are dead, after the things are broken and scattered, taste and smell alone, more fragile but more enduring, more unsubstantial, more persistent, more faithful, remain."

Proust had it right, of course, the power of the senses to trump time and place and to carry one back to a memory unthought of even five seconds ago.

Some twenty years or so ago we stood, you and I, our backs against the sky on a hill crowned by a chapel dedicated to the Virgin Mary, vines falling away all around us like pearls sewn on a wedding dress. We were standing atop La Madone, the town of Fleurie skirting the base of the hill. Spring was late. Buds had not burst and a keen wind stripped the earth. We took in our surroundings in silence. We wanted to linger but the world was cold that day. We retreated and sought out a modest modern house on the edge of the town, the home of

Jean-Marc Despres, the seat of the Domaine de La Madone. I had obviously done my homework – the wines were delicate yet confident, perfumed yet powerful, light yet long, beautifully suffused with strawberry, a serious pleasure.

And for the best part of twenty years I never tasted their like again. I was either misled by more frivolous examples, disappointed by thinner and more acidic examples or misguided by more ambitious examples. Until I refound the wines of Domaine de la Madone in a small out-of-the-way wine shop in Pimlico. I did not know the domaine still existed! Given the quality of its wines, and how none of the major wine merchants stocked them, I felt certain the domaine must have failed, since for what other possible reason were its wines not better known?

But experience has taught me caution. I bought a bottle, excited at the potential but more than aware that a memory from twenty years ago could not just be uncorked like a genie and resurrected. I was wrong. I opened the bottle and, just like Proust and his madeleines, I was transported. The crushed strawberry was the same. It was still there! There was still that balance, the smooth edges, the velvet, the tightrope between pleasure and application. I was breathtaken. We were once again standing on that hillside. We were once again bewitched by the beauty and simplicity of the wine. We were once again 25.

Morgon Côte du Py, Jean-Marc Burgaud 2010
Morgon, Domaine Lapierre 2012

If I were to have my time again, I would drink more Beaujolais, specifically Fleurie from La Madone and Morgon from Foillard. Simple.

Beaujolais is one of those overlooked wine regions. It produces a wealth of good wine but somehow struggles to be taken seriously. In the past this could be blamed on poor production methods (situated just south of Mâcon, it can be a marginal climate for red grapes which, in less than great years, can result in thin, acidic wines). It could also be blamed on Beaujolais Nouveau, a craze of the 1980's and early 1990's when the new vintage (as often as not, not nearly ready for consumption) would be raced over the Channel from the region, a stunt which resulted in the market being flooded with anaemic wines each November. And it could also be blamed on the way the Gamay grape is vinified, by carbonic maceration which produces light wines high on bubble gum and banana, less so on texture or length.

As with almost everywhere, things are changing. Georges Duboeuf has led the way in improving production standards, global warming has helped reduce the number of cool vintages and an increasing number of growers are eschewing carbonic maceration to ferment the grapes in a more traditional fashion. All of this has resulted in, well, more seriousness. This should be a good thing. It should be, and for many it probably is. The wines are deeper coloured, more textured, more ageworthy. Maybe it is just me, maybe I have just not kissed enough frogs to find the princes, but I miss some of the playfulness of the (good) Beaujolais of old. For me, there must be a balance. Beaujolais should not be intellectual or cerebral, it should be carefree and joyful. So by all means (listen to me!) reduce yields, pick only ripe grapes, ferment the grapes with their skins, punch down the cap, extract a little more colour at a slightly higher temperature, maybe even age the wines in a little oak, but please don't overload the wine with ambition.

Why do I blither on like this? The disappointment I suppose of Burgaud's 2009 Morgon Côte du Py. 2009 was a very successful vintage in Beaujolais, much as it was throughout France, and Burgaud is a very successful grower in Beaujolais. And Côte du Py is a highly rated section of Morgon, one of Beaujolais' most famous villages. The stars were aligned, surely? I diligently waited a few years before broaching the first bottle and then diligently worked my way through the case at even pace. Disappointment followed disappointment. The wine was surly. Where was the love? It was well made, clearly. The wine had texture, depth, length. But it never sang. When I got to the last bottle, it had melded but more in the way of a lighter Nebbiolo, a Roero maybe. Beaujolais? Not the wine of love and song that I was familiar with.

So we shall have to see where the 2010 Burgaud goes. It is hopefully a sappier wine, with lift and life that I could never find in the 2009. If not, whack it in a coq au vin.

The Lapierre? It should be good. Lapierre, along with Foillard and two others, Thévenet and Breton, spearheaded the movement to return to more traditional vinification methods. I have not tried other than Foillard's offerings which are sublime. Maybe they do have more substance than the sappy, light versions of Beaujolais we are all used to but Foillard's wines nevertheless have a charm and lightness of touch which belies this serious intent. So Lapierre will, I hope, be in the same mould. I hope. A look on cellartracker suggests that my hope might be misplaced, that the wine may be a little too heavy and grounded for its own good. Still, there is only one bottle.

Since writing this, we have tried the 2010 Burgaud. The coqs can rest easy; there need not be too much coq au vin, at least not with the Burgaud. The wine is, in its own way, beautiful. Not really one for me but there is no hiding its quality. Clearly well-made and well-balanced, it is thought-provoking. It is sombre. The song it sings is serious. It is a wine of reflection, not celebration. It will have its place.

CHAMPAGNE

What can I say of champagne that has not been said before? It must be one of the first wines that all of us ever taste. We are so inured to it, take it so much for granted that I also wonder if it is not one of the most unthinking wines that we ever consume. We are handed a glass, continue our conversation with our neighbour and drink it with barely a moment's thought. And well done to the Champenois for having created this market, a market predicated on high volume, high turnover, high prices, high expectation ("we must have champagne, what will our guests think otherwise?") and low demand for quality. The fact is that half the champagne we drink is probably not fit for purpose and we would all be better served drinking sparklng wine from other parts of the world, Australia, New Zealand, even now (actually, now more than ever) England. That said, I draw the line at Prosecco.

The rules about champagne are simple, or at least should be:

1. Buy it a year in advance. Easily said, but done with difficulty.   Non-vintage champagne, in particular, improves no end for another year or two in bottle once purchased. The acidity mellows, the body broadens, the flavours deepen. I have long resolved (though have yet) to buy in advance this way each Christmas when the supermarkets offer ridiculous deals, often not only the obligatory 25% off but this sometimes on top of initial discounts anyway. The trouble with buying a full year in advance is that the first year requires a double investment, buying for the coming year but also for the year after that.

That is quite an investment, especially at Christmas time.

One evening you sent me out to buy a lemon, I would like to say for our gin and tonic but I am not sure it was that essential. It was Christmas, the offers were in full flow. I queued up to buy the lemon together with six bottles of Moët that I could not resist. The till assistant was having great difficulty removing the security tags from the bottles and a queue was developing.

I turned to the man next to me to apologise.

"I am sorry about this. And I only came out for a lemon. I am not sure my wife is going to be that impressed."

"Aw, that's alright, mate" the Antipodean replied "and anyway, it's a husband's duty to disappoint."

2.   Trade up to vintage if you can. This is particularly the case if you are capitalising on the Christmas discounts. The improvement in the quality of the wine is proportionately greater than the (often modest) increase in price. The quality of the grapes will be better, the wine will have been aged for longer, greater care will have been taken in its production.

3.   Conversely, give up on cheap champagne. Break free and buy better from elsewhere. The quality of sparkling wine from around the world has never been better, often ironically produced by champagne houses which have set up overseas outposts. But if you are British, buy British (or specifically, English). With a changing climate, propitious soils (the same chalk as resurfaces in Champagne) and major investment, I have been endlessly surprised by the quality of English sparkling wine which

is now emerging – the depth of flavour, the complexity of the flavour, the uniqueness of the taste. Even if the prices of these English wines are approaching the prices of entry-level champagne, the quality is higher. And of course there is the pleasure of buying British; this nationalistic loyalty in buying local almost makes me feel, well, French. Look for Gusbourne, in particular.

4.   You already know the fourth rule. If you are drinking cheap champagne in a smart place, ask for a glass of red or white. You may well be surprised by what you are offered.

Bollinger NV
Veuve Clicquot NV
Taittinger NV

I would say about 10 years ago, so on the basis that I am now not far off 50 that must mean at least 15, quite possibly 20, years ago, I received a telephone call from Stephen.

"Hank, hi."

"Hi."

"What are you up to?"

"When?"

"Now."

"I'm at work."

"Can you bunk off?"

"Why?"

"I've got these tickets. Listen to this: *The Union des Maisons de Champagne cordially invites you and a guest to its annual tasting at the Banqueting House, Whitehall where over 80 producers will present their non-vintage and rosé and non-vintage cuvées and a vintage cuvée of their choice for your pleasure.*"

Or at least words to that effect.

Stephen's pigeon hole at the BBC was bang next door to that of one of the BBC's wine correspondents and clearly the invitation had been misfiled. Stephen was not going to undo the error and I was not going to hang around at work any longer.

From memory, we made a pretty good job of it. I cannot recall if we managed all 80 tables or, if we did, if we managed all three samples on each table, but if we failed in any regard it will not have been for lack of trying. And what do I remember from the event? Apart from the unabashed opulence of Rubens' ceiling, the lingering and pervading melancholy at Charles I's demise here and the constant attempts to retain a sense of professional authority in tasting these wines, I remember the two standout tables as being those of Bollinger and Alfred Gratien, both, it turns out, houses that ferment their wine in oak. This lends the wine a roundness and a richness that I, for one, find irresistible. Maybe it is why I am always drawn back to the Wine Society's own label champagne, produced for it by Alfred Gratien. Certainly one to seek out.

And the wine of the show? Bollinger's Grande Année (forgive me that I cannot remember the year). The full package: rich, complex, mouth-filling, sublime. There is always the next wine up the rung to compare it with (in this case, Bollinger's RD) but really, I see no reason to climb any further up the ladder. Leave the RD to the oligarchs and to those who cannot sleep at night. For a special occasion: Grande Année.

Bollinger: you will see there are a couple of magnums in the cellar, together with a few odd bottles. The odd bottles were the subject of a Christmas raid on Tescos, the magnums both prizes for Letter of the Month in Decanter magazine. Like a fool, I have thrown out the edition which contained the first of these letters – a plea for less hubris in the wine world and a remembrance of what wine is there for and the fundamental pleasures it brings – but you will still find the magazine with the second of the letters in the downstairs loo, a tired treatise against vintage hype as the Bordelais line up to skin the world's wine lovers once more with inflated claims and inflated prices for the new vintage. A colleague at work was not impressed that I had won Letter of the Month again: "What on earth was the editor up to? Asleep on the job again?" There's maybe three or four years' difference between the two magnums. I have marked the earlier one with an X. On the basis of rule 1 above, it should be a cracker.

Veuve Clicquot and Taittinger: solitary bottles about which I can tell you little. I prefer Taittinger (it develops an intriguing Burgundian nose with time and brings back happy memories of drinking it with Gran in Brighton – she would always produce champagne before lunch, always, without fail: how utterly civilised) and have rarely drunk Veuve Clicquot, despite the profile of its brand and its ubiquity.

ALSACE

Disney. Is that so terribly unfair? It must be. But whenever I think of our stay in Riquewihr in the summer of 2012 I think of gabled houses, cobbled streets, picture-perfect Technicolor. Even the sky is blue. And the storks nesting in the chimneys? Well I have to remind myself that they were not carrying babies wrapped in swaddling clothes in their beaks.

We stayed at the bottom of the hill, the rooms looking directly out onto the lower vines in the Schoenenbourg vineyard, Riquewihr's most famous grand cru. Occasionally a twee motorised train would drive by, ferrying tourists through the vineyard and across the hill above the town. This captured Claudia's imagination no end, to the extent that we too had to take the same journey. Not to say the view from the top was not a beautiful one. I just felt we were cheating time, that the town had been preserved in aspic. There were few signs of the 21st Century, few signs of the ravages of war that have bothered this region for so long as man can remember. Is that why? Have the ravages cut so deep that all memory of the horrors have been forcibly exorcised and hidden under timber frames and jolly demeanours? Maybe this is unfair as well (Riquewihr itself escaped 1939-45 relatively unscathed) but then many of the opinions I hold about Alsace I feel are tainted by unfairness.

We ate well in Riquewihr, unapologetically rich and full, we drank well in Riquewihr (Bott Frères' Muscat, winged with just a little sweetness, was perfect), all was cheery, all was plentiful. And the breakfast buffet? Can you remember how excited little Claudia was by the buffet? Each morning she would take charge. Each morning, on the first sign of interest or intent from any of us, up she would pop and run around the restaurant, pointing us in the direction of the toaster, of the egg boiler, of the croissants, of the cereals. Our very own private waitress.

Days of happiness, sunshine and carefree existence in a smile-drenched landscape. Just like the movies really.

I am surprised to find we have any Alsatian wines in the cellar, not because they are not, or cannot, be delicious, more on account of the fact that they have not, for whatever reason, formed part of our canon.

In a country obsessed with appellations and terroir, that is to say a country which promotes the geographical origin of the wine as the source of the wine's identity, rather than the grape variety, Alsace is a rare beast. For in Alsace, grape variety is king. A system is slowly developing whereby the vineyard, if a grand cru, might be given equal billing to the grape variety but, for the most part, the defining feature of an Alsace wine is its grape variety and it is this which is most prominent on the wine label (along, of course, with the name of the winegrower).

Most Alsatian wine is white (there is a small amount of Pinot Noir but I have always found it slightly weedy and, for the price, not worth it) and most of it from one of six varieties: Riesling (probably considered king, much more petrolly than over the border in Germany and, for the most part, dry as a bone), Gewürztraminer (unique to Alsace, heady and redolent of lychees and rose petals, a love it or leave it wine), Pinot Blanc (I have always struggled with this – in a region so rich in grapes with strong identities, most Pinot Blancs I have tried seem discreet and unremarkable), Muscat (I love this grape which smells and tastes of grapes – wonderfully fresh and open, a loud trumpet blast of life), Pinot Gris (I come onto this below) and Sylvaner (spicy, grapey, considered the least noble of the six, unfairly in my view).

So if I am so keen on the flavours of Alsatian wine, which I hope the above brief skim over the grape varieties makes clear, why so few Alsatian wines in the cellar? The first problem I have is that, when buying an Alsatian wine, I have no idea if it is dry, medium or sweet (save for the very sweet dessert-style wines which do indicate their character, not least in price). The label is silent. I cannot for the life of me understand why the Alsatians have been so slow to address this. I can think of no other wine-growing region, at least of Alsace's stature, which would allow this. I have no difficulty with the rules of the appellation allowing this latitude and flexibility in terms of how the wines are vinified, but cannot the growers at least give the customers something of a clue? It seems not.

The second reason comes back to the terroir point. Maybe it is the romantic in me but I like to associate, within reason, the wine I am drinking with a place. I like a story or an identity. If the label simply says the wine is a Riesling from Alsace (not a small region) then, really, that is not giving me much to work with or much of a clue. To be fair, the "grand cru" system does lend an identity but sadly at the same time a price. So might the Alsatians one day follow the Burgundian model of a series of village appellations the length of the Vosges, within whose weather window the main villages shelter? Drinking a Riesling from Riquewihr would be more intriguing especially if, the next time, I should be trying a Riesling from Ribeauvillé.

Thirdly I struggle a little with the monovarietal nature of the wines. There is a wonderful grower called Marcel Deiss who has gone the other way, who has championed terroir over grape variety and who blends grapes from a single location and names the wine after the terroir, not the grape. And I find these mixes (edelzwickers they are called) much more interesting that the single grape wines.   For the most part, however, edelzwickers are the cheap seats, they are the entry-level wines. Which is a shame. Why? To borrow the old adage, the whole can be greater than the sum of the parts and I have always found these blends offer a degree of complexity absent in many of the other wines.   Besides, I enjoy trying to distinguish the component parts, the grape of the Muscat, the petrol of the Riesling, the lychee of the Gewürztraminer.

So there you have it.   My tuppence worth of thoughts, most probably deeply unfair.

Pinot Gris Reserve, Trimbach 2013

But despite all the above, this wine is a beauty.

For me, Pinot Gris is the most intriguing of the Alsatian grape varieties.   It has a flavour and a character which is difficult to pin down, like smoke drifting across the landscape.   It is not clean and precise; it is mysterious, evanescent, one flavour subsiding, just as it achieves dominance, to be replaced by another.   There is a depth to it which shows itself best when vinified just off-dry.   The sweetness of ripe apples and an echo of spice.   A slightly heavy texture, a wine that will tread at its own pace.   A wine that sums up the appeal of Alsace perfectly: rich, gourmand, gastronomic.

There are much weightier examples than this one but I like the freshness and balance that this example retains.   It is essentially dry but with that little twist of sweetness at the end to wrap up the palate perfectly.

LOIRE VALLEY

It will have been early 2002, probably January, a partners' quarterly presentation. Judith, one of the firm's senior partners as impressive in stature as intellect, was presenting to the assembled partners. She drew breath and used this opportunity to have a sip of wine. By all accounts she almost choked.

"Christ, this is disgusting, this is properly disgusting. Who on earth chose this?"

James, from the floor, piped up. "Catering are in charge of choosing the wine now."

"Can we change? I do not see why I, in fact why any of us, must be subjected to poison like this."

James continued. "We're making Goulding up in May. He knows a bit about wine, or professes to, so we'll put him in charge."

And so was born my parallel career as wine partner, a post I have held happily for the last 14 years.

Not that it has always been easy. Filled as I was with enthusiasm for my new role I set about introducing all the unsung gems I had discovered over the years, wines off the radar that majored on taste and interest and minored on caché and cost.

One of my first purchases, for client drinks parties, was an Albariño from Galicia. The wine was fresh, light, with entrancing overtones of apricot and white fruits. Except...except that it came in a brown bottle.

A partner cornered me after one drinks party. "Nice wine, Henry, but the colour of the bottle will not do."

"Sorry?"

"A client commented that we must be hitting hard times if we are forced to serve wines out of brown bottles."

I learnt on the job. Nothing too smart but at the same time nothing too off the beaten track. In fact, try to keep it French and keep the name recognisable, so from the main regions.

Two or three years into my apprenticeship, I was asked if I would present a wine tasting to clients.

"Happily" I replied.

"Just don't make it too serious" came the response.

I chose the Loire Valley. I could see the partners were nervous, 40 or so clients in the room and an unknown quantity about to hold forth for an hour or so. I put up a picture of the Loire: wide, slow, reed-choked banks, sandbanks visible near and far.

"The longest river in France" I ventured "and quite possibly the most useless."

I could see the partners' tension break even at this feeble joke; it was not going to be too serious after all.

To be fair, wine tasting, even the subject of wine (unless it is your livelihood), must never be taken too seriously; it will make a mockery of you if you do, not only on account of the main purpose of wine (to spread joy, conversation and communion) but also because an individual's sense of taste is so evanescent that it is impossible to predict how it will perform at any given time (to say nothing of the wine itself). Harry Waugh, one of the great tasters from mid-century, was once asked if he had ever mistaken claret for burgundy? "Not since lunch" he replied. Exactly the right attitude. Never take it too seriously.

So yes, the Loire. The longest river in France (by the time the river, which rises in the Massif Central, reaches the most well-known easternmost regions of wine production, Pouilly-Fumé and Sancerre, it is already half-way to the sea) and yes, possibly the most useless. At least this is one reason proffered as to why the wines of the Loire are not better known and, until the age of the car and the plane, were not exported more. It is not an easy river to navigate and so could not provide an easy outlet for the products of the region.

In any event, I am surprised at how few wines we have from the Loire in the cellar for, if I was forced to restrict myself to one region, I suspect I would choose the Loire. Not only on account of the vast range of wines produced along its length which covers the full gamut of most wine lovers' requirements but also because the region majors on medium. "Medium" is such a cursed word but should be a blessing in the world of wine. The Loire lies pretty far north for wine production and each year it can be a struggle to ripen the grapes properly. But this means the region's wines are not blockbusters or fruit bombs. They are not a meal in the glass, wines you can stand a stick in. They complement food and you can drink more than one glass without feeling full. They are fresh and often require work to tease out all the flavours. They can sometimes be green. And cool. They are not obvious. They are often wines for lunchtimes and clear heads. They are easy to overlook.

I once wrote the following, in fact about a wine not from the Loire, but it gives a flavour of the appeal of the less than obvious and its rightful place at the table, especially in this age of ease, the instantly gratifiable, the immediately accessible:

"Relatively, an unremarkable wine. When the cork was pulled, the wine seemed thin and anodyne. Pleasant (at a stretch) but anonymous. Watered down. On its own like this, the wine would have failed miserably in any blind or solo tasting. But then we drank it with supper. The dry tannins, previously uncharming, added texture to the food and the food, in return, brought out the flavours. And as supper, and the bottle, progressed, the wine came more and more into its own and with each mouthful became more and more interesting and rewarding. Sweet berry fruit (just) and an aroma difficult to pin down. Nothing obvious, everything to be worked for and, even then, only just there, just obtainable. Basically, from the start to the finish, this wine was reluctant to give anything away and therefore held my attention throughout. But it gave just enough, and just enough was exactly what I wanted. Nothing New World or Parker points here and thank goodness. A proper (not great) wine."

And consider Muscadet, one of the great wines of the Loire Valley. It is cheap and it has suffered from overcropping and poor production methods in the past but this should not detract from its appeal and its worth. It is made at the western end of the Loire Valley in a maritime climate. The grape is Melon de Bourgogne (being neither a melon nor from Burgundy), a relatively anonymous grape with difficult flavours to pinpoint. But is there any better wine for seafood? I would hazard a guess not. It is light, not too alcoholic, its subtle flavours allow the equally subtle flavours of the seafood to sing, it has a slight salty tang, it is fresh, it is clear in the glass. It does not stand on ceremony, it is equally at home in a small tumbler as in a fancy wine glass, it is the faithful and perfect companion. Indeed, so good is Muscadet, it is our solemn obligation to drink more of it, at the right time of course and, equally, only good examples (probably from the Sèvre et Maine appellation and best if "sur lie" which means the wine has been aged on its lees to give more flavour, but not too much more mind you).

I have banged on enough. The charms of the Loire Valley are many – the noble sweet wines of Bonnezeaux and Coteaux du Layon, the sing-song freshness of Muscadet, the blackcurrant leafiness and chalk of Pouilly-Fumé, the intellectual challenge of Savennières, the cool charm of red Sancerre, the effervescent joy of Saumur, the appeal of the following. The triumph of medium!

Vouvray, Haut Lieu, Demi-Sec, Domaine Huet 2008
Vouvray, Le Mont, Demi-Sec, Domaine Huet 2008

The Road Not Taken. 1985. I had finished my A-Levels less than three weeks previously, left school and was now travelling round Europe with Johnny. We had caught a bus out to Vouvray from Tours and now, after a morning wine-tasting, were waiting for a bus back to town, in the high heat of the day, down by the banks of the Loire. The sun was busy stilling my fuzzy head and I stared vacantly out across the sandbanks, my mind circling as aimlessly as the eddies midstream. A Whiskered Tern ghosted by, wraith-like. A Little Egret stalked the shallows, its brilliant plumage reflecting the magnesium brightness of the sun, giving no quarter to shadow. A flock of Goldfinches scattered the silence.

"Let's go for a swim."

I stared at the river. I was baking, a little hungover, in no rush.

If I could drink the river, I would have. At least the cool of the water on my skin would free me from this torpor.

"No."

"What? You must be kidding. Come on, it's baking."

"It's dangerous. No." The water still beckoned me, challenged me. The more it did so, the more my resistance rose.

Was it dangerous? The river looked utterly innocuous, only a few dimples on the smooth surface betraying any movement beneath. But something made me nervous and something made me adamant we should not be swimming here. Was it caution or sense that made me hesitate? I have often thought back on this. I am not sure I have ever been a risk-taker. Was that day on the banks of the Loire a snapshot of who I am, who I have become? Should I have seized the moment and embraced life and washed off the day's dregs in the still waters? Or would deep currents of France's longest river have carried us off? Would a different decision that day have changed me? Dramatic, I know, but I have always wondered whether this was the road not taken, if my life would have been different if I had acceded to Johnny's implorings and we had gone for a swim. We tread a tightrope of chance, the path we take a constantly woven thread of one decision over another. Why should I particularly remember that day outside Vouvray? I do not know but, in the there and then of the situation, the decision I reached seemed significant. And for whatever reason, it is a decision that has nagged at me ever since. Sensible or unenterprising? I shall never know.

Vouvray makes dry (sec), medium (demi-sec), sweet (moelleux) and sparkling wine, all white, all from the Chenin Blanc grape. Treat Chenin Blanc with respect – proper ripeness, the right soil, limited yields – and you can be rewarded with some of the longest-living, most concentrated and complex wines in the whole of France. Custard, apple, lanolin, a healthy streak of acidity to keep it honest – the wines are unique. Overcrop and the wines are dilute and they lack the depth and character to support the slight sweetness that Chenin Blanc naturally tends to. We drank just such a Vouvray, light and sweet, not unpleasant but a little too undemanding, at the Lobster Pot in Church Bay all those years ago. In fact we must have drunk more than one because I cannot otherwise explain why we then thought it such a good idea, later that evening and in the dark, to drive your Renault 5 down the ramp and onto the beach. As so often, the good idea rapidly became a bad idea but, with you behind the wheel and me behind the bumper, well the car extricated itself from the sand and we got away. We were not left, with the sweet Chenin on our breath, having to explain away our behaviour to Anglesey's finest.

Huet. Vouvray's most famous producer, this vintage being one of the last being made by its most famous winemaker, Noël Pinguet. And Huet is more than this even: the domaine is also one of France's most famous biodynamic producers. It is curious how everyone appears to have heard of biodynamism without necessarily having an interest in wine (or at least its production) or even knowing what biodynamism is about. The concept of filling a cow's horn with dung and planting it at the end of a row of vines, though, is clearly an arresting one as this is the example that everyone can recount. Is it a fad? Is it the stuff of nonsense? Who am I to say but, despite being the cynical lawyer I am, I cannot help but think there is something in it. The one fact of which I feel certain is that we have little idea how the world works. For thousands of years before us, people sowed and harvested according to the moon and the stars (this being a central tenet of biodynamism, as well as the use of organic material to control pests and succour the soil). Is our generation really so knowledgeable now that we can dismiss these ideas out of hand? To do so, to me at least, smacks as much of the ignorance and hocus-pocus that critics would level at biodynamism.

And there is one other, very persuasive, reason why I am happy to champion biodynamic wines. Those who espouse biodynamism care deeply and passionately about their wines and, given that half the battle of finding a good bottle of wine is finding a good producer to make it, well here you have a ready-made answer. Even if biodynamism at the end of the day does not make any difference, the care and attention that the winegrower expends in growing his grapes and making his wines does make a difference and it will be apparent in the end product.

These two wines are demi-sec from, the wine merchant urged me, one of the greatest vintages of recent years for the demi-sec style. Demi-sec is unfashionable (anything other than bone-dry these days is) but to my mind this style accentuates the unique style of Loire Chenin and adds body and depth without losing the wine's ability to be paired with food (scallops would be a cracker). They will last forever. For what it is worth, Haut Lieu should drink slightly earlier than Le Mont but, really, I would not pay too much attention to that. The wines will be rich but time will moderate the residual sweetness and leave, in its place, smoke and lingering memories of time past. Dominic once produced such a bottle, won at a school fair (Wycombe Abbey obviously produces a better class of raffle prize). The wine silenced me, its quiet beauty and swirling depths reminding me, yes, of the perpetual run of the river to the sea.

Saumur-Champigny, Cuvée Lisagathe, Château du Hureau 2005
Saumur-Champigny, Tuffe, Château du Hureau 2010

I suspect it was 2002. Emily was small but not tiny. We stayed in James and Margaret's house in the Sartre, not far from Angers. Again, I had done my homework and one day we drove to Dampierre-sur-Loire, to the east of Saumur, where the village clings to the chalk cliffs and overlooks the river.

The château was beautiful, intimate and white-washed, steep slate roofs, a pigeonnier and a turret, the delicacy of the civilised exterior incongruously emerging from the cliff behind, the land precipitously dropping away to the front, down through the village, down to the road and, across the road, down to the river. We parked in the courtyard and rang the bell.

Philippe Vatan fitted his environment perfectly, wearing both the culture of the château and the honesty of the farmer lightly. He was a man of measured words, few but not so as to appear withdrawn or surly. We walked into the thousand-year-old cave which debouched onto the courtyard, part of a network all along the cliffs and in which was housed all the equipment and storage of a modern cellar.

You looked after Emily who behaved impeccably as we tried the white (a superbly rich but dry Chenin Blanc with surprising depths), the reds (in those days there were only three cuvées, the estate wine, the Fevettes, which was a little gamy for my taste, and the flagship wine, the Lisagathe) and a sublime sweet wine. I forget what we bought but it was a civilised, polite tasting and we will not have left empty-handed.

Philippe walked us out to the car (that violently green Golf

Estate). It was then he saw the bird book in the backseat and his face lit up. So this was how to crack him! He became animated and we spent a good 10 minutes talking about the birds of the region, where he used to go, what he used to see.

When I drink the wines of Château du Hureau I often think of that visit and wonder if he still has the time to go birdwatching and, if so, what he has most recently seen.

There are wines that divide the wine world. Every expert will extol the virtues of, say, Riesling but there are certain wine styles which (reassuringly for the rest of us?) simply come down to a matter of taste. Take New Zealand Sauvignon Blanc, for example. An overblown, slightly sweet and monotonous style of wine, with little in the way of mystery or complexity, or a wonderfully refreshing blast of confident flavour which can be relied on to deliver the sunshine for which we all yearn? It does not come down to winemaking ability, or even the suitability of the land for the grape, it just comes down to taste. The same can be argued, either way, for a number of different wines, Zinfandel from California (love it), Pinotage from South Africa (I haven't touched the stuff for 20 years on account of that terrible burnt rubber taste) and even Gewürztraminer from Alsace (again, love it).

Another wine style in this gallery of ruffians is Cabernet Franc from the Loire, mainly grown around the towns of Angers, Saumur and Tours. Further east, Pinot Noir produces lighter, softer reds around Sancerre and Menetou-Salon. These wines escape the ire of certain critics, gentle echoes as they are of the great wines of Burgundy not that much further to the east. But Loire Cabernet Franc is different. It is scratchy, sometimes (maybe often) awkward and usually just a little demanding. The raspberry freshness of the wine is complicated by chalky tannins and an occasional herbaceousness which, given the wine is traditionally drunk young and often cool, have to be navigated. There is a green pepper element and the wine is shot through with a metallic taste (Jilly Goolden, in The Taste of Wine, has "cold steel knife" as a typical prompter for the wine). So, as often as not, you have to concentrate. The wine is not modern in any way: it is not fruit-first, it is rarely soft and the names can be obscure.

But I love them. Why? There is something quintessentially Gallic about them – their intransigence and refusal to bow to modern tastes (well, not quite true – I suspect the style has softened a little but red grapes grown this far north in a semi-maritime climate will always require some work). Maybe it is the evocative names (Saumur-Champigny derives its name from "campus ignus" – field of fire – I have no idea why), the unfashionability of the wines and their idiosyncrasies (copied nowhere else in the world), their concomitant value perhaps but also their beauty, the Cinderella nature of the wines that, with age, soften and broaden exquisitely into something much more becoming to modern fashion (not that many ever let them get that far). And I love their versatility, with or without food, but often shining brightest over an informal lunch on a sunlit breezy carefree day.

So, these two wines. Is it sacrilege to say that I prefer the Tuffe to the Lisagathe? Just as there can be no question that Kermit Lynch's Adventures on the Wine Route is the greatest wine book ever written, so there can be no question that the finest wine writer penning his thoughts today is Andrew Jefford. Not only is what he has to say worth saying but he is consummately articulate and he has the poet's touch. Find him online or in his monthly Decanter column. A number of years ago he wrote an article, using a Mosel Kabinett as a case study, on the merits of accumulation and disposition. Wines today, he argued, are almost invariably judged on mass, their worth rated by how much they have, whether of texture, extract, flavour, ripeness, depth, length, colour, longevity, you name it. So the Lisagathe wins the accumulation stakes, being the product as it is of the Château's finest, ripest grapes from its finest vineyard. But Andrew Jefford argues that the pleasure derived from a wine is from its disposition, not its accumulation, in other words how the wine disposes of itself as it is consumed by the drinker: how balanced it is, how the flavours develop and deport themselves, how the wine treats the drinker (with a light touch, leaving the drinker wanting more, or with a heavy hand, imposing itself and leaving the drinker exhausted?). You can see why a Mosel Kabinett is such a good example of the triumph of disposition over accumulation, the lowliest of the QMPs trumping the weightier, more serious wines higher up the classification, and for me it is true of the Tuffe as well. It is a lighter wine, better balanced, perhaps without the depth of fruit that the Lisagathe has but put together with greater harmony. Or maybe the Lisagathe is just in a funny place at the moment but the last bottle I had was all over the place. The tannins were ripe and the fruit was ripe but the alcohol was noticeable and, at that stage at least, the tannins were not providing the framework to carry all the fruit and alcohol. Maybe the wine will improve. Philippe Vatan is such an accomplished winegrower, I suspect it will. The Tuffe is beautiful now and will remain so for a while; give the Lisagathe another five years and let it prove me wrong.

The Tuffe is beautiful now and will remain so for a while; give the Lisagathe another five years and let it prove me wrong.

Chinon, Clos du Chêne Vert, Charles Joguet 2005
Chinon, Clos du Chêne Vert, Charles Joguet 2014
Chinon, Clos de la Dioterie, Charles Joguet 2014

Of the Loire's reds, I will struggle to tell you the difference between a Saumur, a Saumur-Champigny, an Anjou, a Bourgueil and a St Nicolas de Bourgeuil – they are all too similar for my palate to distinguish, perhaps not too surprising given they come from the same grape and pretty much the same soil. Chinon, however, I have always found slightly different. Chinon, famous for its castle and the attentions of Richard the Lionheart and home of Rabelais' favourite wine, is the easternmost of the famous red wine appellations of Anjou and Touraine and, to my mind at least, has quite different a flavour profile. Although the wine is made from the same grape, Cabernet Franc, the flavours are softer, the fruit is warmer, the tannins finer (maybe because the soil is sandier?). It is a friendlier wine, if not in immediate youth, certainly with a few years of age on it. I once unearthed a cache of bin-end Chinon in a now-defunct wine shop on Sloane Avenue. I wish I could remember the grower but the year was 1986. It was on sale at some pittance of a price, 7 years old by the time I got to it. And it was sublime – soft raspberry fruit, palate-wrapping, mouth-filling, soul-enhancing. I can taste it still and its memory alone has always made me gravitate to Chinon on a wine list in the hope I can once again recapture the essence of that pleasure.

Charles Joguet. He took over the domaine in the late 1950's and, by the 1980's, the reputation of the domaine was sky high. The domaine's fortunes then waned through the 1990's and early 2000's following Monsieur Joguet's retirement. Judged on the 2005, however, the domaine is right back where it should be. Joguet makes a number of different cuvées, the two stand-out wines being the Clos de la Dioterie and Clos du Chêne Vert, both the product of old vines in famous vineyards. And in the Clos du Chêne Vert I have rediscovered the taste of the 1986 wine I had all those years ago. Indeed, when the wine finally turned the corner into maturity (it had an awkward upbringing to begin with), it was quite possibly the most exciting wine event of the year for me. The sweetness, the depth, the homecoming! It reminded me of a great, and I mean a great, Saint-Emilion (which increasingly uses Cabernet Franc in its traditional Merlot-predominant blend). I would like to think that the Bordelais now understand the structure and freshness that Cabernet Franc can bring and, when ripe, the swan that it will turn into with age. The wine was sublime.

I must admit to a weakness at this point. Such is the memory of the pleasure that the 2005 wine has brought, the thrill of the discovery, the anticipation of what is to come, that I have just bought a half-case of the 2014 Chêne Vert and, beat this, a half-case of Clos de la Dioterie too. Orrin cautions against living by fear. He likes his food, he says, and uses the example of a lavender crème brulée to make the point:

"Suppose I pass a patisserie and see a lavender crème brulée in the window. Now I would love that, I really would. So I go in and buy it. But why have I bought it? Is it because it is so delicious that I really can think of nothing better than sinking my teeth into it or is it because it is so unexpected, and such a rare thing to come across, that I feel I must buy it as otherwise I will never see one again or someone else will come along in a moment and buy it from under my nose?"

If the doctor buys the crème brulée because he is worried that, if he does not, he will not get the opportunity again, he is living by fear; it is the fear of losing the crème brulée that compels him to buy it. If, on the other hand, he buys it because he can think of nothing more delicious, then he is buying it for the right reason, a reason not driven by scarcity or negativity.

Remember what I said about Vieux Télégraphe? I ended up buying that out of fear, not because I was so smitten with the flavour of the wine which, as I said, can be demanding and require effort. I started buying successive vintages not for the wine itself but to keep the run of vintages going. I started buying it out of fear that if I did not I might miss something special. This is worth bearing in mind. If the bug gets you and you start buying the same wine vintage after vintage, make sure you are buying it for the love of the wine, not for fear of breaking the cycle. There are so many astonishing wines in the world; don't become bound to only a few for the wrong reasons.

I bought the 2014 Clos du Chêne Vert because I have fallen head over heels in love with the 2005, because I love the flavour of the wine, the potential, the depths, the excitement of what is in the bottle. And I bought the Clos de la Dioterie, not ever having tried it, because its reputation is equal (some might say slightly greater, but I will stick with equal) to the Chêne Vert, because I am sure it will deliver just as much pleasure and, well, it might be fun to compare them down the line. Compare them, mind you, not denigrate one at the expense of the other. They will both be magnificent bottles and it would be a waste for one of them to be considered "lesser" than the other.

I hope we shall drink these wines together but whoever ends up drinking them, say 10 or 15 years hence, will experience unadulterated pleasure. The wines have been bought not out of fear but out of love.

BURGUNDY

Burgundy. So big a part of my heart is devoted to Burgundy, I do not know where to begin for fear of missing something. If there is one wine region which has given me more pleasure than any other, if there is one region that I have visited more than any other, if there is one region that I associate more closely than any other with my passage across this planet, if there is one region that, my love, I identify with our journey together, then it is Burgundy. A land of coloured-tiled roofs, of white Charollais (special cows!) in green fields, of intimate landscapes and marginal weather, a land of individuals and of farmers who happen to be winegrowers, a land of the Church and of dukes, of thousand-year culture, of rich food, of bounty, a small-scale land of honesty and of richness, a land of villages of weathered stone and towns of wine, a land (I must say it) home to the greatest wines on earth.

I remember our first visit like it was yesterday. We were catching the Dover-Calais ferry at the crack of dawn so I had come over to your flat the night before. You and Alex were going out to a drinks party. "I promise we won't be long" you said "one drink, one drink only." The pair of you rolled in past midnight, giggling. "One drink, I promise you I only had one drink!" Alex was in little better state. I knew better than to challenge your assertion. Credit to you, you were up at the allotted time and we were off in the dark. The car smelled like a brewery. I knew to hold my tongue. And credit to you, you kept the car on the straight and narrow, the Kent constabulary stayed away and we made the ferry.

In those early days, we eschewed the motorway in France, saving on the tolls. We travelled down arrow-straight avenues of poplars, through dirty towns redolent of industry, past endless cemeteries to the fallen, across Flanders' plains featureless but for church spires on the horizon. If we ever had cause to stop, the air was rich with the song of skylarks and brisk with the business of early spring. It was only when we reached Soissons that the hard graft of travelling would release its relentless grip, the landscape would soften, folds in the land would develop, town names would appear on signposts suggesting the promise to come – Reims, Epernay – and, as often as not, the sun would break through the relentless cloud cover and the wind would ease. We would not stop, mind you, but press on, past Reims, past Troyes, before peeling off and landing exhausted in Chablis. From Chablis it was only then a short hop to the Côte d'Or and its golden treasures where we would wander, happily and with limited purpose, before, a week or so later, doing the whole thing in reverse.

How many times did we make this trip? We made it in your Renault 5, we made it in the green Golf, we made it in the grey Passat. We made it by ourselves, then with Emily in tow (how she used to be carsick), we then made it the four of us with Gus and finally the full complement when Claudia arrived. And each time we had grown up a little, the travels became as much about looking after the children as looking after ourselves, we started using the motorway and losing immediate touch with the countryside we were travelling through, we started to stay in smarter places than we had stayed before (once, do you remember, we had even spent the night in a lay-by to save on hotel costs?), we started planning our trips more, we visited domaines I had researched rather than diving into the first place in each village which promised "dégustation vente", we even started having pretensions to tasting, and buying, other than the most basic wines on offer.

Our life together. We can measure it through our holidays in Burgundy. For me, it is inextricably linked with you.

Whenever I try to proselytise about Burgundy, the most common response I get is that Burgundy is just too complicated. To which I respond that this is just not true. It is true that you can make Burgundy as complicated as you like but it will be off the back of a few very simple concepts which, if you are so minded, are all that you really need to remember.

Let's give it as shot:

1. There are only two grape varieties to worry about, one white, one red. Burgundy is the home of Chardonnay and it is Burgundy's white wines that are responsible for the success of Chardonnay the world over. Although Chardonnay is easy to cultivate, it is the supreme expression that Chardonnay can achieve in Burgundy that acts as the world's lode star and that growers from everywhere seek to emulate. In Burgundy, the great whites speak of the earth (the well-mapped earth). The red grape is Pinot Noir, the allure of which has been made famous by the film Sideways (worth watching, in fact one of those rare films funnier second time than first). Pinot Noir is tricky to grow, thin-skinned, quick to jam if overripe but with troubling tannins and greenness if not properly ripe. Get it right however and it is capable of achieving complete mastery of the consumer's senses and capable of leaving an impression which, in my view, no other red variety can match.

2. There are four regions to be aware of. Chablis in the north (everyone is familiar with Chablis), then the Côte d'Or an hour to the south (the jewel in the crown, home to all the stellar wines of Burgundy – indeed, if people talk of Burgundy, nine times out of ten they will be talking about the Côte d'Or), then the Côte Chalonnaise just to the south of the Côte d'Or (this is really something of a specialist subject so if four regions are one too many to remember, then forget about the Côte Chalonnaise) and finally, about an hour to the south, the large region of Mâcon, the home of increasingly serviceable whites and a few ambitious crus. Technically speaking, Beaujolais forms part of Burgundy as well but nearly everyone views it as a separate region in its own right. As shall we.

3.   As a general rule, all Burgundies will be named after the village in which they are grown. This can be confusing, I admit, because the labels will rarely mention the word "Burgundy". For Chablis this does not pose too much of a problem because Chablis is the only permitted name on the label (and everyone has heard of Chablis). In the Mâcon region, the wine will as often as not be prefixed by Mâcon before the name of the village so, even if you do not know the villages, you will at least have an idea of where the wine comes from. The Côte d'Or is the tricky one. You will only know the wine is from this blessed place if you know your villages. This does all mean that, if you become interested in learning more, then yes you will need to learn the names of the villages in the Côte d'Or (the same applies to the Côte Chalonnaise) but, if you do become interested, well really, is there anything more delightful than this learning exercise?

4.   Finally, there are four levels of hierarchy by which the land on which the grapes have been grown are graded. At the most basic level, a grower might have a Bourgogne which will be made from grapes grown outside the village boundary (or on land within the village but not deemed good enough for the village appellation). Next will be the village appellation, followed by Premier Cru and, at the top of the hierarchy and greatest of all, Grand Cru.

So, were you to visit a grower in Gevrey-Chambertin, say, with sufficient holdings across the village, he might first of all offer you a Bourgogne (and, despite what I have said above, this will just be labelled Bourgogne – the secret then, if you stumble across a bottle of Bourgogne, is to look at the address of the winegrower and, if it is situated in an august village, then it will be worth exploring). You will offer a respectful nod as to how well the vigneron has produced something quite so lovely from such humble stock (truth told, Bourgognes are my happiest hunting grounds, a point I will come back to later).

He will then produce a straight Gevrey-Chambertin, a village wine. This might come from an individual plot within the village or be a blend of several different village sites. This should have a little more body, colour perhaps and length. Here you will nod a few times, appreciatively, showing how clearly you admire the step up in quality. But don't get too carried away, still two more to go and you want to make sure he pours them for you - keep your powder dry, you are a serious punter and are more than familiar with all the great wines of Burgundy, to which you are busy mentally comparing this vigneron's offerings.

The grower will then produce one, or a number of Premiers Crus. The Premiers Crus can be bottled and labelled individually (the grower may show you a Gevrey-Chambertin 1er Cru Champeaux or Gevrey-Chambertin 1er Cru Clos St Jacques) or as Gevrey-Chambertin 1er Cru if the grower has blended his wine from a number of Premier Cru sites across the village, maybe if his holdings in each are not sufficiently great to merit individual bottlings. Here, you will offer a sharp intake of breath, maybe shake your head a little and offer only a few words (less is more in this situation), perhaps no more than "Ça, c'est bon, c'est très bon" with, if circumstances need it, a single raised eyebrow.

Finally, if you have played your cards right, you might

get a taste of the Grand Cru. These are few and far between and their value has sky-rocketed in recent years so the grower will have to have been well impressed with your performance if he is to produce this, which will be his pride and joy. Here the wine does not actually have to carry the village name at all; such is the grandeur of the wine, and its fame quite possibly, that the name of the vineyard will suffice. So you might be offered Mazis-Chambertin, Clos de Bèze or, quite possibly and, as this is a hypothetical situation dreamt up by me as I write, most certainly, the granddaddy of them all, Le Chambertin. I have never tried Le Chambertin but if you get the chance then grab it. And be kind to the vigneron. Even if you do not think much of it, he will and courtesy will demand that you become breathless, that you lose your focus momentarily before fixing on an object in the middle distance so you can collect your thoughts and utter perhaps nothing more than "Mon Dieu, c'est formidable". You could then simply ask "Pourquoi?" and allow the winegrower to expostulate at length on the merits and advantages of the Grand Cru site over all others. You need do no more than nod at this point and let him impute you with all the knowledge that he is now spouting.

The joys of winetasting. And the gems that we discovered on our way.

So Burgundy need not be complicated. It is certainly a region that everyone interested in wine must visit at least once, in fact several times. Even now, with its vaulted reputation, it is a region of small artisanal winegrowers many of whom are desperate and proud to show off their wares. Away from the big players, it is not (yet?) a region of multinational and insurance group owners with closed doors and inflated opinions of themselves. It is a region of farmers with smallholdings, closely (irrevocably) tied to the land, each with several wines to show across the different hierarchies and even across different villages and, even then, in both red and white. You can never get bored of Burgundy – the combinations are myriad.

<u>CHABLIS</u>

So, Chablis. Chablis can only be white – you know that anyway. And, adopting rule number one above, Chablis can only be made from Chardonnay. So be careful not to profess a boredom or dislike of Chardonnay and then praise Chablis to the rafters. And rule four pretty much works as well although, between Bourgogne and Chablis, there is the intervening category of Petit Chablis. I remember the first time we visited a grower in Chablis to taste his wares. Not an august address but a highly visible one, just as you cross the Serein on the way into town. On the table he had different pieces of chalk, Portlandian and Kimmeridgian, named after the Dorset villages of Portland and Kimmeridge and part of the same swathe of chalk that forms the South Downs, disappears beneath the English Channel and then re-emerges in the vinous landscapes of Sancerre, Chablis and Champagne. Do not ask me the reasons why, but Kimmeridgian chalk is deemed to produce finer wine than Portlandian, maybe because the Portlandian strata is found above the Kimmeridgian strata and so on higher ground. Given how cold Chablis gets, and how far north Chablis is, higher ground is at a distinct disadvantage when it comes to ripening grapes. So most Petit Chablis will be found on this higher ground. It can be thin and brutally acidic but, again, in the hands of a conscientious winegrower, it can offer a more than faithful rendition of the bracing minerality (without stripping your enamel) that makes Chablis so unique And Petit

Chablis will shine in warm years when the heat can blunt this rapier edge in the more favoured climats lower down the slopes.

Above Chablis (literally and metaphorically) are the Premiers Crus, the most established ones to the east of the town and a spreading number to the west, and at the top of the tree are the Grands Crus, seven of them wrapping themselves around a hill immediately to the east of the town. It is worth walking up this hill, both to clear your head and to understand the lie of the land. Slope and exposure is everything in Burgundy, to catch the most of the sun and to shelter from the worst of the elements, particularly so in Chablis. Standing at the top of this hill, it is obvious why these are the most favoured sites.

So what should Chablis taste like? I have always found an innate contradiction in the best examples, a generosity and a warmth (you might say, some of Chardonnay's traditional butter and white fruit flavours) tempered by a core of acidity that balances the welcome and sends the gentlest shiver to combat any complacency. Above all, there should be a strong mineral element, even a taste of the sea. Growers will love reminding you that the chalk on which the grapes are grown is formed of many billions of oyster and other mollusc shells, the chalk being the sediment left on the retreat of a shallow tropical sea all those millennia ago. For Harry Yoxall, author of the first wine book I ever read, Wines of Burgundy (published in 1968, it belongs to a different, maybe less accountable or measurable age: a beautifully relaxed and gentle introduction to the region), a good Chablis always reminded him of the forced marches he was obliged to undertake during the First World War, during which the soldiers would suck pebbles to slake their thirst. Perhaps the best description I know comes from Clive Coates (I hope he does not mind me quoting in full):

"The colour should be a full, in the sense of quite viscous, greeny-gold. The aromas should combine steeliness and richness, gun flint, grilled nuts and crisp toast. The flavour should be long, individual and complex. Above all, the wine should be totally dry, but without greenness. The aftertaste must be rich rather than mean, ample rather than hard, generous rather than soulless. Chablis is an understated wine, so it should be subtle rather than obvious, reserved rather than too obviously charming."

Why do I labour this point about the wine's taste? Because there are too many poor examples out there (it is such a sellable commodity) and yet, at its best, it is quite literally one of the finest white wines in France, if not the finest. The great whites from the Côte d'Or can sometimes be too great for their own good. They are born into a life of privilege and greatness is expected of them. For Chablis and its northern clime, it is all just that bit more of a struggle and its greatness, when in evidence, is earned. As with humans, does that not make it that bit more attractive?

Chablis Vieilles Vignes, Saint Claire, Domaine Brocard 2012

However bored you were at our endless visits to winegrowers, I could always make you smile. "Où se trouve les vignes pour ce vin?" and "Les vignes ont quelle âge?" They were my stock questions, each and every time. My sole gambits, my only rolls of the dice. And so predictable to you that I can still see the smile on your face each time I asked the questions.

As often as not, the first of these questions would set the vigneron off, he would pull down a map and with a blunted, scarred finger, dirt still under the nail, repeatedly thump the vineyard or vineyards responsible for the wine. Given that, in those days, we were only ever buying Bourgognes or village wines, I was interested to know where the vines lay, how close they were to more august vineyards, how I could kid myself that these wines had more than a passing resemblance to the better wines next door. And I suspect the winegrower was equally happy playing this game as well.

You would stand by patiently, humouring my deep-seated interest and skin-deep knowledge. And when we came to tasting the wine, it was only you who could judge the wine impartially, uncluttered by misleading knowledge, expectations and reputations, instead sticking to what mattered: what was in the glass.

And both of these questions would have been apposite for this wine as well. Although it is only a generic Chablis, each year the Vieilles Vignes bottling comes from the same set of vines in the Malantes vineyard (not Premier Cru but highly thought-of in any event), planted in 1947. So what is it about old vines? Old vines naturally produce fewer grapes and so those fewer grapes are naturally more concentrated, resulting (naturally!) in a more concentrated and flavoursome wine.

This wine also has a little bit of bottle age. Much Chablis, possibly too much Chablis, is drunk within a couple of years of the vintage (much is made for early drinking). That is a shame. Age brings stature, new perspectives, new flavours, new depths, greater interest and a more faithful rendition of the land on which the wine was grown. In this case, the wine has broadened out, there is an element of butter, the gun flint is deeper, the wine is gentler and less angular, there is more substance, there is more to offer. Really it is very good (this bottling by Brocard always is). As a rule of thumb, drink Petit Chablis within the first two years of the vintage, Chablis two to four years after the vintage, Premier Cru four to eight and Grand Cru, well give it a good six or so to start with and then see how you are getting on.

Chablis 1er Cru, Montée de Tonnerre, La Chablisienne 2010
Chablis 1er Cru, Montée de Tonnerre, Domaine Patrick Piuze 2010
Chablis 1er Cru, Montée de Tonnerre, Domaine Christophe 2010
Chablis 1er Cru, Le Forest, Domaine Dauvissat-Camus 2006
Chablis 1er Cru, Le Forest, Domaine Dauvissat-Camus 2007
Chablis 1er Cru, Le Forest, Domaine Dauvissat-Camus 2008
Chablis 1er Cru, Le Forest, Domaine Dauvissat-Camus 2010
Chablis 1er Cru, Vaillons, Domaine Dauvissat-Camus 2010
Chablis 1er Cru, Le Forest, Domaine Dauvissat-Camus 2011

The last time we visited Chablis was in 2012, the year of the London Olympics, the summer of our road trip across France to the Alps and back after the first of my big operations. We stayed in the Hostellerie des Clos in Chablis, something we could only dream of all those years ago when we first visited. We all of us crowded into in a family suite, the little ones sharing a bed with great excitement, us upstairs and Emily putting a brave face of being in the same room as the other two and cutting out their noise as best she could.

It was the night of the opening ceremony of the Olympic Games and Gus, as self-appointed Olympics information officer, was keen not to miss a minute of it. But we had supper to get to and dragged him away.

I remember little of the food but everything of the wine list. Wines that I could only dream of fell off the page and at prices I could barely hope for. We settled on a bottle of Raveneau's Butteaux, an unattractive name for a Chablis Premier Cru forming part of Montmains. 69 euros (how on earth do I remember this?) against a retail price in England of well over £100 (and who would guess how much in a restaurant). The wine was extraordinary – as Hugh Johnson says of Chablis, mined from the bowels of the earth.

None of this cut any mustard with Gus of course. I do not know if he was simply miffed at being dragged away from the Olympics but he took exception to the fact that he was asked to order his food while sitting in the lounge and not at the table, something I have always quite enjoyed myself. And when he was brought a sorbet as a palate cleanser between courses, well this was completely out of order. He had not ordered it, it should be taken away. I think I ended up eating it.

And do you remember Greeny, Gus's pale excuse of a rag which passed for a comforter? That night he lost it mid-sleep. He marshalled the help of Emily and Claudia but this was not enough and we both had to come downstairs to help. It was eventually found down the side of the bed. A troubled evening for Gus, and he hadn't even been drinking.

There is a school of thought that the apogee of Chablis is not its Grands Crus but rather its Premiers Crus. The sites of the Grands Crus, some would argue, are too blessed, too sun-soaked and, in this warming climate, the sun blunts the chiselled edge of the best Chablis. Wouldn't I love to test this theory. Unfortunately the Grands Crus that I have tried can be counted on one hand. Premiers Crus, however, I have had more luck with, as witness the number we have and as witness, perhaps, the number that there are in Chablis. Whereas there are only seven Grands Crus, all in a strictly defined area on the edge of the town itself, the sites of the Premiers Crus spread far and wide. I am not sure there is anything wrong with this. Although what are considered to be the finest Premiers Crus (Montée de Tonnerre, Fourchaume and Mont de Milieu) all flank the Grands Crus on the left bank of the Serein, there are plenty enough good examples from elsewhere, Raveneau's Butteaux for starters, to indicate that just as propitious land for the grape lies further afield. As ever, I suspect, it is a question of going for the grower rather than the vineyard. In any event, Premiers Crus will, or should, show a greater intensity than straight Chablis, an ability to age, a longer finish, deeper and more complex flavours. As well as sea shells, there should be a greater degree of ripeness and body which fills out the palate. In the best examples, I occasionally and surprisingly get an echo of cheese on the aftertaste, all of which adds to the interest and the complexity. And if you are very lucky, an element of smoke creeps in, from a far-off fire of vine cuttings on a winter's day.

La Chablisienne: There are no great wines, only great bottles.

For a long while I have struggled with the meaning of this expression but I think I finally understand. Let me try and explain. My heart belongs to Montée de Tonnerre. Simple. That is because the best bottle of Chablis I have ever had was with you, my love, at the Chablisienne co-operative on our very first visit. La Chablisienne is a wonderful place to go, especially if it is your first time. The full array of wines is on show to try and it is sufficiently impersonal not to feel obliged either to engage in conversation or to buy anything at the end of it. Of course we did but, for the most part, it was Petit Chablis (which was then, chilled overnight in the boot of the Renault 5 and hauled out for successive picnics on equally chilly days, quite the perfect wine for the occasion), a few bottles of an oaked Chablis (a rare beast, Cuvée Speciale it was called, and not I think made any more) and, as a special treat, just a couple of bottles of Montée de Tonnerre which we religiously and carefully brought back to England for no doubt a couple of special occasions which I have completely forgotten about. But it was that first taste in the co-op, that first taste of something bigger and better than what had come before, that first taste of something that could take you further, that promised unfolding flavours and new sensations, really that is something I have never forgotten. I am not saying that, qualitatively, it is the finest example of Chablis I have ever tried, that may be Raveneau's Butteaux, but it is certainly the best bottle of Chablis I have ever had. So whenever I see Montée de Tonnerre I am immediately transported back to that epiphany. It may not have been a great wine, but it was indubitably a great bottle. There, that is it.

This example, by the way, a solitary bottle, will be good but do not tarry too long. La Chablisienne's wines are not made for long-term cellaring. 2010 was a great year, Montée de Tonnerre is a great vineyard, but do not ask too much of the wine.

Piuze: Things are changing but for a long while Chablis suffered from a lack of competition. Plenty of good growers but few to push the boundaries or focus on the detail to show up the complacency of others, detail such as lower yields, picking by hand, concentrating on the terroir of individual plots and ambition to produce the very best that man can from what nature has provided. Patrick Piuze is one such man. His wines are very fashionable and impossible to find and he is impossible to get hold of. I tried to, when we were in Chablis that Olympic year, but e-mails went unanswered. I think I did in fact see him in the main square when we were having coffee one morning but he was with a mother and child (both, I think, belonging to him) and I thought it might be a little unwarranted to accost him there and then. In any event, I eventually tracked down a few bottles in Reims of all places and this lone bottle is what is left. The last bottle I tried was completely dumb (good wines will often close down for a few years after bottling, as they progress on their slow maturation). Unlike La Chablisienne's offering, this wine will last the distance. Maybe, even, leave it till 2020. Gus will be 18 and may like to share it over the opening ceremony of the Tokyo Olympics.

Christophe: For a long while, Domaine Christophe's Vieilles Vignes offering was the office's "smart" Chablis for client lunches. It is a beautiful wine, encompassing all that Clive Coates looks for in a good example. His Montée de Tonnerre has not yet hit those heights but I am not sure whether this is because that is in the nature of the wine or if it is because it is still a little young. As with the Dauvissat below, I have noticed that Sebastian Christophe's wines take time to shed their unformed, unfocussed fruitiness, their puppy fat, to reveal the core of minerality underneath. Now Montée de Tonnerre will always have a little more fruit and substance to it anyway because of its wonderful location and exposure but are we there yet with this wine or does it still have some distance to go? I suspect the latter.

Incidentally we once went to visit them on their farm up behind the Grands Crus. Sebastian was out in the vineyard but his father was desperate to get stuck in. It must have been a slow afternoon for him (he and his wife were looking after the grandchildren). He collared me, left you to look after Emily who was instructed to play with the other kids and dragged me into the tasting room where he proceeded to open as many bottles as he could despite my hesitation. He wasn't mucking about or wasting time. I think I asked you to drive us back to town.

Dauvissat: What is wine? Many things to different people. Fermented grape juice. Safe drinking water (this was certainly the case in centuries past). A social lubricant to bring people together, to encourage conversation, the exchange of ideas and companionship. A relaxant, the re-boot at the end of each day, the means by which to start again with the one you love. The necessary companion to food, to make the meal whole. A reminder of the joys this planet can bring and the diversity present here on God's earth. A hobby (of course) and for those who think about it more (too?) seriously, a repository of time, place and memory.

Time, the passage of time. For lovers of wine, this is one of the most fascinating aspects of collecting wine, to view the wine's development across the passing of the years. There is little more exciting than broaching the first bottle of a case of wine that has been laid down until deemed ready. And then there is little more fascinating than watching that wine develop over the rest of the case. Stephen Spurrier, talking about claret, advocates opening the first bottle after seven years. It will still be too young, he suggests, but by this time the wine will be beginning to reveal its secrets and will offer you a glimpse of what the future holds. For it is the secondary, even the tertiary, development of a wine that holds most fascination for wine lovers. When a wine is young, it is all fruit, maybe mixed in with awkward amounts of acid and tannin, possibly slightly dominant vanilla flavours from oak ageing too, all of which disguise the true identity of the wine (and therefore of place and time). Time melds these, the fruit stops shouting, the tannins ease off, the acidity knits it all together, the vanilla recedes with the tide. And in the quietness created, other flavours hesitantly emerge and, like the development of man himself, true identity is then revealed. And that is what we wait for.

Alongside François Raveneau, Vincent Dauvissat is considered the finest winemaker in Chablis. He makes wines for the long haul, refusing to stir the lees in barrel. Stirring the lees (natural sediment from the fermentation process) releases more flavour and so is suitable for wines designed to be drunk early; a side effect of doing so, however, is that it reduces the wine's ability to age and to develop further. Please don't ask me why. So Dauvissat's wines, when young, are relatively impenetrable. They are mute and, if not mute, carry a strong flavour of camomile. Some mistake this for premature oxidation (I will deal with this below) but the wines are simply going through a prolonged dumb stage. It has taken me a very long time to realise this. Look at my tasting notes for the 2006 Forest. It has been deeply frustrating and at times completely frustrating although, now with hindsight, a fascinating exercise.

Which brings me on to case size. Should you buy six bottles or 12 bottles when you lay wine down? There are a few factors here. 12-bottle cases undoubtedly give you a longer run at tracking and understanding a wine, especially if the drinking window is a wide one. Thank goodness I have 12-bottle cases of the Dauvissat because it has taken me ten bottles or so of the 2006 to learn my lesson. In the early stages of building up a cellar, 12 bottles will also get you up to a proper fighting weight, in terms of cellar size, that bit quicker. Six-bottle cases begin to make more sense when your collection reaches such proportions that, really, you are not going to tackle it in anything like a sensible way unless you ease off on the numbers. And six bottles also makes sense if the wine is expensive. In fact, it becomes a good mantra to buy less and drink better as time passes.

All very interesting, but what about the Dauvissat? The 2006 is beginning to come into its own. 2006 was not the greatest of vintages in Chablis so it may always be a little fat but the pebbles and oyster shells should emerge. They certainly have in the 2007 which is a much better vintage, less warm so less ripe fruit to disguise the bracing acidity and minerality of the wine. Maybe it is my chemo-affected palate but, if anything, I found myself longing for maybe just a little bit more love, a little bit more flesh and fruit, from the glass of 2007 I had. I have not tried the subsequent vintages. These are expensive wines to buy now (for a while they were underpriced given the price paid for them on the secondary market). I kept going till 2011 but, after that, based on the refusal of the wines to reveal their charms quickly, and the rising prices, I eased off. Like Butteaux, Le Forest is a small part of Montmains. Vaillons is another highly thought of Premier Cru on the right bank of the Serein. They will all be good. In time.

Chablis Grand Cru, Valmur, Domaine Moreau-Naudet 2009

I am afraid your guess will be as good as mine on this one. I used this wine for a winetasting I did a few years ago now, comparing Moreau-Naudet's Chablis, Premier Cru and Grand Cru all from 2009. 2009 was a ripe vintage and so not best placed to showcase Chablis' verve and bite. So unsurprisingly, quite apart from being very young at the time, the Valmur (one of the top Grands Crus) seemed fat and a little bland. There is one bottle in the corner of the rack. Keep an eye on cellartracker. Others' tasting notes might reveal when it is best to broach it. I suspect that time will blunt the warmth of the vintage and that the vineyard's true character will come through. By 2019 there should be something there. See if you can hang on till then unless, of course, together we have got there sooner.

COTE D'OR
BLANC

I am sticking with white for the moment. The reds will follow.

So if Chablis and Mâcon, north and south respectively, book-end the white wines of Burgundy, the jewel in the crown, indubitably, is the Côte d'Or, the golden slope where all the great white wines of Burgundy are to be found.

The Côte d'Or can be split into two, the Côte de Nuits and the Côte de Beaune. The Côte de Nuits runs down from Dijon to somewhere south of Nuits-St-Georges where the Côte de Beaune then picks up the baton and runs south, past Beaune, to just north of Chagny (where the Côte Chalonnaise makes its brief appearance – home of the appellations of Mercurey, Rully and Givry though we agreed, of course, to ignore them to keep things straightforward).

Given that the Côte de Beaune lies to the south of the Côte de Nuits, you would have thought that the Côte de Beaune was warmer and therefore better suited to red grapes (red grapes needing more warmth and sunshine to ripen than white grapes). This is not the case. Although there are very august red wine appellations in the Côte de Beaune (Volnay, Pommard, even Beaune), the Côte de Beaune is actually better suited to Chardonnay than to Pinot Noir. The slopes are gentler and the exposure more south-east than east.   Given how far north Burgundy is, every scrap of sunshine is needed for red grapes, none perhaps more important than the first rays of the day to banish the overnight chill, so east is good, south-east less so.

The escarpment is also more broken on the Côte de Beaune, allowing cool winds to creep in, unwelcome to Pinot Noir, often essential to retain the freshness of Chardonnay.

All of which is bringing me, ever so slowly, to the question of terroir. I have tiptoed carefully around the topic to date, not wanting to drag you down with this concept but I am afraid you cannot talk of Burgundy without talking of terroir. The issue has to be confronted. Two chapters in Harry Yoxall's Wines of Burgundy are headed "Some Optional History" and "Some Compulsory Geography". He had it right. We have to concentrate.

For "terroir" read "microclimate", in other words the combination of the different elements of the environment which affect the production of the grape in that particular spot. When we mow our lawns we all recognise patches where the grass grows thicker, or dries out quicker, or doesn't grow so well, even in a tiny West London garden. It is the same with grapes. Grapes grow differently in different ground and the quality is better or worse or, even if no different qualitatively, quite often different in character depending on where the vines are to be found.

And for "Burgundy" read "the high temple of terroir". Look once again at the World Atlas of Wine. Look at any of the maps for the Côte de Nuits and the Côte de Beaune. Every square foot of the main slopes has been graded and evaluated according to the quality of the grapes it produces in the most extraordinary detail. And this has been done empirically, over the course of literally thousands of years. It started with the Romans, stuttered along during the first millennium and then took off with the arrival of the Cistercians in the 12th Century who encroached onto the uncultivated slopes of the Côtes and began the serious business of parcellation and gradation.

Equally important, this has been done with conviction. How else, for example, can you stand at a crossroads in Puligny-Montrachet, survey in one corner a Grand Cru vineyard, Bienvenues-Bâtard-Montrachet, on the other side of the road a Premier Cru, Les Pucelles, and to your back two village vineyards, Les Meix and Rue Rousseau? No more than 10 metres, maybe, separates these four vineyards and yet the value of the wine they produce can have a differential of 10 or even more between the various plots.

Of course, the great variable in this concept of terroir is the skill of the winemaker which frankly counts above all else. In terms of the constituent parts of terroir, however, although I would love to be able to talk about Earth, Wind and Fire, really it is a question of earth, air and water. So taking these in reverse order:

Water: as ever, it is a question of having neither too much nor too little but rather just the right amount. And different vineyards perform better or worse. Some, whether it is because they are in a weather window or perhaps on too steep an incline so the rain runs off, get more drought-stressed than others. Others, perhaps because they are at the bottom of the slope or on the valley floor, suffer more flooding than others. It is easy to see why the finest vineyards are found mid-slope, because this is where the balance between over- and under-water supply is best in balance.

Air: is the vineyard susceptible to frost, to the katabatic winds that creep down off the high ground and settle in the valley bottoms? If so, then a late frost can devastate a year's crop and leave the vines with not enough time to produce and ripen a second harvest that year. Or maybe the vineyard lies in a sunpocket and through the extra warmth so generated ripens its crop earlier than surrounding vineyards (a distinct advantage in this northern climate). And how quickly does the cold morning air warm up? Is the vineyard on a steep east-facing slope so that it quickly captures the morning sun as soon as it has risen? Or is it on a shallow south-facing slope and so rests in shadow until later in the day? All of this will have an effect on the ability of the grapes to ripen.

Earth: and what of this? On the Côte d'Or the underlying bedrock is essentially limestone. At the top of the slope this is very near the surface but, as the hill falls away to the valley floor, it is subsumed first beneath a layer of chalky marl and then, increasingly, beneath clay. Grapes grown on limestone produce a very different flavour profile to those grown on clay – the tannins are finer, the wines are a little nervier and maybe more elegant whereas wines grown on clay have more obvious, blunter flavours with less filigreed tannins.

Burgundy is a myriad of all different combinations of these factors and it is what makes the region so fascinating to anyone who is seduced by its wines. Burgundy has no more of a monopoly on terroir than any other square foot of earth on this planet. What it does have, however, is two thousand years of history of mapping out the relative merits of each square foot and a product to showcase the differences between these square feet.

Pernand-Vergelesses 1er Cru, Sous Frétille, Pierre-Yves Colin-Morey 2008
Pernand-Vergelesses 1er Cru, Sous Frétille, Pierre-Yves Colin-Morey 2011
Pernand-Vergelesses 1er Cru, Sous Frétille, Pierre-Yves Colin-Morey 2014

Pernand-Vergelesses. We came here on our first ever visit, desperately seeking out villages off the beaten track which might offer a glimpse of the glories of Meursault, the Montrachets and even Corton.

You drove your Renault 5 up the steep hill, through narrow streets, past the church, past the coloured roof tiles to the walls of Domaine Dubreuil-Fontaine. We parked outside and entered with just a little hesitation. We need not have worried, the man positively grabbed us and only just stopped short of hugging us. We tried his whites, we tried his reds. He was surprised we turned down the opportunity to try his top wines, his Grand Cru red Corton and white Corton-Charlemagne (what on earth were we doing?!) and we brought his red and his white Pernand, humbler wines from the cooler side of the hill.

Then we climbed the hill behind the domaine, up to the shrine of the Blessed Mary, Nôtre Dame de Bonne Espérance. From here we looked south along the valley floor, the vineyards of Pernand and Savigny climbing the slopes, Beaune sprawling in the middle distance. Ile des Vergelesses, Pernand's finest vineyard, lay in the kidney of the slope. I pointed it out to you and bored you about how each village on the Côte d'Or has commandeered the name of its most famous vineyard as a suffix to the village name. Except that the villages of Puligny and Chassagne were reluctant to cede Le Montrachet (Burgundy's finest Chardonnay vineyard) to the other so both have used it, the vineyard lying half in Puligny, half in Chassagne.

So yes, I have always had a soft spot for Pernand. I am always reminded of those first tentative steps, nervous of the reception that we might receive, arriving unannounced at a domaine, and our (or my?) reluctance to try Dubreuil-Fontaine's top wines. Was I just too timid, worried he would recognise the ignorant I was? Or was I just too honest, in no way being in the market to afford or buy those top wines? In any event, it was a pretty poor performance. One more puzzle.

In recent years, I have discovered a wonderful source of Pernand from the magician who is Pierre-Yves Colin-Morey, his wines as focussed and full of intent as his character, reserved in youth, even in maturity measured and ever so slightly withheld. Sous Frétille lies just beneath the statue to the Virgin Mary, looking out on that self-same view as you and I did. As to be expected, from a relatively cool site (quite high up, a southerly exposure) and a relatively cool producer, the wine gives slowly, is not over-generous and merits concentration. Above all it is mineral, age bestowing more in the way of hazelnut and caramel than anything so soft as gentle fruit flavours (there is even a touch of Chinese Five Spice if you will believe me). It is not without fruit, by any stretch, but appreciate its reserve, far more noticeable than in the warmer wines to the south. Give the 2011 and 2014 time to unravel; give the remaining bottles of 2008 the attention they deserve.

Corton-Charlemagne Grand Cru, Domaine Follin-Arbelet 2009

At university, medieval history was my thing. The different world governed by different mores, the power of tradition, superstition, religion, the small scale of the conflicts and the wide significance of the consequences (the making of history being such a privileged pastime in those days, undertaken by the few), the mystery, the unknown, the romance of the stories, the romance of today's ruins and buildings from that era and, if I am honest, the scarcity of sources and the resultant paucity of research that needed to be undertaken by, frankly, idle undergraduates.

So it was natural that we should have to visit the vineyards responsible for Corton-Charlemagne, the first white Grand Cru of the Côte de Beaune, wrapped around the southern and eastern flanks of the vast Corton hill, a wine of huge stature and statement, capable of extraordinary complexity, always retaining that slightly reserved cool, mineral element found in Pernand (some of the vineyard lies in Pernand) but everything just on a bigger, much bigger scale. A wine of serious proportions and unlimited ambitions.

We picked up a track, coming out of Pernand, that followed the curve of the hill around to the east. It then turned steeply uphill, between low stone walls, surrounded by vineyard, before settling at a higher level and tracking the contours of the hill round to the north, the wooded crown of the hill above us shadowing our perambulation. It was hot and impossibly bright, the sun bouncing off the chalk slopes. The vines were still bare, twisted with age and the potential of the coming year's harvest. It was hard under foot, no grass cover, bare chalk, awkward stones. Half way round the hill we stopped beneath the shade of a solitary tree, just above Clos du Roi, beside a vigneron's hut. Away to the east the Alps sketched a hazy silhouette on the horizon, snow still visible on the higher parts. We continued on our walk and were soon back into the woods. I heard, then saw, my first Crested Tit and together we watched a red squirrel tumble and gather along the boughs of a pine. Through the wood and round the other side of the hill, we made our way back to the village, through vineyards less singular and less blessed but more varied and more beautiful, folded as they were into the waves of a small valley.

The story of Corton-Charlemagne is well-known, if almost certainly made up. The land belonged to Charlemagne, the first Holy Roman Emperor, the most powerful man that Western Europe had seen since the Roman emperors 500 years before.

The land was planted to red grapes. Charlemagne loved his wine. And he had a white beard. He also had a wife who, despite being married to the most powerful man in Western Europe, was not afraid to reprimand him on a regular basis. As will be familiar to many, Charlemagne's wife got after him about his drinking habits. She could tell exactly when he had been drinking because his white beard would soon be stained red. Tired of this unwanted attention, Charlemagne ordered the grubbing up of the vines and their replacement with vines producing white grapes. Henceforth he would only drink white wine so as to avoid his wife's detection. It is likely that Chardonnay vines were in fact only planted in the 19th century but this story cannot detract from the allure of the vineyard, that this land might once have belonged to Charlemagne himself.

Although the reputation of Burgundy is waxing wonderfully at the moment, all is not entirely well in the land of White Burgundy. The problem is premature oxidation. It started with the 1996 vintage, a white wine vintage brimming with such promise (even if the acidity for some was just a little lively). One of the great traits of White Burgundy is its ageability which brings with it complexity only hinted at in the young wine and, over time, a peeling away of the layers to reveal the nuances of each vineyard. The trouble with 1996, and subsequent vintages, was that these wines started falling off a cliff after no more than five years in bottle. Five years! For wines that were designed, and priced, to last 20. They developed oxidised flavours (the smell of sherry is a good prompt here – delicious in sherry itself but fairly devastating in a Premier Cru from Puligny-Montrachet) and a deep golden colour. What on earth was happening? At first, the Bourguignons stuck their heads in the sand and denied there was any problem. Hardly sensible. But when they did come to admit the problem, they were flummoxed as to the cause. Was it a lack of hygiene in the cellar? Was it too much bâtonnage, the stirring of the lees? Was it the corks? Too much skin contact? Too high or too low a fermentation temperature? Everyone came out with different theories, no one really knew. And no one really does know, even now. It is likely something to do with the cork since, in a case of 12, only a number of the bottles will be affected. So it was not a case of whole batches, rather individual bottles and the only difference between individual bottles is the cork. At least this is what logic would dictate, hence the fashion now, amongst the more conscientious growers, including Colin-Morey, to seal his bottles with wax to double the protection afforded by the cork against oxidation.

This is all relevant here because we only have the one bottle of Corton-Charlemagne, albeit in the form (what a magnificent form) of a magnum. Corton-Charlemagne should take many years to reach its best, to develop the twists and turns of a bewitching complexity, to surrender flavours of cordite, hazlenuts, butter, nutmeg and lanolin. But if the risk of premature oxidation hangs over the bottle, what on earth to do? The answer must be to risk it, to allow the wine time to fulfil its potential because if it does reach its potential, the joy will be much greater than the disappointment of premature oxidation or unformed flavours if we were to open it earlier than we should. So there, I have managed your expectations, you have been warned. But play the long game and go for the reward. And you can of course, we can of course, keep an eye on cellartracker to see how others have fared with this wine (just remember to take all their views with a pinch of salt; not everyone is an expert). As mentioned above a few times already, 2009 was a warm vintage for whites. It was nevertheless a good vintage for whites (though not as stellar as it was for Red Burgundies) so long as the vigneron could hang on to some acidity and not allow the wine to be overwhelmed by overripe white fruits. Given the vineyard's altitude and the slightly cooler microclimate than further south, I have high hopes that this wine will have managed just fine with the vintage. And Follin-Arbelet is a man who knows what he is doing.

Auxey-Duresses, Les Ruchottes, Pierre-Yves Colin-Morey 2012

Yet another example of my ignorance is that I have never really been sure where Auxey-Duresses is. It lies off the main drag of world-beating, world-famous villages that line the Route des Grands Crus which trickles down the Côte d'Or from north to south. Past Corton and Pernand, the white wines of the Côte de Beaune take a back seat for a while to the reds of Savigny-lès-Beaune, Beaune, Pommard and Volnay before arriving with a fanfair in Meursault, Puligny-Montrachet and Chassagne-Montrachet. I know that Saint-Aubin lies just behind Chassagne, but where on earth is Auxey-Duresses? The answer is (having just looked at a map), behind Meursault and, to get there, you have to take a break from the beaten track and head west for a couple of miles into the hinterland. I am afraid that is as much as I know about Auxey's geographical location, as much I know about this wine. I bought it because of the reputation of the grower and the recommendation of the wine merchant I trust. There is something quite liberating in this. My expectations are nil. I am relying on others. It will be fun. And carefree. And knowing nothing about the wine or the village, and assuming I am here to drink it, I shall be like you and shall impose no preconceptions on the wine. I, you, we shall drink and judge the wine for what it is in the glass. No history, no baggage, no problem. Lovely. Maybe in a couple of years.

**Saint-Aubin 1er Cru, En Remilly, Pierre-Yves Colin-Morey
2010**
**Saint-Aubin 1er Cru, En Remilly, Pierre-Yves Colin-Morey
2012**
**Saint-Aubin 1er Cru, Chatenière, Pierre-Yves Colin-Morey
2012**
**Saint-Aubin 1er Cru, En Remilly, Pierre-Yves Colin-Morey
2013**
**Saint-Aubin 1er Cru, En Remilly, Pierre-Yves Colin-Morey
2015**

For the record, these are wines bought out of love, not fear. Saint-Aubin used to be cheap; it is not any more. Is this a bad thing or a good thing? It is only a bad thing where price is driven by fashion or scarcity. If by fashion, then leave to their own devices the fools who buy these wines to satisfy their own lack of self-esteem. If by scarcity, well we know the answer now, again leave the wines alone. There will be others just as good, not as scarce and half the price elsewhere.

Saint-Aubin fits neither of these categories. The wines are not scarce nor are they particularly (or at all?) fashionable. The village sits just behind Chassagne-Montrachet, just the other side of the hill indeed from Le Montrachet itself. But the exposition of the land, and the soil of the land, is not at all bad. I would hazard a guess that the prices have risen for Saint-Aubin as much as they have (though, for the record, they still represent good value compared with the wines of Meursault and the two Montrachets) because ambitious winegrowers have realised just how much potential there is in Saint-Aubin's whites. And that is borne out by the wines I have tasted. Again, without having the curse of trying a Saint-Aubin against, say, a Meursault of equal standing, I have been struck by how complete and complex these wines can be and have been left asking not so much whether White Burgundy can be any better than this but do I need White Burgundy to be any better than this? To which the answer is no, I do not.

En Remilly is generally considered to be the finest vineyard in Saint-Aubin, being (no coincidence here) the closest to the Premiers Crus and Grands Crus of Puligny and Chassagne. It is in fact an extension of Le Montrachet, the most revered white wine vineyard in the world, but without of course quite the exposure and lie of the land of the great vineyard itself. The examples I have had, including the 2010 here, but not the more recent vintages which remain untasted, show tremendous body (fatter, for example, than the Pernand Sous Frétille from the same grower) and some of that wet dog smell which is the trademark of proper and exciting White Burgundy. The 2010 is mouth-filling with an almost Sauternes-like richness and flavours of burnt matchstick and white peach. Really, really good stuff. I have no doubt the other vintages will follow in this vein. As for Chatenière, I can tell you little but it is a vineyard in the same mould as En Remilly so will likely produce a similar, rich offering. Something to look forward to.

Bourgogne Blanc, Domaine Antoine Jobard 2011
Bourgogne Blanc, Pierre-Yves Colin-Morey 2013

It is probably fair to say that the wine from which I have derived most pleasure in my 30 years or so of wine-drinking is Bourgogne. You will recall that Bourgogne sits at the bottom of the hierarchy, below village level. So a Bourgogne will be produced from vines outside the village boundary (maybe only a couple of yards) but it can also contain declassified fruit from a higher appellation (village or even Premier Cru) if the winegrower is not happy to put that fruit into the higher wine. So if you can find a conscientious grower who produces a Bourgogne from vines that lie near the village then you will be onto a winner, an absolute winner. Red or white, a good Bourgogne will offer way more than a passing resemblance to the more famous wines of the area and with just as much of the character of Burgundy. I have such inordinately happy memories of so many Bourgognes from such good domaines – Digoia-Royer, Roumier, Maume among red, Darviot-Perrin, Pierre Morey, Matrot among white (and these are only a few). To begin with, we had no choice but to hunt among the Bourgognes, being the cheapest wines we could find, but in time I came to seek them out from choice. Why is this? Because of the character the wines impart, the eternal appeal of the underdog, yes, I will admit, the eternal appeal of value for money, the knowledge that as much skill and knowledge goes into a Bourgogne as into the rest of a good producer's range, the memory maybe of where we started.

Jobard: you could argue that there is no finer example of a Bourgogne than Antoine Jobard's mini-Meursault. Again, produced from vines grown just outside the village appellation, Jobard has made something of a name for himself with this wine and the 2011 does not disappoint. It has all the marks of a good Meursault – wet dog, hazelnuts, rich peach, flint, smoke – and it screams of its place; this wine could not come from anywhere else. There is one magnum, on the top shelf of the wine rack. Embrace it now.

Pierre-Yves Colin-Morey: this wine is in a different key to the Jobard. It is tighter knit, not so generous or front-loaded in its gifts. It is made from young fruit from Saint-Aubin and Puligny-Montrachet and it takes time to come round. Expect something more refined, maybe, more reserved but ultimately with just as much to say. I would leave it a year or two and then gently tip your toe into the case.

MACON

Mâcon. We have all drunk Mâcon and some of it has been pretty atrocious. Victoria Wine, in the good old days, used to do a Mâcon-Villages which was anodyne to the point of being tasteless and thin to the point of being paint stripper. But we persevered because Mâcon has always been a bolt-hole, whether on a restaurant's wine list or in a vain search for respectability as we desperately search for a well-priced wine that we can honestly and without shame present to a host. Mâcon: the largest of the regions of Burgundy (again, ignoring Beaujolais) and given to over 90% white wine production.

Chardonnay is the key grape here and, in keeping with the basic rules about Burgundy, there is something of a hierarchy. At the bottom of the pile remains Bourgogne (but this is such a different beast to the Bourgognes of the Côte d'Or that care should be taken before taking the plunge – they are not the works of love of small producers from hallowed ground but, for the most part, mass-produced products of large négociants from indifferent terroir). Then comes Mâcon which is supposedly inferior to Mâcon-Villages (which must be produced from grapes grown in one or more of a number of entitled villages) which in turn should be inferior to wine produced from a number of named villages which can add their name as a suffix to Mâcon, such as Mâcon-Farges or Mâcon-Chardonnay (yes, there is a village called Chardonnay). At the top of the tree come the villages which do not even mention Mâcon, such as Saint-Véran (which I have always found slightly bland and ever so slightly underwhelming), Vire-Clessé and Pouilly-Fuissé. There are no Premiers Crus or Grands Crus to worry about; it is simply a case of understanding where the village fits into the hierarchy. Whether this makes it easier to understand or more difficult, I cannot say. There are in fact plans to introduce

Premiers Crus though whether these plans will ever get off the ground I am not sure. The French have a spectacular way of cocking up the most well-meaning proposals. Just look at the 10-yearly plans to review the Saint-Emilion classification system or the planned reclassification of the Médoc's Crus Bourgeois. As soon as perfectly sensible proposals are tabled, there is uproar from the aggrieved parties who have been excluded, a law suit is launched and the various governing bodies are then forced into cancelling the planned redesignations. Perhaps this is unfair, perhaps it is an exaggeration, but the Mâcon and Premiers Crus – don't hold your breath.

If my enthusiasm for the region sounds lukewarm, then I am doing it a disservice. When well-made (and, in common with the rest of the wine world, as standards rise this is more and more the case), a Mâcon wine can produce a burst of sunshine and uncomplicated pleasure that is impossible to resist. The wine can be full-bodied and generous. Whereas too much acidity used to be the problem, now the conscientious growers are concerned about too little acidity on account of global warming and the increased efforts of the vignerons to pick ripe grapes and extract as much flavour as possible. A well-made Mâcon is, or should be (to adopt an expression I abhor) a "good drop": honest, upfront, devoted to pleasure.

As ever, some producers are pushing the boundaries. Reduced yields, greater care in the vineyard, biodynamism, hand-harvesting, planting on north-facing slopes (to prevent over-ripeness) and, in the cellar, blocking the malolactic fermentation (preserving a brighter level of acidity in the wine), ageing in oak, bottling different parcels separately, any number of different techniques really, are producing wines of greater concentration, expression, ageing ability and typicity. Coupled to this, there has been an influx of gifted winegrowers from the

Côte d'Or (led by Lafon and Leflaive), attracted by the land prices and the potential of the region. Mâcon is a region on the up and, in the right hands, delivers a lot for the price of the bottle.

Pouilly-Fuissé, Vieilles Vignes, Domaine de la Soufrandise 2012
Viré-Clessé, Les Hauts des Menards, Domaine André Bonhomme 2012

Soufrandise: This domaine has not yet gone down the route of bottling different parcels separately, instead holding to the belief that the whole can be greater than the sum of the parts. It is also a matter of expediency since, in common with many growers in Burgundy, holdings can be scattered far and wide, some of them very small in size: it is just not feasible to bottle them all separately. I was happily getting into the habit of buying this wine annually because it is a reliable, joyous expression of the bounty that the finer parts of the Mâcon can offer. It is rich and golden, filled with Burgundy caramel, and retains that unmistakeable tang (some liken it to vomit which is probably unhelpful) and cracked cordite of good White Burgundy. Pouilly-Fuissé has traditionally been viewed as the apogee of the Mâcon and Domaine de la Soufrandise does nothing to dispel that impression.

Bonhomme: Goodness, another wine about which I know very little. This was an impulse buy and, in common with all impulse buys, there was something deliciously cavalier and abandoned about it. I had heard of Bonhomme before but never tasted his wines. This wine is a rare beast, only some 2,000 bottles being produced annually for a world population of 7.4 billion. How could I refuse? I recall the promotional literature saying that the wines take a good while to express themselves. And the care of the winegrower is obvious in the way each bottle is individually capped with wax (to prevent premature oxidation as well, maybe, as to suck in buyers like me). Unlike Domaine de la Soufrandise, André Bonhomme produces a number of different bottlings for certain of his more valued plots, as here. I read the vines for this wine are over 85 years old. The potential is clearly there. I have not tried it and cellartracker is silent on the subject. Best wait a few years more.

COTE D'OR
ROUGE

And so to the reds. Coming back to the rules of Burgundy, we can keep things equally simple for the red wines of Burgundy. If we ignore Beaujolais, the only grape of any import is Pinot Noir and the only region of any import the Côte d'Or. Chablis does not produce red wine (save in a couple of very specialist satellite appellations) and, as I have mentioned, Mâcon produces no more than 10% red. The Côte Chalonnaise does produce some (especially in Givry and Mercurey) but, for current purposes, we can focus solely on the Côte d'Or and its Côtes de Nuits and de Beaune.

Pinot Noir is often referred to as the holy grail of grapes. It is picky about where it will grow, it is then tricky to vinify and it can be tricky in bottle. It can produce desperately disappointing thin, green and stalky wine but at the same time it can produce the finest expressions of *vitis vinifera* (the vine responsible for all the great grape varieties) the world knows, wines that explode out of the glass, full of body and life (despite the wine's seemingly slight frame), wines with a panoply of flavours that others can only dream of, filled with love and fruit, wines that appeal to the emotions as much as to the intellect. It is a thin-skinned grape but with surprising degrees of tannin (it can be challenging when young) and it will faithfully express its origins. Look again at the maps of the region - given the patchwork that is Burgundy, the appeal of this attribute is obvious. To become a disciple of the wines of Burgundy is to launch on a life of fascination and comparison, to immerse yourself entirely in the infinite variety of life and its endless capacity to surprise, to embark on the pursuit of perfection and the inevitable experience of disappointment (but occasionally hitting the heights where words are meaningless and emotions sweep all before them). I mean this. You might think this is puff and hyperbole but I mean it, I really do. Coming back to Sideways, listen to the main character's paean in praise of Pinot Noir, far more accomplished than the few words above (and below).

So let's move from north to south, starting with the Côte de Nuits, traditionally considered the stronghold of Red Burgundy, home to Gevrey, Vosne and Nuits, before moving on to the Côte de Beaune with the (hardly lesser) villages of Volnay, Pommard and Beaune. What a wonderful concentration of riches and beneficence. Royal wines indeed.

Marsannay, Les Longeroies, Domaine Bruno Clair 2005

"Go on, get it!"

"Tackle him!"

"Pass it! No, not him! Someone on your own side!"

"Shoot!"

"Urgh…"

And then after the game:

"Well done. Your lad did well."

"No, he can't tackle. Yours played a blinder though."

"No, he never passes the ball.   I tell him every time, he just won't listen."

It is a curious feature of the relationship between a father and his son, given how strong that relationship traditionally is, that the father should often be the son's worst critic. Look at any touchline on a Saturday afternoon and the array of fathers imploring their sons to tackle harder, pass the ball sooner, shoot for goal now. Others' words of encouragement and praise for the son's performance are as often as not met with regretful denial as they are with grateful acceptance of the compliment well-meant. Why this should be, I do not know. Is it the father's insecurity that somehow the son's performance reflects on the father's worth? Or a sign of the father's absolute love for and pride in his son that his son be the best possible at what he does (and the father's inevitable disappointment when he cannot hit those Olympian heights)?

This will all seem a long way from Marsannay but I am always reminded of the point because an earlier incarnation of this wine, the slightly unfashionable 2000 vintage which has turned out to be an absolute charmer, defied this trend and led my father to praise the wine unreservedly and at length. You may think my father was only praising the wine (maybe he would say the same) but, for me, I took it as praise of me, even if only having the wherewithal to have rooted out this wine and served it to my father when all the planets were aligned. But given how often I produced wonderful wines for my father which he then, however gently, criticised (something he would not have done with other hosts), I remember this occasion as a signal triumph, as we sat outside for an early spring lunch, washed in sunshine that was just enough to defeat the chills of a not long gone equinox.

Marsannay is the first village of the Côte de Nuits, perpetually threatened by the southern sprawl of Dijon, with no Premiers or Grands Crus. It is unfashionable but, in the hands of accomplished growers, quite capable of producing Burgundies honest to their place and within reach of those without the means for the more famous villages of the Côtes. Some might say they are earthy, some might say they lack the aromatics and delicacy of others but I say they carry a strong flavour of baked beans (at least Clair's Longeroies does) and I find them quite delicious. It is sometimes said that with age Marsannay will develop elements of sous bois, undergrowth, the scent of rotting leaves softly trodden underfoot on an autumn walk through damp woods. I once asked Bruno Clair when he thought his Longeroies showed best, hoping he might develop a misty far-off look and with a conspiratorial but magical gleam declare that 10 years would bring an explosion of tertiary flavours, of those damp autumn mornings and fruitfulness. With typical Gallic aplomb he shrugged his shoulders and replied "Just when the grapes are picked". Hmm, I thought, not much help there then. But this 2005 is delicious and, whether or not it ever develops elements of sous bois, I am not sure there is anything to be gained by waiting around to find out. Keep going.

And reverting to my father, I do not know if it was the Heinz element of the wine that he particularly appreciated; given that I was ahead in the day's stakes, I suspect I did not ask him.

Gevrey-Chambertin, Vieille Vigne, Domaine Fourrier 2005
Gevrey-Chambertin, Vieille Vigne, Domaine Fourrier 2008
Gevrey-Chambertin, Vieille Vigne, Domaine Fourrier 2009
Gevrey-Chambertin, Vieille Vigne, Domaine Fourrier 2010
Gevrey-Chambertin, Vieille Vigne, Domaine Fourrier 2011
Gevrey-Chambertin, Vieille Vigne, Domaine Fourrier 2013
Gevrey-Chambertin, Vieille Vigne, Domaine Fourrier 2014
Gevrey-Chambertin, Domaine Maume 2010

Slices of memory, slides of the past. Whenever I think of Gevrey-Chambertin I am inevitably drawn to that first trip we took, our first exposure, our first landfall in a new land. Walking up the wooded cleft of the Combe de Lavaux behind the village, hunting for Black Woodpeckers, leaving the steep slopes of Clos St Jacques at our backs, unaware of its gifts. Our first introduction to l'Ami de Chambertin, the pungency of the cheese's washed rind startling us before drawing us in. The Bourgogne Blanc discovered at Domaine Heresztyn, an intoxicatingly rich and surprising expression of Chardonnay this far north. The vineyard stumbling on into the middle of the village, surrounded on all sides by houses. Eyes wide open, wandering the streets randomly, streets that ended suddenly in the vineyards, wondering this one or this one, this way or that. And oeufs en meurette! Donkeys' balls! Might it be that Gevrey was our first introduction to these as well? My memory fails me here. Maybe that was Meursault.

Not having done the sums, I suspect Gevrey-Chambertin is the largest red wine village in the Côte d'Or, as well as being the first meaningful village you reach on the Côte as you head south from Dijon. It is also one of the most august. Its noblest expression is to be found in its Grands Crus, the most famous of which are Chambertin and Clos de Bèze (sadly I have tried neither), but there is much wine of village level which is very commendable (and sometimes quite pricey). Flavour profile? Gevrey is at the fuller, meatier end of the spectrum. When people talk of Red Burgundy, they often talk of gamey notes, malt and darker fruit profiles. This is the land of Gevrey. Sometimes it can be too much of a good thing (though not for Napoleon, for whom Gevrey was his favourite wine). One of the most beguiling aspects of Pinot Noir is the sweetness of its fruit, particularly strawberry. When you can combine the gaminess and the sweetness, well then you are getting close to the Promised Land. Without the fruit to back it up though, the gaminess and savoury notes can sometimes be a bit top-heavy, lacking the foundations of welcome and mouth-filling pleasure to fill out the wine and give it the balance of the best examples.

Fourrier: these wines are impeccable. My first introduction to them was the 2002 vintage and I could not get over how balanced, sweet and generous they were. Yes, they had the typical feral top notes but they also had the requisite fruit, even in the lowliest examples, to produce a mind-altering experience. Really, they are that delicious. Jean-Marie Fourrier is a thoughtful, ambitious, articulate winemaker with a remarkably pretty wife from Norfolk. He inherited ancient vines from his father in the mid-1990's and soon set about implementing changes, particularly in the cellar. His wines are gentle and scented but with no lack of stuffing. The tannins are there but almost imperceptible. The wine fills out in your glass, in your mouth, in your mind and leaves you with a silly grin, convinced at last that all is well (how rewarding to be a pedlar of such happiness). His wines offer the classic "peacock's tail" character of good Red Burgundy, which is to say that the flavour fills out on your palate, spreads its wings (or, I suppose, its tail feathers) and overtakes all your senses to permeate every part of your being.

These wines are expensive now, Fourrier being one of the

fashionable new names in Burgundy. They are not overly expensive to buy, however, at least not at this level but they do then double in price, possibly more. Have I bought them through love or fear? That's a difficult one because I really do not know. Drink them if you will, we certainly should, but if they end up being sold? Well, don't sell them all; there is too much beauty at stake.

And if you do not sell these wines? I have given you no clues as to the differences in the vintages. And consistent in my inconsistency (I have, after all, for other Red Burgundies) nor shall I. I talk later of vintage charts and vintage chart mentality but, for whatever reason, it is in the red wines of Burgundy that I feel the least attachment to the relative merits of vintage. Why here I wonder? Because in Burgundy, perhaps, there is no clearer exposition that winemaker is king. 10's, 50's, maybe even more winemakers might work the same plot of land and the comparisons in ability and the end product are there for all to see. Burgundy shows clearer than any other wine region the importance of the winemaker's ability and that it is his or her skills which will overcome all but the very worst that nature can throw at a year. So all the vintages we have will be different but they will all be eminently (beautifully!) drinkable, some a little slower to come round perhaps, some a little weightier, others a little more acidic, some more floral, some more charming, others more taciturn. Red Burgundy (and White Burgundy before the days of premature oxidation) lasts much longer than people give it credit for. Enjoy them at your own pace. The 2005, though, you might struggle to find. The two cases of six lie behind layers of junk at the back of one of the recesses, the same place you will find one of the Vieux Télégraphes, alongside some St Josephs, jockeying for space with that unready case of Prüm 2011. Behind the Christmas decorations.

Maume: now this is a case for drinking, without doubt, probably starting on its 10th birthday. This is a wine at the other end of the spectrum from the Fourrier. This is meaty and gamey in spades, it is a wine that smacks of character and idiosyncrasy and shouts of individuality and a road less travelled. It is one of the eternal appeals of Burgundy that it is a region of so many small winemakers that you will always find vignerons who do things differently, their own way, meaning that there is never any chance that the wines of the region will all begin to taste the same (Bordeaux, stand up maybe?). This wine is about malt and marmite, even the touch of merde that Red Burgundy is so often associated with, but always with fruit to back it up. The one thing that puzzles me about Maume is his practice of adding cultivated yeasts to the grape must ahead of fermentation. If the raison d'être of Burgundy (which I feel it must be, given the importance that is attached to terroir) is to reflect as faithfully as possible in the finished wine the gifts of nature from each particular plot and each particular year, then is it not counter-intuitive to introduce an outside agent into the equation which will modify the taste accordingly? I once had a slightly surreal conversation with Jasper Morris, author of Inside Burgundy, about this. I had gone along to Berry Bros to pick up my signed copy when it was first released (it is a book of great detail, maybe its only shortcoming the author's reluctance to express an opinion on the relative merits of the winegrowers he profiles). No doubt to Jasper Morris's horror he suddenly found himself having to talk to me and, don't ask me why, I alighted on the subject of cultivated versus natural yeasts (natural yeasts being those naturally found on the skin of the grape and which, in most cases of high quality bespoke wine, will be used to trigger the fermentation process). Jasper Morris is clearly knowledgeable and, equally clearly, soon lost me completely. I tried to beat an orderly retreat but I do wonder if he had a quiet chuckle after we had parted company, as I did, at the random and really quite obscure conversations that you can from time to time quite unexpectedly find yourself in. Anyway, wonderful wine to be enjoyed. What's more, enjoy it while you can. The domaine was sold in 2011 and the wildness and idiosyncracy of the offerings will no doubt disappear.

Morey-St-Denis, Clos Solon, Domaine Fourrier 2009
Morey-St-Denis, Clos Solon, Domaine Fourrier 2010
Morey-St-Denis, Clos Solon, Domaine Fourrier 2011
Morey-St-Denis 1er Cru, Clos de la Bussière, Domaine Georges Roumier 2009

Read any book on Burgundy and they will all say the same of Morey-St-Denis – overlooked, without a clear identity of its own, only ever defined by its shortcomings in comparison with its neighbours, Gevrey-Chambertin to the north, Chambolle-Musigny to the south. So it is something of a puzzle and something of a mystery. It is a tiny appellation, over half of which is taken up with Grands Crus and Premiers Crus. It should be a jewel (rather it is, like all these villages on the Côte d'Or, but it should have the reputation of one). Or, if it is not, it should be cheap (but it is not). People say it is not as tannic and manly as Gevrey nor as feminine and perfumed as Chambolle. My limited experience of the village's wines places it closer to Gevrey than the villages to the south, retaining a deal of Gevrey's feral and meaty aspects.

We did visit the village once and called in, I fear, on a terribly august grower for the house was grand and its prospect was over a vast expanse of unbroken vineyard. It was early in the day, the sun slowly warming the back of our necks as we rang the bell. The grower, or the grower's wife, was very polite and, despite the hour, was more than willing to pour us samples. Either the wines were impenetrable or it really was just too early in the day for our tastebuds to have woken up. In any event, we retreated fairly quickly without any purchase, none the wiser, as puzzled as when we entered. But then there's nothing wrong with a mystery.

Fourrier: I have just tried the 2009, but I should caveat "tried" by declaring that my palate is in no fit state really after the chemotherapy. Still, the nose revealed a lot of the wine's character – tobacco smoke, malt, mushroom and strawberry. Only Burgundy can do this. The wine shows a deal of the 2009 vintage's generosity, fruit and low tannin and acid. A lovely triumph.

Roumier: Roumier is one of the great names of Burgundy, his wines are impossible to get hold of and really I don't know how I managed to secure even six bottles of this. The Wine Society receives an annual allocation and, after years of trying, clearly the celestial bodies aligned in 2011 when the wines were first offered and I was one of the lucky ones. I have not tried it, I do not know if I will. These wines are worth a lot on the secondary market now so do we drink or do we sell? This is a conundrum that all wine lovers are faced with. For some it is easy: never sell. So long as the wine was bought to be drunk, drink it. Pay no attention to the secondary value. Embrace life and its pleasures. Money is the devil's work. I am increasingly drawn to this attitude (how can I fail to be?) but money also makes the world go round and there may be occasions (there have been occasions) where the money is needed elsewhere and then, however much a shame it might be to do so, it is not a sin to sell. There. I have answered my own question. So long as there is not a crying need for the money elsewhere, these wines should be drunk. They will be dark and beautiful and taste of the earth.

Chambolle-Musigny, Domaine Georges Roumier 2012

Chambolle, Chambolle, Chambolle. The sun will have been shining (it always does in Brighton; why else would the town have such a name?), I will have had my back to the window and the sea, the wine will have been poured into the cut-crystal wine glasses that my grandmother always favoured and the sunlight, streaming over my shoulder, will have scattered refracted rays of garnet and ruby across the table. I will have picked up the glass and smelling and tasting the wine for the first time, will have become lost in silence. I had never smelled nor tasted wine like it before. I did not know wine was capable of such expression, of stopping time and shutting out existence this way. I was engulfed in bemusement and wonder. The scent was of an autumn bonfire, the palate of overripe strawberries and the two fed off each other, each in turn accentuating the pleasure of the other. And all within a texture of deep and utter comfort. This was my epiphany, the moment my interest in wine ceased to be solely intellectual and became something more elemental, something that rooted wine and the pleasures it can bring deep into my soul. At that moment I became aware of the poetry of wine and how it can alter the senses. It was the first time that I experienced how something as fleeting and ephemeral as the taste of wine can alter time itself and offer a glimpse of a timelessness that so often, in our rushed existences, we never stop to notice.

The wine was Robert Groffier's Chambolle-Musigny Premier Cru Les Sentiers. I cannot tell you the vintage but, consumed in the early 1990's, let's indulge ourselves and claim it was 1985, such a great vintage for Red Burgundy. It is the single most memorable bottle of wine that I have ever had and the person I have to thank for it is James D'Albiac, to whom this book is dedicated.

It was my father who introduced me to wine. As a family, there would always be wine with lunch or supper and my father would inevitably want to spend at least a moment or two discussing its merits before moving onto politics and world affairs, the staple of any conversation around the table. In time we moved on from the Mesa d'Ouro of late 1970's Lisbon and when we moved to New York in 1979 my father developed a taste for Californian wines. These, I remember, plus Beaujolais (particularly Brouilly for some reason), white Bordeaux (which I have never lost the taste for) and clarets from Saint-Estèphe (Château Meyney being a favourite). But (and this is no criticism of my father) my father's salary was that of a civil servant and, once I had developed my interest, I became impatient to try grander things. And so it was my uncle, James, who introduced me to the poetry of wine, to the heights of Burgundy and the rigours of Claret, as often as not via the wines with which he would constantly replenish my grandmother's cellar. Whenever I (we) visited Brighton, my grandmother would pull out a decent bottle, knowing how keen I was on the subject, and it was this way that I slowly expanded my vocabulary. What wines we would drink (Beychevelle, Calon Ségur, Ducru-Beaucaillou, Pillot, Groffier, Chevillon) and how often I would bless my uncle's generosity, not that he would ever say anything about the wines; never assuming such knowledge or presuming to impose it, he would let the wines do the talking. Everyone deserves such an uncle (or such an aunt). If you cannot find one, then be one yourself if you possibly can. Inform and indulge the next generation. Bless them with this knowledge and experience. Light up their lives with these, God's gifts. In any event, James, should you ever read this, then thank you; thank you for all the wonderful bottles that you have so generously given me over the years and the blessings they have brought.

Chambolle-Musigny is traditionally described as being

"feminine". I have not had the pleasure of drinking enough of it or of its neighbours in the Côte d'Or to opine on whether this description is merited or not. As ever, I suspect it depends more on the winegrower than on the terroir. "Feminine" suggests something lighter, something scented, something lifted. Beats me. Whether the Roumier (yes, another planetary alignment at the Wine Society) will present this I do not know. The only Roumier wine I have had was a case of utterly memorable Bourgogne from 1999. Although it was only a Bourgogne, it was a superbly constructed wine, generous, filled with the ripeness of the vintage, maybe without the length, depth or filigree of Roumier's best wines, but with a strong start, middle and finish, rich but not top-heavy, warm but still agile. I have high hopes. But leave a little while.

Vosne-Romanée, Domaine Georges Mugneret 2009
Vosne-Romanée, Domaine Georges Mugneret 2010
Vosne-Romanée, Domaine Georges Mugneret 2011
Vosne-Romanée, Domaine Georges Mugneret 2012

Now this properly is a wine bought out of love, I would even go so far as to say unconditional love if the price had not been steadily creeping up over recent years to the point I am not sure I can any longer keep pace.

It is a truth universally acknowledged that the jewel in the crown of the entire Côte d'Or, indeed of the whole Pinot-Noir-producing world, is the village of Vosne-Romanée, a relatively nondescript little village if not for the swathe of Grands and Premiers Crus that surround it and make it quite possibly the most expensive real estate in the world. Indeed the saying goes that there are no ordinary wines in Vosne and that even the village wines are something special. At the top of the tree is Romanée-Conti, a bottle of which can easily fetch a five figure sum. I do not know a single person who has tried it though they must be out there somewhere. At the bottom of the tree are wines such as this. And if this is the bottom of the tree then I shudder to think what Romanée-Conti, Romanée-St-Vivant, Richebourg, La Tâche, Grands-Echézeaux and others must be like because, as I have recorded in the cellar book, I struggle to think how Red Burgundy can get any better than this Mugneret Vosne. Although this is only a village wine, it has such depth and length and nascent complexity that I am nervous each time I pull a cork that it will not live up to the expectations the last bottle only served to augment. The nose is redolent of spice, nutmeg and clove; the palate filled with violets and strawberries. It is phenomenal wine, rich, full, velvet, a celebration of life and all its gifts. I speak only of the 2009, not yet having broached any of the other vintages, but have tried enough of Mugneret's wines to know that they will not disappoint.

Looking back now over the last 20 years of collecting wine, and 25 years of learning to understand Burgundy, if I were to restrict myself only to drinking the wines of only one village on the Côte d'Or it would have to be Vosne; if I were to start again and concentrate on one village only it would have to be Vosne; I daresay that if I were only to be allowed one more glass of wine on this planet it would have to be Vosne. Vosne, I am yours, I am hooked (line them up and I will sink them).

These wines will offer unconditional love whenever broached. But there is no need to hurry, no need at all.

Hautes-Côtes-de-Nuits, Le Clos Duc, Hervé Murat 2010
Hautes-Côtes-de-Nuits, Le Clos Duc, Hervé Murat 2012

Not that I should get carried away. Not that any of us should get carried away. We do not have the salaries to support a Vosne-only fix and anyway where is the joy in depriving ourselves of all the other wonderful wines in the world, some not even a kilometre or two away?

Land prices on the Côte d'Or are stratospheric. This can cause chaos on death given the complexities of the Code Napoléon and the strict inheritance rules whereby all members of the next generation are equally entitled. If this then involves two or even three siblings having to be bought out, how can the heir keen to maintain the family domaine possibly afford such a buy-out? Will this spell the end of family domaines as the big insurance companies move in, the only ones who can possibly afford the prices? Hopefully not, but prices are high and land is at a premium. Which in turn forces newcomers to start slowly, with meagre pickings on the edge of things, forced to cut their teeth on humbler appellations. Which is not to say, given ambition and attention to detail, humbler wines.

Hervé Murat was just one such example of a new vigneron starting out. He had his own vines in the Hautes-Côtes and bought grapes or rented vines from others to augment his collection with some more august offerings (including Chambolle and Morey). Doubtless he hoped in time to afford to buy some vines in such places but, in the absence of these, his wines from the Hautes-Côtes were the ambassadors for his ability.

There are two Hautes-Côtes, happily and logically the Hautes-Côtes-de-Nuits and the Hautes-Côtes-de-Beaune which respectively shadow to the west, on higher cooler ground, the Côte de Nuits and the Côte de Beaune. As the crow flies, Le Clos Duc is not far at all from the hallowed vineyards of Vosne-Romanée but, in vinous terms, it is many miles. Gone is the unbroken slope of the Côte d'Or, of east and south-east facing vineyards on gentle limestone slopes that maximise drainage and exposure. The Hautes-Côtes are the land of expediency, of heterogeneity where vineyards are broken with woodland, meadows and arable, where vineyards are planted where conditions combine to provide something half suitable. There is no silver spoon up here. Grapes need a long warm growing season to ripen, to make up for the rollercoaster of climate and exposition. But they do, and they can do so with very impressive results. Indeed, if global warming continues this way, then there may be untapped benefits to be had from some of these cooler sites (Pierre-Yves Colin-Morey thinks as much, having expanded his range to take in some Hautes-Côtes-de-Beaune, to produce a fresh, nervy white from Nolay). All part of the addictive complexity of Burgundy.

The last time I had the 2010 it was in a bit of a sulk. Wine is a living thing and goes through stages. Typically, it will be bursting with fruit when young, then the tannins will assert themselves and push the pleasure to the back of the cupboard. The wine will remain in this sulk until the tannins in turn mellow and the fruit, less primary now, more developed, takes centre stage once again. At this stage, you would say the wine is mature, more complex that its earlier incarnation, with more to offer, more to say, the structure of the wine offered by the tannins now hidden, albeit there. So, this wine: in a sulk. I would leave it for a year or two and then see. There is no hiding the potential of the wine however – from the (ever so slightly) heavier bottle than usual, the fruit and extract that was there at the beginning and, of course, the ambitions of Hervé Murat and his plans to make something of and for himself. Horrible label, mind you.

And so what of those plans? Sadly it didn't work out for Hervé and, for reasons I do not know, he was forced to sell up. These wines are now wines of the past. His loss, our loss.

WH Auden was not a man who admired the grand gestures. When Neil Armstrong first set step on the Moon on 20 July 1969, Auden did not share the rest of the world's elation. It was, he thought, a hollow and vacuous achievement that did little to contribute to human happiness, a task that fell to others:

Our apparatniks will continue making
the usual squalid mess called History:
all we can pray for is that artists,
chefs and saints may still appear to blithe it.

He might have added winemakers. Thank you, Hervé.

Nuits-Saint-Georges 1er Cru, Les Porêts, Domaine Alain Michelot 1999
Nuits-Saint-Georges 1er Cru, Les Poulettes, Domaine Gachot-Monot 2009
Nuits-Saint-Georges 1er Cru, Les Poulettes, Domaine Gachot-Monot 2015

We have now wended our way down the length of the Côte de Nuits which ends with the wines of Nuits-Saint-Georges, traditionally, along with Gevrey, considered the darkest most manly wines of the Côte d'Or. Maybe they are beefy. In my experience they are less savoury than the wines of Gevrey, dark and rich but with a softer fruit profile. And it makes a difference which side of Nuits you are on. The vineyards to the north are very close to Vosne and, I would argue, are very close in style as well. Try (if you are lucky enough) a bottle of Mugneret's Nuits-Saint-Georges Premier Cru Boudots and, quite apart from being in for an utter treat, you will notice the similarities to his Vosnes, hardly surprising when you learn the vineyard borders Vosne Malconsorts, one of Burgundy's finest vineyards.

And I suspect the wines of Nuits were once a deal manlier than they are now on account of the Grenache shipped up from the south to bolster the anaemic wines of the north. But the world is a different place today – wine is now of a value (both in Gigondas and in Nuits) that vignerons can afford to do things properly and, although tales of fraud and deceit do occasionally surface (and make me smile when they do), well, I think Nuits can get by on its own these days.

Michelot: I know little about this wine other than it was given to us by Max and Virginie when they came here for lunch one day. We had tried it once at their house (Max having been given a case by a grateful colleague) – it was soft and ripe, as you would expect from the generous 1999 vintage. It is a smart enough wine and I was a little surprised to be offered another bottle when they appeared for lunch. I had already opened the wine for that day (a Tempier Bandol I think) and so we were not going to have the opportunity to drink it together. That is my first rule when someone brings around a decent bottle – open it there and then if you possibly can, or at least offer to. That or save it for another occasion with the giver. My second rule (maybe this is terrible) is never to take a smart bottle around to someone unless either I am happy and reconciled to the fact that I will not be drinking it, then or at a later date, or unless I have prepared the ground and am safe in the knowledge that the wine will be consumed that visit. With friends this can be done easily enough, either by direct and open honesty ("Shall I bring round X? I will if we crack it open. It might be fun"), which obviously only works with very close friends, or by slightly more indirect methods ("I was just wondering what we were going to be eating this evening? I have a lovely bottle of Y and was wondering if it might suit if I brought it along?"). Either way, it requires forethought or, I suppose, levels of generosity which I fear I may not have. How bad. In any event, I would drink this bottle soon.

Gachot-Monot: I was first put on to the wines of this producer through his Côte-de-Nuits-Villages Les Chaillots, a lovely generous open wine without pretension but capable of knocking the spots off others with supposedly higher reputations. Seek it out if you can. This wine, although clearly from smarter terroir (higher up the slope, away from the flat valley floor, in fact no more than 50 metres from Michelot's Pôrets), is cut from the same cloth. It is open and easily accessible (and all the better for this; this is not damnation by faint praise) and has surprising lift for the warm 2009 vintage, maybe because of the vineyard's altitude. The last bottle we had, well you told me off for finishing it (it was meant to be an alcohol-free night in the house) until I pointed out that I had only opened it because a friend of yours had unexpectedly dropped by and had accepted the offer of a glass of wine and that, after she had left, we had then shared the bottle equally between us. So I was only doing my duty. The wine is as ready as it will be. To be accepted at face value and enjoyed for what it is: complete pleasure.

And the 2015? The next great vintage of course (psst, they come round every year). Madness for me to be buying it but my taste returned, and in the briefest scintilla between this event and the doctors' orders to abstain, well I managed to taste another bottle of the 2009. It had the lift and generosity I recalled but this time something else, a deep exhilarating timeless core that underpinned everything. I stared into the large glass, past the rim not yet tawny, through the heart of garnet, deep into the immutable core and glimpsed, I kid you not, something of the universe beyond. I could not but smile, smile like the uninitiated fool I am. The secret of life is not the preserve of the smartest addresses. It lies where you look for it. This is why I bought the 2015.

Pernand-Vergelesses 1er Cru, Ile des Vergelesses, Domaine Chandon de Briailles 2002

Now we enter the Côte de Beaune, the southern half of the Côte d'Or, the home of lighter reds, grown on shallower slopes in cooler climes. None the worse for that mind you; Burgundy's great appeal is the contradiction it offers, both in the glass (the iron fist in the velvet glove – how can such a light wine pack such a punch?) and to the world at large (bigger is not necessarily better, despite today's mind-set persistently arguing to the contrary).

That said, and this is not arguing against myself, this wine has always proved something of a disappointment. Quite apart from an unacceptable number of bottles being corked, it has always tasted just a little green and just a little slight. Ile des Vergelesses is considered Pernand's finest vineyard (hence the suffix), at least for red wines; some of the Corton-Charlemagne vineyards within the village boundaries clearly being superior for white. I have even heard it argued that Ile des Vergelesses should be promoted to Grand Cru. Not on this showing. Despite the beauty of the label, the strength of the vintage, the reputation of the grower, this wine does not suggest Grand Cru lineage. In its defence, you might say it is an old-fashioned wine, in other words a wine that places structure and balance above fruit and body. The last bottle we had, with John and Sally at La Trompette (coincidentally West London's finest restaurant bar none), admittedly struggled coming, as it did, after a bottle of Fourrier's mind-blowingly rich Gevrey-Chambertin Clos St Jacques 1er Cru 2007 but I expected a little more of a fight. At least until the cheese arrived, by which time the wine had woken up and, curious how different foods can do this to different wines, completely changed the light in which we viewed the wine. Its structure, previously awkward and a little unyielding, provided a perfect platform for the soft and fatty cheese which in turn would have sent the fruit of any friendlier wine packing.

I am not a huge believer in the necessity to match food and wine, too much can be made of it, but that is not to say that I cannot appreciate that certain foods will suit certain wines better. So maybe save it for the cheese and hope this last bottle is not corked.

Beaune 1er Cru, Theurons, Louis Jadot 2005
Beaune 1er Cru, Clos des Couchereaux, Louis Jadot 2009
Beaune 1er Cru, Clos des Couchereaux, Louis Jadot 2012

Franc de goût. How I love those words. Frankness of taste is the awkward, unwieldy and literal translation. It is an expression used to describe the wines of Beaune. Unpretentious and frank is what it means; a wine that lays its cards on the table, has no sides and, to paraphrase a pretty mediocre television advert, does what it says on the tin. The wines of Beaune are broad, expansive, generous. Beaune - my word, it is even an easy name to pronounce: a single syllable, two consonants bookending a long "o". Franc de goût. Not simple, not lesser. Just an open and honest articulation of a beautiful wine.

Beaune is the beating heart of the Côte d'Or. Whereas all the other villages the length of the Côte are given over to the production of wine, Beaune is as much given over to the business of wine. It is the home of the Hôtel Dieu, one of the most photographed and therefore typical buildings of Burgundy (Gothic gables, polychrome tiled roofs), it is the home of the Hospices de Beaune whose annual charity auction sets the tone for the following year's prices and it is the seat of all the major négociants, for so long the power behind the business, the serious wine business, of Burgundy.

A word about négociants. They exist in other regions of France (and elsewhere in the world too) but nowhere are they so prominent as in Burgundy. Given how small the holdings are of so many of Burgundy's vignerons and how diverse they are, often spread across different appellations, it has never been economically viable for these growers to set about vinifying their own wine. Burgundy being the temple of terroir that it is (and the different prices that can be obtained for grapes from different sites), it is not sensible or desirable to lump all the grapes together in the same vat and to produce one blend entitled only to the name of the lowest appellation going into the blend. But then a vigneron might not have enough grapes from one appellation even to fill one barrel and, if he owns vines across a number of appellations, well then clearly the poor man has a headache. So the answer for such a vigneron is to sell his grapes to one of the big houses, the négociants, who will acquire wines from all over the region, and from all the smaller vignerons, in sufficient quantities to be able to produce meaningful amounts of wine from the different appellations. Many of these négociants will be familiar. Louis Jadot, Joseph Drouhin, Bouchard Père et Fils, Louis Latour, Chanson, Champy: these are the big ones. And they fulfil a very useful role. Some consumers are sniffy when it comes to négociant wines, thinking they cannot reach the levels of single domaine wines. As ever it depends who you are talking about but the quality can be very high and, in a region as complex as Burgundy, the négociants are able to provide a level of consistency and in sufficient volumes to satisfy the world's demands. Besides, many of these négociants will also have their own vineyard holdings and so, to all intents and purposes, operate as domaines in their own right as well.

You might think this is all very interesting but you might also be wondering why I am banging on about this so much. For two reasons: first to impress on you the extent of the range of wines that négociants are able to offer, buying as they do from all over the Côte. And secondly, because there is a négociant house, Patriarche Père et Fils, maybe not quite in the same league as those mentioned above but which was instrumental in my first exposure to the wines of Burgundy. And what an exposure it was.

In the spring of 1988, Stephen, Jibba, Jim and I set off on a road trip across Northern France. Having taken in the battlefields of Picardy and, among many others, the cathedrals of Laon, Reims and Metz, we lost Jim to his father in Strasbourg before turning south to Burgundy. Our first footfall was in Dijon but our first meaningful experience was in Beaune. Jibba was interested in the art so headed off to the Hôtel Dieu; Stephen's and my priority was wine and so we headed off to a dégustation chez Patriarche, advertised as the largest cellars in Burgundy. We would meet an hour later, back at the car. Stephen took the car keys.

It all started well. We paid our few francs for the tasting, were given a tastevin each (a shallow quaich-like dish out of which we were to taste the wine) and told to follow the arrows down into the 13th Century vaults. We followed these arrows for a while, I recall, past endless arrays of stacked bottles and blind corners until we emerged into a slightly more open area where bottles, open bottles, were arrayed on various tables. We picked up a leaflet itemising the wines on offer for tasting. Immediately two things struck both of us: the list was a good 30 wines long, so a certain amount of endeavour was going to have to be expended to taste them all, and, secondly, we were quite alone. No other visitors, no one to answer questions or moderate consumption. Stephen gave me a look.

When Shergar won the 1981 Classic Trial at Sandown, his prep race for the Derby, the celebrated racing journalist Richard Baerlein implored his readers that now was "the time to bet like men". Shergar's win was so impressive that Richard Baerlein could conceive of no way that the horse could fail to win at Epsom. The horse duly did, by 10 lengths, easing down on the line. Now I cannot recall if Stephen used the same words, I suspect not, but his look was clearly imploring the two of us that now was the time to drink like men. And we duly did. We left not one bottle untasted and, by the time we reached the last 10 or so bottles (including no doubt various Grands Crus), I am afraid that we had also dispensed with the services of the tastevins, finding that the neck of the bottle delivered the wine so much quicker to our throat than any shallow silver dish ever could.

I recall nothing of the individual wines (the first one may in fact have been a Chablis) and, needless to say, we recalled nothing of the march of time as we emerged blinking into the April light. Our allotted rendezvous with Jibba had, suffice to say, long passed. Stephen had the car keys, these were the days before mobile phones and so Jibba had had no choice other than to wait by the car for our return. Our reception was not a good one. Not that it bothered me. I collapsed into the back of the car in a catatonic stupor and was only half conscious of Stephen's attempts, through broken sequences and slurred syllables, to repair the situation.

Jibba drove us south that afternoon, doubtless past or through the great villages of the Côte de Beaune, not that I will have noticed. I do recall, however, that we found a farm track that evening that carried us high up onto a field overlooking La Rochepôt, the château's coloured tile roof standing out in the distance, clinging to the valley slope. We set up camp for the night. I slept in the car, Stephen continued his efforts to mend bridges and I experienced the single worst headache I have ever suffered.

Beaune: you will be forever associated with this memory. And, of course, with wines such as these. My love, you will immediately notice two things: first they are all Premiers Crus. It is a curious feature of Beaune that most of the wines you see are Premiers Crus; a village Beaune is a rarer sight. If you look at a wine atlas you can see that the Premiers Crus cover a vast swathe of the eastern and southern flank of the Montagne de Beaune to the west of the town itself. Is it all deserving of Premier Cru status? Others will be better placed than me to opine on this but I have not had any experiences to suggest otherwise. Some Premiers Crus are perhaps more structured than others but, just as similarly, some Premiers Crus are fleshier and deliver more immediate pleasure than others. To each their own.

Secondly, they are all from Louis Jadot. They are not négociant wines, blends of the grapes of many, but rather domaine wines, from vines belonging to the house of Jadot itself.

A third feature which you will not immediately recognise is that, in the world of Burgundy, the Premiers Crus of Beaune offer some of the best value of all. Why? Difficult to say. The snobbishness of some to embrace the wines of négociants, the major peddlars of Beaune? The fact that there are no Grands Crus in Beaune, only a plethora of Premiers Crus? Or maybe the very franc de goût of the wines and their perceived lack of intellect? In any event, we consumers are those who stand to gain. Keep an eye on the wines of Beaune: they are better than the market will give them credit for.

On reflection it is odd that I should associate that road trip around Northern France in the spring of 1988 with such fine wine. Our standard fare, I recall, was a vin de table called Le Villageois which came in litre-size plastic bottles with plastic lids. I recall it did the job admirably and cannot be sure that I did not from time to time, on the second or third bottle, announce Le Villageois delicious.

And so to the wines in question.

2005: it is so often a feature of great vintages that they take a blessedly long time to come around, perhaps no more so than 2005 which was blessed with surfeit of everything: fruit, tannin, acid, the works. The wines are now showing their wares but less so chez Jadot where the winemaking style has always been one of high extract for a long life. These two cases of six sit quietly at the back of the cellar, behind the Christmas decorations, biding their time until the reviews (on cellartracker as much as anywhere) turn friendly and the wine world's frustrations at unyielding tannins and disjointed components melt into conciliation and a harmonious whole. The wines will last a long time. And Theurons is one of the finest of the Premiers Crus.

2009: another "great" vintage but a friendlier one than 2005, one that can be broached earlier. So drinking but very much primary. The tannins are still noticeable. The wine has yet to soften properly and develop, as it will, flavours of fudge and strawberry, it has yet to wrap itself around you and convince you of its love. It will happen though.

2012: not yet tried. And no rush.

Pommard 1er Cru, Clos Blanc, Domaine Albert Grivault 2005

Each January the growers of Burgundy descend on London for a mad week of tasting the new vintage. I used to attend Justerini & Brooks' tasting religiously until I realised that there was not actually that much pleasure in tasting such a young wine and that, in any event, I was not sufficiently accomplished a judge to pick the gems at this early stage. All except this one, that is. Even when I tried it in early January 2007, I could sense a lovely wine in there – perhaps there was more fruit than others were offering at that stage and maybe, after all, I could sense the balance between the various components that everyone says is such an important feature to identify in a young wine (if it does not have balance young, it is unlikely to have balance when mature – or so they say). Or maybe I just got lucky. In any event, this is a delicious wine – soft red fruits, mature (yes, mature despite being 2005), rich, of good length, very much alive and kicking but with wistful, melancholic aromas of decay and autumn, a wine at ease with itself.

I have only one criticism of the wine – too many have been corked, one or two horrendously and one just winged. When a wine is properly corked, it is easy to detect. The wine smells damp, it smells of a cellar or of wet clothes pulled from a sports bag days too late. There may still be fruit in the background but overwhelmingly the wine smells of mould. Sometimes, however, it is not so obvious. The wine might simply smell flat or finish short – it does not sing, fruit does not leap from the glass. The foolproof way to tell if a wine is corked is to smell the end of the cork that has been in touch with the wine as soon as it is first pulled from the bottle. If the end of the cork smells of wine, the wine will be fine. If the end of the cork smells of cork instead (remember it is the end of the cork you smell, not the side; it is not a cigar) then the wine will be spoiled. And the wine itself might not smell corked to begin with, it might smell fine, but if the end of the cork smells of cork, not wine, then the wine will be corked and within five minutes or so the wine will smell as such. Trust me, it works. And if you are in a restaurant, don't hesitate to send it back. Can you remember, my love, the occasion I sent back three cheap bottles of white that evening in Ronda? Three in a row. Even I was becoming uncomfortable by the time I did it for the third time. The waiters just look stunned, even slightly bemused. You were a little uneasy yourself. I don't blame you. It was an unlucky run.

Volnay Domaine Vaudoisey 2010
Volnay 1er Cru, Clos des Chênes, Domaine Vaudoisey 2010

Everything about Burgundy is on such an intimate scale – the villages, the distances, the size of each grower's holdings – that I am always surprised by how steep some of the escarpments can look. In a land of gentle slopes and subtle gradations, to come across terraces supporting the vineyards and the heights of some of the hills forces a mental correction every time. Or so I thought as I walked with Gus from the car in Volnay to the cellar door of Monsieur Vaudoisey and, looking north to the far horizon, over and beyond the vineyards of Pommard, took in the size of the Montagne de Beaune and the stonework supporting some of the more elevated vineyards on the hill's southern flank.

You and the two girls had elected to stay in the car and Gus, sensing impending male responsibility, chose to accompany his father into the cellars. We had a distance to travel that day, over to the Alps for a week's summer stay in Chinaillon, and we could not spend too long dallying on the Côte d'Or.

Gus took to the task admirably despite his tender age of 10. Chez Vaudoisey we worked quickly through the generic Volnay, Gus declaring an interest in trying the wine (his subsequent expression, on trying the wine, betraying his preference at this age for Sprite) before moving on to the Premiers Crus. I could not decide between the Mitans and the Clos des Chênes but in the end settled for the latter, that and a few bottles of the Volnay to accompany the endless Reblochon we were about to encounter up in the mountains.

We walked back to the car through the mid-morning sun of a fresh July day, our provisions in our arms. The land was alive, a carpet of vines and the bright green promise of the future surrounding us on each and every side, nature's gift in the offing, this year like every year. My son was at my side and my heart sang.

Not that the village Volnay we have in the cellar is the same as was under my arm that day in 2012. The Volnay in the cellar was in fact bought from Marks & Spencer a year or so later, a surprise discovery really, that one of the country's main supermarket chains should stock wines from such a small producer. Not a usual sight.

I said early on that the secret to eternal happiness is to discover a wine merchant you can trust and to join the Wine Society. Between the two of them, 90% of your wine needs should be covered. Every now and again, however, we will all have to fall back on supermarkets. In which case, if you are living in the United Kingdom in 2016, restrict yourself to Marks & Spencer and Waitrose. These two seek out interesting wines and interesting growers (even if Marks & Spencer are unwilling to tell you who they are, which I always feel they should as they have nothing to lose in such disclosure), the range is wide and their ethos is not to stack high and sell cheap. As for the others, the Tescos, Lidls and Aldis of the world, I would say leave them alone (certainly a wine is only ever worth its discounted price so don't believe you are getting a bargain when the price is halved; you are simply being skinned if you pay the full price) but then wine is to everyone whatever everyone wants it to be and, if the wines of these supermarkets flick your switch, then so be it. Don't give up on such wines, at least not to begin with. But maybe try wines from an independent merchant or from Waitrose or Marks & Spencer and maybe, just maybe, you will think there is more out there to discover. The world of wine is such a wonderful, rich and varied place; if you are inclined to agree, it would be such a shame not to explore it.

I will stop preaching. Do what you will. Of these wines, the Volnay is a lovely wine at the moment, with some of the silk and balance that Volnay is famous for. It is not meaty like Pommard or the wines of the Côte de Nuits but wields its power through control and careful aim. Too many Volnays that I have had have been just a little weedy and light; there is none of that here. It shows the precision of a surgeon. It is bright, sappy, lifted and delightful, strawberries, almonds and coffee all wrapped up in a lace-like frame. And the Clos des Chênes, Volnay's top Premier Cru, should do likewise, albeit on a bigger scale. I have not tried it since that day with Gus four years ago (the bottles safely transported back from the Alps and now asleep in the cellar). I suspect though that, by the time it is fully mature, Gus will have put away childish things and will have developed a taste for Volnay over and above Sprite. Drink it with him; he will appreciate it and maybe even recall that visit those years ago.

Côte-de-Beaune-Villages, Domaine Michel Lafarge 2002

One solitary bottle left, I feel from a different lifetime. An impenetrable wine for so long (so long!) I despaired of it ever yielding its charms. I began to lose hope as I methodically worked through the case of 12, the wine being stubbornly mute for the first six at least and then only slowly coming out of its sulk. The last bottle I had, I see, was in 2014 – "will never set the world alight" I wrote and, on a previous occasion, "all about this wine is a mystery". "Almond and berry" I managed to elicit on one attempt; on another, "gentle echoes of smoke and coffee".

And I had such high hopes: Lafarge, one of the top growers in Volnay; 2002 a successful year; and, although only a Côte-de-Beaune-Villages, literally only a row away from the Volnay village boundary so, to all intents and purposes, a Volnay.

What a puzzle. At least the last two bottles gave some hint of the wine's heritage, sharing the delicacy of Volnay but a delicacy, perhaps, bordering on the underwhelming and betraying the desperation of the taster to detect some validation of his 12 years' patience.

And maybe this is a good place to leave Burgundy. Part of the region's frustration and part of the region's almost mystical allure is its unpredictability. This has got better over the last 20 years for all the right reasons – better viticulture and care in the vineyard, better winemaking in the cellar – but I would be lying if I did not admit that part of Burgundy's appeal is its complexity (despite my attempts above to keep it simple), the endless variations on a theme, the contradictions of paleness and depth, of lightness and strength, of savoury and sweet, the elusiveness in particular of Pinot Noir, the inescapable feeling that the wine is often turning a corner ahead of you and disappearing out of sight, keeping you guessing, keeping you moving forward to get a better glimpse. I adore Burgundy, the promise it affords, the expectations it creates, the dreams it fosters and, when it all comes together, the utterly sublime experience it provides. As I said, to each their own. For me, Red Burgundy is the single greatest red wine on earth.

BORDEAUX

Sui generis. Of its own kind. Bordeaux may well be France's most important wine region (though that itself is worthy of an essay: important to whom?), it may well be the world's most important wine region, but it is also unique and unlike any other wine region in France or, indeed, the world. For in Bordeaux, wine has become secondary to the greater force of the market. In a sea of dross, the reputation and identity of Bordeaux is forged by the select and golden few, by perhaps no more than 100 châteaux who define the region and, many would argue, fine wine itself. And it is an identity that has ceased to bear any relation to the product in the bottle but instead has latched itself onto the world of high fashion and finance. The wines that matter, the classed growth clarets in particular, the wines that hold the DNA of Bordeaux, that for over 150 years have been the guardians of the region's identity, have now become so sought after as symbols of wealth and privilege that they have become investments in their own right, not to be drunk, other than by oligarchs and bankers, but instead to be bought for financial return.

Witness the most recent en primeur campaign, when the wines of Bordeaux are first offered as futures (they have not yet been bottled), and in particular Cheval Blanc, one of Saint-Emilion's finest. 12 bottles of the 2015 are yours for £5,600 (before taxes). If that is what the market will bear, then that is what the market price will be. But read the merchants' puff accompanying the emails offering this wine. They do not look to seduce you with rhapsody or elation at the quality of the wine; instead, they look to persuade you to invest in a case because its price is sure to go up in the future and, this way, a canny purchase now will secure you a healthy profit in the future.

Bordeaux is business, very big business. It is the land of suits rather than dungarees, insurance companies rather than smallholders, commerce rather than pleasure, returns rather than consumption, gain rather than soul. It holds the world's rapt gaze. It influences the world's fine wine market to such an extent you could just as well argue it is the world's fine wine market. It is not a land for romantics.

And so it Is a land of split identity. A select few determine the culture and identity of the region, one of the biggest wine-producing regions in France (second only, in fact, to Languedoc-Roussillon), while those who produce the vast majority of the region's wines, which contribute nothing to the sheen and allure of the region's finest, struggle to carve out an existence and sell their wares. Look at the wine shelves of any French supermarket and row upon row will be dedicated to the wines of Bordeaux, but not to the unaffordable classed growths. Instead, the shelves will be stocked with endless variations on a theme, of too often poorly-made wine, produced on a shoestring and on the back of no reputation, by growers desperately trying to eke a living in a saturated market. Which is the real Bordeaux? The shiny shoes and glitzy cars of the lucky elect or the mud-coated boots and faltering tractors of the silent majority? The ultra-glossy and over-engineered wines of Pauillac and Pomerol or the pedestrian, stubborn, spiky wines of Bordeaux AC and Bordeaux Supérieur AC? Bordeaux is capable of such beauty and refinement and, at the same time, of such industrial disappointment that I cannot think of any other wine region which embraces such dichotomy and extremes. Democracy has not come to Bordeaux: it is the land of haves and have-nots. The Ancien Régime has been replaced by the Nouveau Régime and the inequality is just as great.

And nor is it the land of terroir. There is no parcellation of the land into different grades of quality. So long as the land falls within the appellation boundary, the wine its grapes produce is as entitled to be labelled Château Lafite or Château So-So depending on which château owns the land. It is the châteaux which are graded, not the land, a fact which must be utterly counter-intuitive to the Bourguignons further north.

But see below and the wines I have bought over the years. Do my criticisms of Bordeaux and my reservations make me a hypocrite? I am a child of my father's generation and he of the generation before and, raised as we have been in this country, it is inescapable that we have been raised on the wines of Bordeaux. My father and his father before him will have known of few other wines than those hailing from Bordeaux. Maybe a smattering of Burgundy, a supply of Hock, a risqué wine or two from the Rhône but, essentially, their diet will have been Bordeaux which has, for so long, enjoyed such a close relationship with the burghers, middle and upper classes of Britain. So if they cut their teeth on Bordeaux it is only natural that, learning at my father's table, I will have done so likewise. Yes, my father will have drunk Portuguese wines in Portugal and American wines in the United States but his mainstay, the lode star to which he inevitably returned, the yardstick by which all else was measured, was Bordeaux.

Times change. That bond is weakening now. The revolution started by the New World (and so ably assisted by Oddbins) in the 1980's has slowly altered the drinking patterns of the British public, so that the historic link with Bordeaux has been substantially weakened. My buying patterns have changed over the years and, whereas I would in the past have unthinkingly bought a case of Bordeaux to lay down almost every year, I now hesitate or else am distracted by other regions of the world, offering better value perhaps, or different experiences, or maybe even better memories. What I have described above is a work in motion, a spinning off the central axis, a spiral away from the mainstream. Bordeaux's principal role in the wine universe may yet be re-established, who can tell, but at present, to many consumers and sommeliers, it is a region in flux, one of confused identity, muddled message and creeping irrelevance.

Which is a shame.

WHITE BORDEAUX

It is a curious feature of Bordeaux that, given how popular the region's wines have traditionally been, the wines themselves are often of a style that are not particularly consumer-friendly. The reds I will come on to in more detail later but the dry, slightly austere profile of the best examples of red Bordeaux does not always sit happily with the modern taste for instant accessibility and gratification. The sweet wines, although the flavour is to everyone's taste when they actually get round to tasting them, are out of favour because of the unpopularity of post-prandial wines in general. And Bordeaux's dry white wines? I think they are some of France's finest so I am always at a loss to understand why they are not more popular. Only one bottle in ten in Bordeaux is white. Maybe their distinctive taste is, well, just too distinctive.

My father loved these wines. Château Bouscaut was his favourite and I remember my first taste of it. Grapefruit, overwhelmingly a strong scent and flavour of grapefruit, plus preserved lemons and something petrolly, a little oily. The texture was waxy and the finish ever so slightly bitter. All supported by a full body of oak and a hint of peaches. What was not to like? Clearly something because it was never a wine that my mother appreciated; indeed, the pattern of conversation became predictable each time my father gleefully opened a bottle. But I was not complaining: here was a wine of strong personality and identity, with depth and length, a clear message to deliver and refreshingly unique.

Successful white Bordeaux is a relatively recent phenomenon, the secret being lower fermentation temperatures to accentuate the nettle-like grassiness of the Sauvignon Blanc and oak ageing to coax out and encourage the glycerol and weight of the Sémillon. The combination of the two is bewitching. I adore the gunflint and elderflower of Sancerre's and Pouilly-Fumé's pure Sauvignons from the Loire but find the extra body given by the Sémillon in Bordeaux just that bit more stimulating and rewarding.

The great majority of Bordeaux's white wine is produced in the south of the region, why I am not sure. Nor can I easily find out from the books I have. Maybe because that is where the sandier soil is, soil that perhaps suits white grapes better than red, maybe because the gravel and clay to the north can be more profitably put to use in growing Cabernet Sauvignon and Merlot. The finest region for white wine production is Pessac-Léognan, which lies along the southern suburbs of Bordeaux, of which you will see we have none; I wish we did. Pessac-Léognan then leaches into the bigger region of Graves to the south, of which you will see we have some. And Graves leaches all around into Bordeaux Blanc, of which we have a very little.

Lune d'Argent, Clos des Lunes, Bordeaux Blanc 2012

I have always been hugely disappointed by this wine. It should be so much more than it is. It is made by Olivier Bernard of Domaine de Chevalier, one of the region's most gifted winegrowers, Domaine de Chevalier's white wine being one of the very top white wines not only in all of Bordeaux but in the whole of France. Clos des Lunes is a bold new venture. The vines actually lie in Sauternes, famous for its sweet wines, but Monsieur Bernard believes the region just as capable of producing great dry whites as well. The wine is not entitled to the Sauternes appellation because it is not sweet and so it must fall back on the lowly appellation of Bordeaux Blanc. But as I have said before, follow the winegrower, not the appellation. And last but not least, the wine is beautifully packaged.

So why the disappointment? For the simple reason it tastes of nothing. It never has and, so far as I can tell, it never will. Occasionally I get fleeting glimpses of grapefruit and peach but the scents are as soon carried off like words on the wind. Most of the time, the wine is mute, anodyne, unyielding, neutral and (sorry) tasteless. What to do? Retain the faith. Domaine de Chevalier's white wine is famous for the length of time it takes to blossom. Maybe Clos des Lunes requires a similar length of time. Leave the last few bottles. Maybe try one a year and see if there is any development. If not, well it is one less wine to worry about buying again.

Clos Floridène, Graves 2013
Clos Floridène, Graves 2015

By contrast, I have been endlessly surprised and filled with wonder by the wines of Clos Floridène. This wine is another experiment, very similar to that of Olivier Bernard, this time the maker of dreams being Denis Dubourdieu (one of France's most respected wine professors, known particularly for his work on white wines and, within this, for his work on Sauvignon Blanc) and the virgin territory on which he has worked his magic being Pujols-sur-Ciron, perhaps no more than three or four kilometres from Clos des Lunes.

But here, for the time being at least, the similarity ends. The wine shows levels of depth and intensity that belie its price (at least certainly its release price) and the wine is filled with such strong flavours (yes, of grapefruit and peach) and with such harmony and balance that it is often spoken of as being one of Bordeaux's finest white wines. I agree entirely. As I write this, I wish I had bought a case every year. I wish many things but few wishes could guarantee such happy pleasure. Try the 2013 soon and maybe the 2015 on its fifth birthday.

As well as the flavour the wine provides, I am also tickled by the fact that Denis Dubourdieu was able to identify and then extract such an experience for the consumer from a previously overlooked plot of land. Burgundy's Côte d'Or has been mapped out to the tiniest detail, of course, endlessly scrutinised over the centuries so that no doubt can remain as to the potential of each sod of earth. But I have often wondered where other undiscovered gems lie, land that is as capable as Romanée-Conti itself of producing world-beating wine. It lies hidden, patiently awaiting its turn, its dormant potential to be unlocked by an enquiring mind with a spade and a vine, its promise to blossom and flower and seduce unnumbered generations. Where does this land lie? It must lie all around us, unknown to all, entombed in silence till ignited by a

Promethean spark. The blessings this planet can bestow and man's ability to exploit these gifts to produce something as civilised and as blessed as wine: it is endlessly bewitching. And something for which we must be eternally grateful.

Château Rieussec, Sauternes 1999
Château Rieussec, Sauternes 2008
Château Rieussec, Sauternes 2011

It is hopelessly ironic that, as the prices of top red Bordeaux continue to soar, the prices that can be fetched for Sauternes, the very most difficult and expensive wine to produce in all of Bordeaux, continue to drift listlessly and, in some instances, fall to almost insulting levels. For make no mistake, Sauternes is difficult to make and a risky process at the best of times. Once they have reached maturity, the grapes are left on the vine in the hope that September, October and November bring not rain (a usual supposition) but humid nights and warm sunny days, in the hope that autumn mists springing from the river (the Ciron is actually little more than a stream) blanket the vines and cover them with noble rot that desiccates the grapes and concentrates all the flavours in their shrivelled form, in the hope that this noble rot does not, if the weather is damp, turn to grey rot and destroy the grapes, in the hope that, in anywhere between five and 10 passages through the vineyard, the many pickers can extricate, berry by berry, the nobly-affected grapes from the clusters and in the hope that these grapes can together muster enough juice to create a meaningful amount of wine. The production of Sauternes is a labour of love, time-consuming, risky, expensive.

So Sauternes and Barsac, neighbouring appellations that lie perhaps 30 or so miles south of Bordeaux, are the home of some of the world's finest sweet wines. Some would say the finest. I would reserve judgement, the sweet wines of the Loire, not to mention the Trockenbeerenausleses of the Mosel's steep slaty slopes, being of equal standing in my book. But it is inescapable that the sweet wines of Sauternes are stellar, combining a richness, a freshness, a complexity, a depth and such a panoply of intermingling flavours that it would take a blinkered curmudgeon to deny their status and worth.

Worth. I have used the word intentionally. Whereas many might justifiably rage against the absurd prices of the top clarets, bearing, as they do, little correlation to the quality of what lies within the bottle, they might equally rail against the demeaningly low prices that Sauternes and Barsac can currently command. Of course, the market will set its own price and so such an exercise is ultimately meaningless but I cannot help but feel a tinge of sympathy for the Sauternais at the return (if indeed they measure their life's worth by such criteria which, of course, I hope they do not) they receive for their labours. Unless such meagre return is of their own making: witness Rieussec.

Rieussec is owned by Lafite-Rothschild which, of all the wines of Bordeaux, has probably profited most from the explosion in prices now paid for the region's top wines. For some reason, it is popular with the Chinese and so, until recently at least, there have been no brakes on the price's upward trajectory. To such an extent, however, that to get their hands on an allocation of Château Lafite, wine merchants have been obliged to take an allocation of Château Rieussec. You want 10 cases of Lafite? Then you take 10 cases of Rieussec as well (I am guessing on the proportions). And you take these 10 cases at a price that we set, not what the market sets. The result, as it always is if you look to manipulate the market (a lesson I am far from convinced that the Bordelais have yet to appreciate), is a correction in the secondary market. The market becomes flooded with unwanted Rieussec (unwanted! How can anyone not want such a jewel!) and the price of the wine halves. This is a travesty. The trouble is, however, that, once gone, it is very difficult for a price to recover. If you know that you can pick up a case of Rieussec for, say, £250, it is going to take a great deal of demand and scarcity to drag the price up to, say, £400 where it should more properly sit. So the price has sunk and the state of the market for Sauternes is such that Rieussec's star, one of the absolute jewels of the region, has waned to a shameful level. The wine has not waned in quality or even reputation, these remain supremely high, but it has certainly waned in price.

You might ask why I am complaining and I struggle to come up with an answer. Who profits after all? We, the consumers profit, picking up the wine for a relative song. Maybe I would just prefer to see endeavour and quality properly rewarded where it is properly due. To which you may well argue that Rieussec's fate is a rare sliver of silver lining in the debacle that is current Bordeaux pricing. And you may well be right.

1999: the dying embers of one of my father's cases. The wine is fully mature now, a reflective expression of nature's gift, the exuberance of youth and the fire of its early ambition now fully melded and wrapped around a core of sweetness and gently-reminding acidity to keep the whole in order. It is lovely wine.

2008: this is medicine. I am not sure why I say this other than this is the basis on which the wine was sold to me, an elixir, a pick-me-up to be consumed between treatments, a glassful of goodness, of sugar, of bright light, of life itself. This wine, from a slightly less than perfect year (or so they say), is absurdly rich and bursting at the seams with all sorts of plans for the future. Like a young puppy, almost, and a big one at that. The wine positively glows and pulls you in all directions.

It is a wine to be enjoyed now or left for the future (Sauternes can last forever). I like it now for all the exuberance and joy it brings.

2011: now this is meant to be a good year. Rieussec is traditionally one of the richest Sauternes. Others, often from Barsac, major more on balance and citrus; Rieussec, on the other hand, is full throttle. 12 half-bottles, in its original wooden case, sitting patiently and silently on the floor of the cellar, in the corner, probably smarting at the indignity of its position, both physical and financial.

Château Haut-Theulet, Monbazillac 2009

Of course the greatest kindness that James D'Albiac showed us was not in the steady stream of great bottles regularly bestowed but rather in the steady offer of La Chevalerie, year after year, set back in the quiet Norman countryside of the Cotentin.

We would inevitably arrive late in the day, the disappearing sun in the west, the kids bursting to get out of the car. We would stop at the bottom of the drive, the chatter of the children dissipating into the evening air as they ran ahead of us, between the lines of apple trees planted by Margaret for James. One or other might be distracted by the rope swing halfway up the drive but, for the most part, they would stream ahead, through the white five-bar gate into the courtyard, where my mother would open the door and light would pour out as the children rushed in.

I never ceased to get a thrill climbing that drive. A large, imposing farmhouse (maybe it was too grand to be considered a farmhouse), clad in grey stone bleached by 500 summers, bright white shutters on all the windows muting the building's formality and disguising its imperfect symmetry. And looking out of the windows, fields of tall corn falling away, the solemn ring of a church bell, muted bellows of far-off cattle, a fading light and the silence of nightfall.

We had such summers there. Days bracketed by slow mornings and late nights, the daily communion with the boulangerie, idle happy hours in a climate only a little better than England's but softened by a more clement latitude. A subtle landscape, born of water and low elevations, its kindness belying its violent past of 70 years ago, each crossroads and building, each hill and holloway, hiding tales of conflict and war. But we passed by blithely, concerned only at the gradient of the hill we must climb on the bicycle or the speed with which the little ones then freewheeled down the other side.

In the afternoons we would often go to the beach, driving along quiet roads through a green landscape of empty fields and crowded hedgerows. Carteret mostly, with its faux gothic mansions, closed up for 10 months of the year, clinging precipitously to the corniche that wraps around the hill above the harbour. A town devoted to summer. Moules et frites. Muscadet. Kites. Sand dunes. Wide empty beaches. We would always stop in the town on the way back and sit on the quayside, ice creams in hand, sand and sun on flagging shoulders, a creeping quietness, the tiredness of oxygen, the peace of contentment.

In such a way, we passed countless summers, in such a way we watched the little ones imperceptibly grow, in such a way we were blessed.

And what does any of this have to do with wine? Two reasons. First, I am surprised that this is the only bottle in the cellar which comes from one of those holidays. Most holidays to

France, surely, finish with a car load of wine coming back, don't they? It must be that we rarely did. And that is perhaps because of the second reason for this gratuitous remembrance, namely that for all the blissful idyll that La Chevalerie provided, we rarely drank well there. We would drink deeply, and well into the night each and every night, there always being a willing accomplice to the next bottle, but rarely did we drink well.

It seems the British (I cannot comment for other nationalities) have a curious habit when going abroad, a slightly self-destructive habit, of seeing how low can they go, in other words how cheaply they can drink. It is, as I said, a curious habit but I have lost count of the number of occasions at La Chevalerie when guests or family members would arrive back from the supermarket trumpeting a bottle (or worse, bottles) that they had picked up for a matter of euros. This benefited no one. We would be obliged to drink the bottles but their taste and general contribution to well-being would invariably be in direct proportion to their price.

Why we do it, I do not know. In an effort to stem this tide, I did come up with a number of golden rules for buying wine at supermarkets. Some were willing to take these rules more seriously than others:

1. Make sure the wine is "appellation contrôlée". I have never thought much of this moniker but, to qualify as appellation contrôlée, the wine must meet certain basic standards of production. It is not a guarantee, but it is a start.

2. Make sure the wine is bottled at the point of production, so "mis en bouteille au château" or "au domaine". This was one of Kermit Lynch's bugbears in Adventures on the

Wine Route. The wine will unduly suffer if carted elsewhere for industrial bottling, or so the theory goes. But bottling at the domaine will show an element of care on the part of the vigneron.

3. Make sure the winegrower is an individual, not a co-operative. Granted, some co-operatives are wonderful and a good source of inexpensive wine but you need to know which these are; many co-ops are not so wonderful. Look for the name of the producer. If it is an acronym or a series of initials, then beware, it will be a co-operative.

4. Believe the gumpf. Words are cheap, of course words are cheap, but if the winegrower has gone to the effort of talking about his soils, or the grape varieties, or the methods of production, or whatever, then chances are that he believes in these things and is willing to pay attention to them. And even if the talk is not of technical stuff, if there is passion on the label there might equally be passion in the bottle. This is an example from Italy, actually, but beat this if you can, taken from the back label of a cheap but delicious negroamaro from Salento:

At the passing away of the harvest, red is the night that turns the grapes into wine. The red moon and its grapes of stars watch us – at the dreaming time – repeating the ancient miracle. Red are the hands, our land, our passion, red is the night that turns the grapes into wine.

Irresistible.

5. Look for medals. Some competitions are more august than others – the Concours Général Paris is the big one (its stickers carry an oak leaf on them) and the Concours des Grands Vins Mâcon is another – but chances are that,

if a wine has won a medal (and there will be a little sticker on the bottle proclaiming such), then the wine will be halfway palatable.

So looking at this bottle of Monbazillac, in front of me as I write, (such a deep golden colour; I am tempted to open it now!) it is appellation contrôlee, it was bottled at the château, it is the product of an individual château, the back label talks at length about the wine, its flavour and ageing potential, it won a silver medal at the Paris Concours in 2011 and it won a Coup de Coeur in the Guide Hachette des Vins in 2012 (Guide Hachette being one of France's top annual wine guides and Coups des Coeurs being the guide's "heart stoppers" each year). So it should be good and, if it is not, well then I am the fool.

Monbazillac, by the way, is another sweet white wine, in the same mould as Sauternes (noble rot, Semillon and Sauvignon though perhaps with a little more Muscadelle) but without quite the reputation of Sauternes. It also lies in the Dordogne rather than Bordeaux so forgive me for including it here. It will continue to age well but, given that I am after all British, I will not have paid a great deal for it at Super U so do not tarry too long a while.

RED BORDEAUX

And so we come at last to what many (not me) consider the greatest wine on the planet. Again, it is not a difficult region to understand unless you want to make it complicated:

1.   To begin with, divide the region into three: the Médoc (often called the Left Bank), which sits to the west of the Gironde as it flows north from Bordeaux to the sea, the

Libourne (often called the Right Bank), which sits to the north of the Garonne to the east and, to the south of Bordeaux, the Graves.

2.   There are two main grape varieties in Bordeaux: Cabernet Sauvignon (blackcurrant, green pepper, sandalwood) and Merlot (softer, plummier flavours). There is a third, Cabernet Franc, our friend from the Loire, but for the most part it only plays a supporting role so can be ignored for current purposes.

3.   As a general rule, the Left Bank is the domain of Cabernet Sauvignon, the Right Bank the home of Merlot and the Graves an equal mix of the two.

4.   And within these areas, divide again by two, between the "Cru Classés" and the others. When people talk of classed growths they are referring to wines that have, under various classifications, been graded as better or worse than their neighbours. The most famous classification is that of the wines of the Left Bank that was carried out in 1855. Over 60 châteaux were graded into five classes and, although the classification is over 150 years old, it has stuck. At the top of the tree are the First Growths, Châteaux Lafite-Rothschild, Margaux, Latour, Haut-Brion and Mouton-Rothschild (actually added later). These are then followed by the Second through to the Fifth Growths. A Second Growth may be better than a Third Growth but just as equally a Fourth Growth may be better than a Second Growth; the picture now is very different to what it was in 1855 and, as ever, much if not all depends on the skills of the current generation. However, these classed growth statuses are jealously guarded and a review is as unlikely as First Growths ever being affordable again. Which is not to say

that on the Right Bank they do not try. Every 10 years the Saint-Emilion classification is reviewed and every 10 years, it seems, the disappointed châteaux launch law suits to have the revised classification set aside. In 2015 the legal attempts to have the 2012 classification rendered null and void failed but I suspect 2022 will bring its own suite of suits. The classification of the Graves region took place in 1955 and has, fingers crossed, remained pretty stable since.

5.   On the Left Bank, there are four major appellations to remember: heading south, Saint-Estephe, Pauillac, Saint-Julien and Margaux. These are the big ones, with most of the classed growths. We'll come across others. On the Right Bank, it is easier: the two main ones are Saint-Emilion and Pomerol. And in the Graves, well really there is just one major appellation, Pessac-Léognan, which broke away from the larger Graves in 1987.

6.   And finally, when people talk of claret they are talking about red wine from Bordeaux, whether from the Left Bank, the Right Bank or Graves, whether from the more illustrious appellations or from Bordeaux AC itself. Simple.

And what of claret itself? It took me a long time to learn this but if you are looking for fruit don't go looking for claret. You will find fruit (I would say "certainly" but that is not always the case, especially among the cheaper, meaner examples) but it is not what claret is about and it will be a very expensive way of experiencing fruit if that is what you are after. If Burgundy is sensual and appeals to the emotions, claret is cerebral and appeals to the intellect. This may be a hackneyed view but, in my mind, it still works. Claret is about structure. It is a dry wine that is as much about the process as it is about the end product. So it is not so much about the flavour in the mouth, the pleasure that is delivered as the wine slips down your throat, it is as much about the construction of the wine as you first sip it, its framework, its balance, the interplay of all the component parts, yes the intellectual exercise. It is not a session wine. Without wanting to sound too ridiculous, it is a wine for rumination and reflection, a wine for Sartre rather than Rabelais, for Descartes rather than Rimbaud.

RIGHT BANK

Château Moulin Saint-Georges, Saint-Emilion 2004
Château Moulin Saint-Georges, Saint-Emilion 2010

An impossibly pretty label. Understated, washed a pale lilac, a garlanded frame surrounding the simple statement of château, owner and vintage. The pleasure is all mine.

It took me a while to investigate the wines of the Right Bank. Why? My first experiences of claret were of the Left Bank so, knowing only a little, I was keen to know a lot which meant building on the meagre foundations I had laid and investigating the wines of Pauillac and Saint Julien at the expense of Saint-Emilion and Pomerol. And the wines of the Right Bank suffer a little in reputation in comparison with the Left Bank. Merlot ripens earlier than Cabernet Sauvignon, it is an "easier" wine, the tannins are not so harsh, the rigour is not so great. If claret is about asceticism, the wines of the Right Bank belong to a kindlier order than found across the Gironde. And the winemakers are less classical, perhaps, more modern in outlook and ambition, the new kids on the block who push their (often recently bought) inheritance to its maximum potential, sometimes brassy, sometimes overblown, sometimes almost

New World in the levels of fruit, alcohol and manipulated tannins. The wines of the Right Bank are capable of dividing the critics unlike any other region, ironic for such an established wine-growing part of the world, the divide often running mid-Atlantic between the more reserved European taste and the more open (welcoming?) American taste.

So when I bought, and we later broached, the first bottle of Moulin Saint-Georges, I did not know what to expect. A New World fruit bomb? Unlikely. The château (in fact there is no château), so let's call it the domaine, the domaine is owned by the Vauthier family who, less than 200 yards away, are also responsible for Château Ausone, quite possibly the Right Bank's most expensive wine. The Vauthiers are winegrowing aristocracy and tread a perfect line between the classicism of claret and the generous fruit of Merlot. I need not have worried.

200 yards. Over £500 a bottle for Ausone 2004 and £30 a bottle for the Moulin Saint-Georges of the same vintage. Do you see a familiar pattern at play here? Cherchez le vigneron. Just as in Burgundy seek out the Bourgognes of the great growers, so in Bordeaux seek out the lesser châteaux of the great growers.

The wine, from vineyards on the slopes immediately to the south of Saint-Emilion itself, is wonderfully constructed, the richness and promise of ripe Merlot within a corset of tannin and structure lent by the limestone on which the grapes are grown, so generous but not overblown, sweet but fresh, a panoply of open and welcoming flavours coupled with Bordeaux's trademark reticence.

2004: this wine works better than any other I can recall with Christmas Day. Given the quantity and the extent of the conflicting flavours on offer, a full-blown Christmas lunch or dinner will kill most wine at 20 paces (even assuming a fresh and enthusiastic palate which is not always the case by the time the turkey makes its appearance). This wine, however, has wide arms within which to gather and welcome all the flavours on show, it has a depth to absorb all but the most direct hits and a lovely soaring sweetness with which to clear the car crashes of overlaid textures and competing tastes that Christmas so joyfully brings. It is a delicious wine with plenty of time left. Treasure the remaining bottles and the happiness they contain.

2010: from a behemoth of a vintage, indeed one day it may be called the mother of all vintages. A wine to lay down and forget about until you are unexpectedly reminded of its existence. Like most wines from 2010, it has a surfeit of everything, all supposedly in balance. I feel slightly intimidated just thinking about it. Christmas Day 2025 perhaps. Or maybe 2030. Jeepers.

La Petite Eglise, Pomerol 2012

The pickings from the Right Bank on offer here, they really are quite poor. One representative from Saint-Emilion, one from Pomerol and one from the satellites. Ah well, others' gain.

Pomerol is very fashionable. It is the apogee, perhaps, of Merlot's expression, the heights of Saint-Emilion taken a stage further by an extra layer of richness and velvet (delivered by the appellation's clay soils) and the scent of truffles. Dense, chocolately wine, utterly seductive, perhaps tiptoeing away a little too keenly from Bordeaux's signature streak of austerity.

La Petite Eglise is the second wine of L'Eglise Clinet, one of Pomerol's finest. Second wines are not an entirely new phenomenon but they have certainly taken off in the last 20 years or so. Châteaux owners would say their purpose is simple, to leach off the less than perfect vats so as to ensure the consistent high quality of the château's "grand vin", being the flagship wine of the estate and simply bearing the name of the château: Château Latour or Lafite for example. The second wines will be given separate names – Les Carruades de Lafite or Les Forts de Latour in these cases. So the second wines will contain the less than perfect lots and, yes, can be laudable, their purpose to protect the quality of the grand vin yet still provide the château owner with a source of income from the lesser wine.

But recently I am not sure that second wines have not been used for another, perhaps less honest, purpose. The law of supply and demand is an easy one to understand: so long as demand outstrips supply, the price will remain high. If supply is bountiful, however, then the price will naturally decrease until it finds an equilibrium with demand. But what if a château owner is reluctant to reduce his prices (or is keen to maintain high prices: two sides of the same coin) in the face of increased supply? One way is by artificially reducing the amount of grand vin available by siphoning off wine that would previously have gone into the grand vin into the second wine (and which is frankly good enough for the grand vin). I need to tread carefully here because I do not want to be sued for accusing any of the big châteaux with enormous pockets and aggressive lawyers of such skulduggery but is it not ironic that, in an age of ever-improving winemaking techniques which are steadily improving the quality of what goes in the bottle, the amount of wine going into the second wine seems to be increasing? It could not, could it, simply be to restrict the supply of the grand vin so as to artificially prop up its high price so as to encourage consumers to buy each new vintage secure in the knowledge that the price of the wine will not go down? Could it? 2010 is considered one of the best vintages in history, not least for the homogeneity of the wines produced across the board. Nature was generous and bestowed all parts of Bordeaux with a perfect growing season. It was not a case of some lucky winners and a few unlucky losers as fickle nature favoured some areas over others. No, everyone was blessed and, as all vignerons claimed that year, there could be no excuses for making bad wine. So why, if that was the case, did one famous château only put 40% (40%!) of its production into the grand vin, the second wine accounting for 55% of production. Why? To protect the quality of the grand vin? Unlikely. In a year as blessed as 2010, a vineyard manager would be sacked for negligence if only 40% was deemed good enough for the estate wine. To build the brand? Conceivably. Why not create new markets and new identities for all the wine produced on the estate; the accountants, the modern high priests, will love it. Or to keep the price of the grand vin suitably high? That is for others to say. In any event, it all seems very confusing and I am not sure the châteaux owners have properly worked it out for themselves either. This year, for example, 2015, a more heterogeneous vintage where there was variation across the regions, Château Cheval Blanc is releasing no second wine at all, the whole production going into the grand vin.

Anyway, enough. The mantra is to buy the second wine in a good vintage and the grand vin in a less than good vintage. 2012 was good in Pomerol, quantities were small and so I invested. I have never liked the appeal of second wines: why pay for something that is second best? It is different to buying a Bourgogne of course because the Bourgogne comes from a defined vineyard and will contain the best grapes that vineyard is capable of producing. But I did buy this wine, on the back of an eye-opening set of reviews if I recall properly. All in good time, the wine will be wonderful, of that I have no doubt.

Production in Pomerol is so small, the owners of L'Eglise Clinet will not be engaged in the more convoluted shenanigans surrounding second wines. And Denis Durantou, the winegrower, is inordinately gifted. I would like to think you may even get that faint scent of truffles in due course and that the wine will make you forget yourself, even just for a short time.

Château Puygueraud, Côtes de Francs 2005

A pompous old fool sat opposite me at a formal dinner and, in his pompous old way, he held forth. The topic was wine; in fact it was claret. He was a claret man through and through: formal dinners were his milieu, he projected self-confidence and self-adulation, his slightly flushed cheeks and slightly stretched waistline suggested affluence and settled opinions incapable of challenge; he no doubt believed his own PR. He was the Establishment and he was warming to the topic.

"Of course, the price of claret these days is becoming prohibitive. You can't do without it but, really, these prices do make you wonder."

"Poor petal," I thought "what life must be like without a steady stream of Angélus", one of the most egregious examples of Bordeaux's over-pricing.

"But what I have discovered," the man continued "and what I now buy a case of every year, it really is the most wonderfully charming and honest bourgeois claret, is Château Puygueraud."

Happily skipping along to my own soundtrack of prejudice, it was as if someone had scraped the needle across the rest of the record and brought the tune to a sudden and discordant silence.

Who was the fool now? Who had imbued one man's passion for the subject, and his frankly well-informed views on the problem in hand, with pomposity and elitism? Who had painted an idle caricature of the man and made him an easy receptacle for all his own prejudices and conceits? It was me who was the fool, it was me who was guilty of all that with which I had so derisively tarnished the other. The love of wine takes many shapes and forms. There is no monopoly on taste, there is no right and wrong in preferences. The love of wine is democratic and universal; it welcomes all, those with no knowledge as much as those with a surfeit. There is snobbery, of course, but the joke is on the snob. It is as valid to have a passion for Blue Nun as it is to swoon over Le Pin. Wine is a centralising, civilising force. We are all equal before wine. Wine brings friendship, community, pleasure and has no place for prejudice or conceit. Easy words to write maybe, not such easy sentiments for some to put into practice. But never be ashamed of your tastes: each taste is as valid as the next so long as it is honest. As I said, I have an absurdly soft spot for Chilean Cabernet Sauvignon. Maybe my pompous old fool would have been horrified at this admission but I suspect my pompous old fool, his interest piqued, might instead have wholeheartedly agreed with me or at least have resolved to try it himself one day. And if he had detested the stuff himself, I am sure he would not have thought any worse of me for enjoying it so much. Love of wine is a blessing and recognising it in each other brings so many gifts and shared pleasures.

So what of Puygueraud? My pompous old fool was bang on the money. The property is owned by the Thienpoint family, also responsible for two of Pomerol's finest properties, Vieux Château Certan and Le Pin. The family knows how to make wine. Puygueraud may not share the same blessed soil as VCC and Le Pin but it is capable of delivering just as much pleasure. Yes, the tannins are a little coarser and the wine will not have the gloss, the complexity, the allure or, in time, the translucent truth of its stellar cousins but the wine delivers all that is promised of it, a sense of place, the true taste of Merlot and an echo of class.

And this, I think, is where Bordeaux needs to look to if it is to preserve its position as the lode star of the firmament. The prices now commanded by the top wines of the region are at risk of rendering the region irrelevant to the majority of the world's wine consumers. There is so much good wine in the world today, there is so much competition, so many untold-of pleasures to discover and in which to revel, that Bordeaux cannot run the risk of becoming irrelevant. We all lose if that happens: we the consumers for the particular delights and rewards that Bordeaux brings and the region for the loss of commerce and livelihood. So the future, in my view, lies less and less in the classed growths and more and more in the region's other wines, the Crus Bourgeois of the Left Bank (I will come on to these) and the wines from the satellites on the Right Bank, "satellites" because they hover over above and around the twin peaks of Saint-Emilion and Pomerol.

Château Puygueraud lies within the Côtes des Francs (now renamed Franc Côtes de Bordeaux in an attempt to unite most of the different satellite regions under the moniker Côtes de Bordeaux). The appellation is capable of producing beautiful, age-worthy, identity-ridden wines that do not cost the earth, derived, like the wines of Pomerol and Saint-Emilion, from Merlot. And the other satellite appellations, such as Fronsac, Canon-Fronsac, Côtes de Bourg, Côtes de Blaye, Castillon and Lalande-de-Pomerol, are just as capable. But who is going to tell the consumer and how is the consumer going to be convinced? What is going to stop the consumer buying

Meerlust's Merlot, for example, instead of a wine from Castillon when his favourite Saint-Emilion finally tops £40 a bottle? There is work to be done and it will be hard work. It cannot simply be a case of wine merchants listing various cheap options when each new vintage is offered; no one likes to think they are buying cheap when more expensive options are offered at the same time: the comparison is too stark. The wines need to be offered at different times to the big guns, preferably when mature (or at least in bottle) and preferably when available to taste. I realise this will require roadshows and I realise that wine merchants will not jump with glee at the prospect, because the margins will necessarily be smaller than with the Cru Classés. So maybe it must fall to the trade bodies for these wines to organise the roadshows and events. And not in Bordeaux, either, but in Tonbridge Wells or Leeds because that is where the real consumers are.

And there is something else that these wines can offer which the Cru Classés are at risk of losing: identity. I have often puzzled over John Lennon's line in Come Together: "got to be good looking 'cause he's so hard to see". That is until I tried a classed growth not so long ago that was so polished, was so smooth, was so glossy that it disappeared down my throat having barely challenged my senses. The smartest wines in Bordeaux are becoming so manicured that they are losing their identity. Where is the friction that forces the taster to confront what is in his mouth and to resolve the conflict and, in doing so, to paint a picture of the wine in question? I call it identity, others call it authenticity. The pleasure of consuming a wine is invariably greater for some effort in understanding the wine and it is this identity and authenticity which wines like Puygueraud have not yet had polished out of them. The classed growths run the risk of being so manipulated that they become invisible.

Have I ranted enough? Unlikely, but I must move on. The

wines of Bordeaux have such a strong identity that they must be preserved. It is in everyone's interest.

And all over a bottle of Puygueraud which, incidentally, is nearly there if not quite. After all, it is from 2005…

LEFT BANK

Château Potensac, Médoc 1990

Now we must cross the river, the swollen Gironde, leaving behind the wooded valleys, the polyculture and the limestone and clay of the Libourne for the grey sweep, the viticultural monoculture and the gravel and clay of the Médoc. It is a different world across the river. Low-lying, featureless, the climate tempered by the Atlantic. And the serious business of Cabernet Sauvignon, a grape difficult to ripen, a grown-up game. Except that in the north of the Médoc, beyond Saint-Estèphe, there's not much of a game about it. Vignerons eke out an existence up here, they do not coast on the tails of millionaires. To ripen properly Cabernet Sauvignon needs gravel, gravel to drain well, gravel to retain heat and to nurture the thick-skinned late-ripening Cabernet. But up here, in the northern reaches of the Médoc, cold clay is more in evidence than gravel and this means either unripe Cabernet or riper Merlot instead. It is a balancing act. How much do you push for the true identity of the Médoc, virile blackcurrant-scented cigar-box-scented capsicum-tinged Cabernet, at the risk of under-ripeness or how much do you play the percentage card and plant Merlot which is more likely to ripen? Life is not easy.

But some succeed very well. Like the satellite appellations on the Right Bank, the successful wines will not share the sheen, the clarity, the single-minded purity that lies at the core of the great wines further south but they will be well-constructed, capable, with a less-articulated message perhaps but full of mouth and full of flavour (and you might say, in some cases, with more interest and authenticity). Potensac is one such. I recall in the late 1990's drinking a surfeit of Potensac 1994, such a surfeit indeed I suffered room spin and had to retire. 1994 was a difficult, awkward, vintage, by no means a write-off but one where the vigneron had to work hard to produce anything charming. There was a higher fruit in the Potensac somewhere but it was hidden behind a heavy structure and I worked diligently all evening to extract, it, each mouthful requiring concentration and swilling to catch fleeting glimpses of cassis and sandalwood before disappearing once again behind tannin and something more savoury. The 1990 is better than that. An infinitely more generous vintage, the fruit comes easier even if the wine retains a certain sturdiness and stolidity. Potensac is owned by the Delon family which also owns Léoville-Las-Cases in Saint-Julien, a wine often talked about as a First Growth in nature if not in name. Léoville-Las-Cases is absurdly priced now. I would not say Potensac offers a sneak of its aristocratic brother but the wine certainly benefits from the same skilled winemaking to extract all the character and class possible from this humbler plot.

Château Sociando-Mallet, Haut-Médoc 2003
Château Sociando-Mallet, Haut-Médoc 2010

Moving south from the cold, clay-predominant Médoc, nature begins to relent as do the administrators. Gravel banks creep in, Cabernet Sauvignon begins to exert the upper hand, the wine improves and the appellation becomes Haut-Médoc, in place of plain Médoc. In fact, the appellation of Haut-Médoc then runs intermittently, when not interrupted by other appellations, all the way down to Bordeaux. But the wines become more singular, texture replacing structure, flavours becoming more focused, tannins finer, the wines lighter on their feet, their purpose clearer.

Long considered a candidate for an upgrade to Cru Classé status (not that the 1855 classification will ever be revised), Sociando-Mallet is a masterpiece of over-achievement on the part of the château's owner Jean Gautreau. Many years ago, Monsieur Gautreau identified the gravel mounds on which the vines of the property now grow as prime territory for Cabernet Sauvignon, in fact as prime as the gravel mounds that lie just to the south, across the border in Saint-Estèphe, which are home to the vines of Château Montrose and Calon-Ségur, two of the region's finest. Monsieur Gautreau does not lack ambition and vinifies the wines as seriously as the more famous châteaux to the south, with long fermentations (to extract as much flavour and substance as possible) and ageing in new oak barrels. The wines are built for the long haul but when they do come round they are deeply impressive. It is not a case of making a pearl necklace out of a sow's ear; the grapes really are good enough to stand this level of elevated winemaking and the results are astonishing.

That said, Sociando-Mallet has always reminded me of a dilemma to which I still do not know the answer. I only found out how good Sociando-Mallet is during a golf match down at Royal St George's, home of one of Britain's finest links courses and of one of Britain's finest golf club wine lists (how wine lovers adore poring over wine lists wherever they come across them; you never know when you are going to uncover an underpriced gem and they do appear in the unlikeliest of places). The master of ceremonies that day was our senior partner, as modest in his golfing talents as he was immodest in his talents as a human being. The dining room at Royal St Georges was bathed in Sandwich light, carried in off the Channel by a fresh easterly and now borne by our flushed faces after the morning round. Late swallows swept the perfect lawn outside the large windows.

"And what wine would sir like to order?" The waiter was immediately putting the senior partner on the spot. He looked across the room to where the Wine Trade Golfing Society were enjoying their lunch.

"We'll have the same as them."

"God bless you" I thought.

"Good choice" purred the waiter.

With the assurance of a confidently-clipped 7-iron, the senior partner thought no more of it and continued to make assured progress through his starter. Of course, he had no idea what wine our neighbours were drinking but he was not senior partner for nothing and his gambit was a calculated one.

The wine was Sociando Mallet 1989 and I shall never forget it. It was rich, dark, a gentle expression of power and balance from beginning to (long) end. And it offered all that wines from the Left Bank should – blackcurrant, cigar box, pencil shavings, green pepper, sandalwood.

If the wine did not leave me speechless, it certainly left me distracted and it certainly left me keen to get another glass on board as soon as possible. Trouble was that the remnants of the bottle were by now at the other end of the table. So what. I drained the glass with something less than indecent haste and caught the eye of the waiter.

Another bottle appeared and my glass was soon refilled. I put my nose into it and took a deep breath, keen to wallow once again in the bottle's miracle. Except that I recoiled. Gone was the purity, the translucency of perfection; in its place was trichloroanisole, better known as TCA, even better known as the compound which causes spoilage in wine. The bottle was corked, horribly corked, unmistakeably corked, so corked even my unborn daughter would have called it corked. I was just about to complain to the waiter when, horror of horrors, his glass having been refilled as well from the same bottle, the senior partner took a swig, smacked his lips and declared in a suitably loud voice, not (sadly) sotto voce to himself, "what a wonderful wine this is".

What was I to do? Show up the senior partner? Bite my tongue and move onto water? You tell me. None of the options available thrilled me. In the end, I chose the least of the three evils. I bit my tongue and drank the glass through. Even corked Sociando Mallet 1989 was better than water. And with one eye on my career, and a heart filled with gratitude at his initial call when asked to choose the wine for lunch, I was not about to risk embarrassing the senior partner.

2003: the heatwave vintage. Some regions of France coped better than others with the extraordinary temperatures. Châteauneuf-du-Pape, you will recall, survived well, used as its vines are to high temperatures. Bordeaux? Maybe not so well. The most propitious, well-drained, warmest sites suffered in the extreme temperatures, producing jammy, forward wines with hard tannins and bitter high alcohol. The less propitious sites, on the other hand, often coped better, precisely because they were naturally cooler sites and with higher levels of clay which retains water better than gravel. So the further north you were, the better. I have not tried the 2003 Sociando yet. Quite why I

am not sure. It is 13 years old now. I have high hopes for it –
am I nervous to find out? Will the vintage heat and bluntness
have impacted too much on the wine? Tasting notes suggest
there is no rush, that the wine is only now entering onto its
drinking plateau where it should remain for some time. May it
be the same for me.

2010: to be left a good long while but I would be disappointed
if this was anything other than bang on when the time comes,
an experience as life-enhancing as the 1989, at least the first
bottle.

Château Phélan-Ségur, Saint-Estèphe 2002

A word about Cru Bourgeois. This is a category that subsists
on the Left Bank below the Cru Classés, a category of largely
honest and sometimes special wines. It originated in the 1930's
and has recently been going through the same turmoils as other
classifications. In the early 2000's there were plans to create a
super-category of Crus Bourgeois Exceptionnels, nine or so
châteaux that were considered to be a cut above the 250 or so
Crus Bourgeois, a super-category to include Phélan-Ségur,
Potensac, Poujeaux and Chasse-Spleen (see below). It all
seemed very sensible and for one, possibly two, vintages it all
worked swimmingly. But then there was a legal challenge and,
hey presto, the project was shelved. The current classification
system involves an annual tasting and Cru Bourgeois status is
only bestowed on those wines each year which are deemed
worthy. So maybe it will be a system worth following from
2015 onwards. Personally I find it all rather exhausting but,
technically speaking at least, if you see a label which records
the château as being a Cru Bourgeois, technically it should be a
cut above your standard Médocain fare. Technically.

Anyway, back to the wine. We are now into Saint-Estèphe, the northernmost of the smartest appellations of the Médoc. Its reputation is for producing slightly heavier wines than the appellations to the south, meatier, less perfumed perhaps, more substantial. This is on account of the greater proportion of clay in the soil, or so it is claimed. That said, Saint-Estèphe is no slouch, home as it is to such high-flying estates as Cos d'Estournel and Montrose. Phélan-Ségur does not reach the giddy heights of these two but is an estate with a solid reputation, which makes me slightly disappointed that I have always been slightly underwhelmed by this wine. Maybe it is my expectation, maybe it is the vintage.

Expectation. The curse of too much knowledge which can get in the way of the experience. If I can set expectation to one side, the wine might be allowed to speak for itself. It once did.

Silence of the Lambs is not a film I particularly enjoyed, that is until the very end. Hannibal Lecter, as the film amply points out, is as fastidious in his eating habits as he is in his methods of killing people. Everyone can recall his recommendation of Chianti with human liver and fava beans though few, I hope, have put it to the test. But it is the final scene that I remember best. He is on an overnight flight and, rather than eat the airline's standard fare, he very carefully unpacks his own Dean & Deluca prepared dinner which includes a half-bottle of Phélan-Ségur. A small boy leans across and engages Lecter in conversation. He is interested to know what one particular sweetbread is. Lecter is reluctant to let him try it but eventually allows him half a fork of human brain, reminding him how important it is always to try new things.

It was this half-bottle of Phélan-Ségur that I recalled, travelling up on the train from London to Edinburgh with Tom one time, as I unpacked our very own bottle of Phélan-Ségur to accompany our lunch. I had to call on the man in charge of the buffet trolley (let's call him the *chef du chariot*, an august title for such an important and undervalued job) to provide a corkscrew which he delightedly did. His background was in catering and he was enthralled to see something finer than Echo Falls or Gallo Blush on offer. And maybe it was the chef du chariot's enthusiasm for the bottle which made me recalibrate my expectations for the wine. In any event, the wine rose to the occasion beautifully. Circumstances can conspire to make a wine seem grander or poorer and, in this instance, the surroundings in which the wine found itself forced me to re-evaluate the wine and to appreciate what a work of art it was: dark, chocolatey, rich in berry, a dry tannic twist. Classy. My expectations were altered by the environment and for once I could see the wine in its proper light, not simply damning it by comparison with other finer bottles or other more illustrious vintages.

There are only a few bottles of the wine left now and they won't improve any further. They should be drunk and enjoyed for what they are, not criticised and marked down for what they are not.

Château Capbern-Gasqueton, Saint-Estèphe 2005

This was a find. Owned by the same family and made by the same team as Calon-Ségur, one of the other greats of Saint-Estèphe, but at a fraction of the price (of course), this wine has it all – depth, balance, flavour, fine tannins. Cassis, cedarwood and tobacco in spades. A remarkably good, remarkably strong offering. And, in case you are interested, a Cru Bourgeois. Pair it with roast beef one Sunday – life will seem simple after that.

Château Latour, Pauillac 1967

One bottle. One bottle given by cousin Claire when I was first diagnosed. Her kindness brought tears to my eyes, happier tears than I had previously been shedding. And still I have not broached it. For the last 18 months because my palate has as often as not been compromised by chemotherapy, before then maybe because the opportunity had not properly presented itself. 1967 was an atrocious vintage but, by all accounts, Latour made a good wine that year. The wine is obviously not going to improve any further, in fact quite the opposite, so really we should crack on with this. If it falls to you, don't decant the wine, let it breathe in the glass if it needs it. If it is a weak wine, then it will fall apart quickly if decanted. At least in the glass you can capture it before it vanishes. And if is stronger than that, then what a pleasure to experience its stretching and awakening from 49 years' slumber, a sleeping beauty perhaps. And remember Kermit Lynch's trick. Upend the bottle to mix the sediment with the wine perhaps 10 minutes before serving. It's an old man of a wine and will need all the help it can get.

1967 – the year of my birth. Will the wine transport me back to a time before memory? I think not. I used to believe that wine could capture all four dimensions, that opening a bottle would unleash not only place (which I do believe) but time as well. But whenever I tried to be transported back in time, well it has never quite worked. It has never worked for the simple reason that the wine has aged as we have, the quiet seep of oxygen through the cork and into the bottle ageing the wine as surely as oxygen has aged us. So I (or you, my love) will be meeting a contemporary, a fellow passenger. Not to say that this shared history will not provoke a moment or two of reflection. It will, and it is this that is the time that is captured: an unaccounted moment when time unfolds and ever so briefly holds up a mirror.

I have enjoyed thinking of the wine in the cellar, knowing it is there waiting to be uncorked. The delicious question is what to serve next to it? It is easy enough to work out what to serve with it, something plain to allow the wine centre stage (roast lamb or roast chicken maybe). I am not a great one for food and wine pairings – my only rule of thumb is to work out which has top billing, because the other should not get in the way of the star attraction. But what to serve next to it? Another claret, for sure. A decent enough wine to step into the breach if the Latour is corked, oxidised or, for whatever reason, undrinkable. Otherwise a faithful lieutenant that will not upstage the Latour but will keep up standards. And, warming to the subject, best go for something from the Left Bank to continue the Cabernet Sauvignon theme. Anyway, a dilemma to while away a few indulgent moments. On such silly thoughts are many wine lovers' minutes spent. Maybe a Léoville Barton will do the trick…

I have never tried Latour before. It is said to be the manliest of the Left Bank's five First Growths (the others being Lafite-Rothschild, Mouton-Rothschild, Margaux and Haut-Brion), with a core of iron running through the cassis and cigar box scents and flavours. Somewhat serious I expect, not a bundle of laughs, possibly intimidating. Nor have I tried Margaux. But I have tried Lafite once (at university, a bottle lifted by a friend from her father's cellar without permission I think, an early 1970's bottling, quite glorious and endlessly developing on the palate), Mouton once (the vintage was 1992, a bad one, the wine was enjoyable but nothing more than that) and Haut Brion once (1997 – again, not a wonderful vintage but utterly seductive and delicious). So not a great return on the First Growths but I am not sure it is too much of a hole in my education.

Latour lies in Pauillac, along with two of the other Firsts, Mouton and Lafite. And on account of holding three of the five Firsts, Pauillac is considered the jewel in the crown of the Left Bank appellations. It all comes together in Pauillac – the gravel banks, the proximity of the river (which tempers the climate and provides the extra degree of warmth to allow the Cabernet Sauvignon to ripen), the drainage, the aspects, the concentration of great châteaux. Many would argue Cabernet Sauvignon finds its greatest expression in Pauillac – virile, deeply coloured, powerfully scented, almost imperial, confident beyond compare. It certainly is wonderful stuff.

Château Batailley, Pauillac 1996
Château Batailley, Pauillac 2000
Château Batailley, Pauillac 2005

The wines of Château Batailley have long been the cornerstone of the archetypal middle-class Englishman's cellar. Reliable year in year out, solid, dependable, not subject to the vagaries of fashion, good value but with that inescapable touch of class to merit attention and loyalty amongst its followers. It is, after all, a Cru Classé from Pauillac. My father loved it and you, my love, your father loves it and his father before him loved it. It is as English as cricket on a summer's day. Which, come to think of it, is ironic not only on account of being French, of course, but named after a battle at which the English were roundly defeated by the French during the Hundred Years' War. No matter, I have always thought of Batailley as a corner of a foreign field.

I know your grandfather loved Batailley because he wrote as much in his cellar book: Batailley and Talbot in Saint-Julien (it is coincidence I think that Château Talbot is named after the last British governor of Bordeaux, John Talbot, but it is yet further evidence of the shared history between Bordeaux and Britain). A cellar book is a curiously revealing document. It is not easy to write about wine. If taken in the wrong spirit, it can make you look silly (chasing evanescent flavours with clunky fixed descriptions) and it can make you look pretentious (anthropomorphising grape juice, not least). But it provides a history which is not obvious to begin with but which, stretched over time, comes to remind you not only of the wines you have drunk but the places you have been, the people you have known, the events you have celebrated, the tastes that have changed, the circumstances that have changed, the vinous dreams and ambitions you have had, the person you are. And if you are lucky enough that your financial position has improved over the years, it reminds you of the pleasure you derived from supposedly lesser wines in earlier years, such an important lesson which should never be forgotten.

Looking through the cellar books, I am reminded of what we drank the night England won the Rugby World Cup in 2003 (Dubreuil-Fontaine's Savigny-lès-Beaune Aux Vergelesses 1er Cru 2007 - the name more of a mouthful perhaps than the wine itself – "a relatively simple palate which tailed off quite quickly"), of the bottle Mum and I shared the night Claudia chose to arrive two weeks early (Bruno Clair's Marsannay Les Longeroies 2000 - you were still in hospital – "God bless little Claudia" I wrote "headstrong I fear") and of what we drank the night we found out about this blasted illness (the finest bottle we had in the cellar, Francois Lamarche's Echezeaux 1997 - "clarity, purpose, priority, power and balance"). I am reminded of these and other pinpoints in time - holidays, dinner parties, birthdays, anniversaries, times spent with friends gone and new – postcards to the future, fragments shored against ruin.

In any event, and as I was saying, Château Batailley is not as fashionable as other wines in Pauillac. This is not to say it is shabby, quite the opposite. A new generation is at the helm now and has ambitions, both in terms of quality and in terms of price. This may or may not be a shame. Batailley has always been quite a soft wine, not too challenging or austere (which is not to deny its Pauillac identity), gentle and forthcoming, filled with all the typical flavours of Left Bank: claret, blackcurrant, pencil shavings, green pepper, quite beguiling really. But ultimately friendly and reliable. And it is this that will have impressed my father and your father and your grandfather – a wine without pretence that has consistently produced wines typical of the appellation at a fair price and with a touch of stardust. What can be wrong with that?

1996: a wonderful vintage at Batailley. Cool and clear with a steely purpose. My goodness, 20 years old now. That is sobering. Not a wine to improve any further so really one to polish off with a happy smile.

2000: surprisingly soft for such a lauded vintage. I suspect the wine will continue to develop a little but again, why hold back?

2005: untried. Time to check now if it's ready.

Château Léoville Barton, Saint Julien 1988
Château Léoville Barton, Saint Julien 1994
Château Léoville Barton, Saint Julien 1998
Château Léoville Barton, Saint Julien 2000
Château Léoville Barton, Saint Julien 2002
Château Léoville Barton, Saint Julien 2005

Saint-Julien is a tiny pocket of an appellation, at least by Bordeaux standards. It barely measures four kilometres by four kilometres. Like Saint-Estèphe and Pauillac to the north, it lies flush with the Garonne, the most treasured aspect. Indeed, so bespoke is the appellation, over 80% of it is given over to classed growths.

If Pauillac is the emperor, perhaps Saint-Julien is the poet. It is the same idiom, the wines are even in the same key, but perhaps the wines from Saint-Julien are less strident. They can be equally austere when young but express themselves more quietly. They require greater interpretation, perhaps a tad more concentration. You may think all of this nonsense but my experience suggests that there is a difference, however difficult it might be to distil into words. The bold statement of Pauillac is replaced by the more subtle suggestion of Saint-Julien.

Barely two years after I had started our cellar Emily appeared on the scene. I was keen to buy a case of wine to mark her arrival though, even now, I cannot determine if the case is for her or if the case is ours to drink with her. How I would love the latter. In any event, I was still (as I remain now) learning the ropes. 1998 was a fantastic vintage on the Right Bank (the weather did not turn until after the earlier-ripening Merlot had been picked) but slightly more difficult on the Left Bank, as October brought trickier weather to the Médoc and interfered with the final ripening of the Cabernet Sauvignon. Given these conditions I should sensibly, perhaps, have chosen a Saint-Emilion or Pomerol to mark our first-born's birth. But in my ignorance I was worried that a Merlot-based wine might not make it to Emily's majority so I stuck with the Left Bank. And why Léoville Barton? Long championed by the wine press, it is a Second Growth, it has a high reputation and, just as importantly, it has an enlightened pricing policy for the quality on offer. The choice was relatively easy.

As for the earlier vintages, they came later; naturally.

1988: Léoville Barton is one of three Léovilles in Saint-Julien, all Second Growths, all once part of the larger Léoville estate which was broken up in the 19th century. The biggest and most ambitious of the three is Léoville-Las-Cases which almost crosses swords with Château Latour on the boundary between Pauillac and Saint-Julien. The most aggressive of the three in terms of pricing and aspiration, Léoville-Las-Cases shares many similarities with Latour; it is often talked about as a First Growth in waiting. Léoville Poyferré, the third of the Léovilles, is perhaps the plushest, a gentler rendition. Which leaves Léoville Barton, perhaps the most traditional, the most British even, of the three. In fact, it was Léoville Barton which taught me the lesson that claret is not about fruit. Léoville Barton is a phenomenally dry wine; it is important to realise this otherwise you will be disappointed when you try it. It only yields its charms slowly, over many years, when the softer fruit comes gently peeking from behind the sandalwood and cigar. All this makes the wine difficult to appreciate young and tremendously long-lived. Dad gave us this case, an act of great kindness given it is the single smartest case he ever purchased. We are down to the last couple of bottles; once again, I am reluctant to polish them off but really there is nothing to be gained from hanging on to them any longer. The wine is now at full maturity (it wasn't when my father first delivered the case), all components resolved, the wine at peace, all its hand revealed. Maybe drink them with James and Claire. We have shared a couple of bottles with Rachel and Hugh a while back and well, being his father's son, they are as much James' as they are mine. And he likes claret.

1994: another gift, from a kind client on his first learning of my diagnosis. "Make sure it is ready to drink!" were Robert's instructions to his wine merchant. A fascinating, intellectual wine (so classic claret, in other words). 1994 was a difficult vintage, none too generous, but Léoville Barton pulled it off very well. Linear. A clean line through from start to finish. No surfeit of fruit spilling off the sides but with sufficient cassis to mitigate the green pepper austerity and render the journey a pleasure. This wine could be made nowhere else.

1998: untried, Emily only just now turning 18 (and with no taste for red wine whatsoever). The other reason I chose Léoville Barton this year is because it was apparently a great success in this challenging vintage. One respected commentator even suggested that, after the First Growths, it stood head and shoulders above its peers. Well, time might tell.

2000: the year of madness. The year en primeur went bananas, Léoville Barton caught firmly in the cross-hairs.

Just as you cannot talk about Burgundy without talking about terroir, so you cannot talk about Bordeaux without talking about en primeur. As I might have briefly mentioned before, en primeur, a blessing and a curse in equal measure, is the system whereby, in the spring following the harvest, the wine is first offered for sale. The wine is a long way off being bottled or ready for export, still at this stage gently maturing in its oak barrels. The system really took off with the 1982 vintage and was designed to be mutually beneficial to producer and consumer alike. The producer would receive, in effect, an upfront payment for its goods not yet delivered and, in return, the consumer would buy the goods at a discount to reflect the early payment. And for those wines which were in short supply (rarely a problem in Bordeaux where the quantities produced are vast – up to 25,000 cases a year for Château Lafite, for example), en primeur also offered an opportunity to get in early and secure precious allocations. So far so good.

But then things changed. On the one hand, châteaux owners

saw the prices their wines were commanding on the secondary market and began to begrudge the consumers the profits they were making. And on the other hand, the consumers' ranks were infiltrated by investors who saw what a killing could be made in relatively short order. And if you add in the appeal of the first vintage of the new millennium, and the fact that 2000 was an extraordinarily good harvest, then things were bound to spill over. And they did. It was pandemonium. The wine world went crazy for the new vintage. People surged into the market, wine merchants were inundated, châteaux owners and their courtiers were bombarded on all sides, prices inevitably rocketed. Except of course Léoville Barton. Having produced, by all accounts, one of the finest wines the château had ever produced, Anthony Barton, the proprietor, refused to capitalise on his achievement by asking a price the market could properly bear. Instead he asked what he thought was a reasonable price (to such an extent that his more rapacious neighbours accused him of being a saint). And this only fuelled the frenzy further. Léoville Barton 2000 became one of the most sought-after wines of the vintage. We were lucky. We bought six bottles through the Wine Society and Rachel and Hugh did likewise for us, so we ended up with a dozen. The madness of it all though. The irony of course is that there is no trouble now finding the wine (albeit at a greater price) and other wines are considered more fashionable or desirable. But the wine will come good. The wine is for the long haul, the very long haul, but I am sure all the astonishing and rave reviews that the wine received in 2001 will hold good in 2030 and beyond. An exciting prospect for the future.

And what of en primeur now? In all honesty, the system is pretty much broken although it limps on year to year and the wine merchants try to make the most of it. The châteaux owners are reluctant to concede any value to the consumers who in turn are reluctant to part early with their cash, not least since the prices as often as not come down once the wine is actually bottled and available on the open market. Meanwhile vast stocks of unsold wine build up on the quaysides of Bordeaux. It does not require a degree in economics to guess where this might be heading.

2002: the year of Gus's birth. Untried, of course, but another difficult vintage on the Left Bank (though easier than on the Right). The wine will be dry, the wine will be good. It will go down as a "classic" vintage I suspect: not over-generous but generous enough, typical of its type, a fine example of the middle order. So long as the wine is judged, and drunk, on its own merits, however, it will be a delight.

2005: and finally to Claudia. She struck the jackpot. A stellar vintage, for Léoville Barton just as for all of Bordeaux. Most likely a monster of a wine that will keep going for as long as any of us are. Not to be broached for decades. My only note of caution would be not to allow the reputation of the wine and the vintage to become a millstone around the wine's neck. Ensure there is sufficient levity and distraction in attendance, at least for the first bottle.

Château Moulin Riche, Saint-Julien 2010

After the giddy heights of Second Growths, it seems almost indecent to drop to the level of a mere Cru Bourgeois but I suspect this wine will deliver as much pleasure as any of the above, in its own unassuming way.

Moulin Riche is a relative rarity in Saint-Julien, being one of the 20% not a classed growth. That said, it is made by a classed growth, namely Léoville Poyferré. Moulin Riche used to be the second label of Léoville Poyferré but is now treated as a separate wine in its own right from an inland vineyard, away from the riverside and its gravel mounds. 2010 a wonderful year, Léoville Poyferré an accomplished producer, the vineyard firmly within Saint-Julien's boundaries – all is set for a glorious experience and, just as enjoyable, years of keen anticipation of a wine that promises to punch above its weight. There was once a useful chaser called Moulin Riche. I never backed it but always loved the idea that the owner must have had many happy experiences with the wine to call a horse after it. As good a reason as any to invest in a case, in any event.

Leave the wine for another five years or so. Then derive that greatest of pleasures: the first taste from the first bottle of a case long laid down. How does it measure up to the expectation? All those years' worth of guessing and hoping what the wine might be like. What treasures will it reveal? What promises of the wine and the years to come? Cheat time. Peer into the looking glass and predict the future.

Expression de Margaux, Ulysse Cazabonne 2010

"Hank."

"Stephen, hi."

"What day is it?"

"What day is it? Umm, Thursday."

"No, what type of day is it? A fruit day or a root day?"

"Ah, let me check." I checked. "It's a fruit day."

"I knew it. That Margaux, it's absolutely singing. The best

bottle yet."

This conversation surprised me. Not because the wine might be good but because Stephen is a cynic. What was he doing buying into fruit days and root days and all that nonsense? Fine for those of us whose doubt in most things allows a degree of belief in most things but somewhat of a surprise for someone whose belief requires proof.

I have mentioned biodynamism before but that's been in connection with the production of wine, whether in the vineyard or the cellar. Biodynamism goes further than that however. It can also dictate (or so it is held) how a wine will taste on a particular day. Days are divided into four types: fruit days, flower days, leaf days and root days. These categories identify which days are best for planting the particular types of plant. But they also, it turns out, identify which days are best for tasting wine. Fruit and flower days are good, leaf and root days are bad.

I do not know the science or reasoning behind these propositions, maybe it is something to do with the moon again, but I do know that, empirically, these theories seem to be borne out by experience. Wine tastes different on different days – that is the result of my 30-plus years of drinking wine. And wine tastes better on fruit or flower days – that is the result of my 10-plus years of being aware of this distinction in the types of day. And it is not that I have been aware of the type of day before drinking a wine. So often I have been puzzled why a wine is not showing as well as it has on previous occasions. And so often I have then discovered that we are drinking the wine on a root or leaf day. I am not saying this is always the reason why a wine tastes different (my mood, for example, might equally be to blame) but the coincidence is telling and I would be arguing against myself were I to ignore this. Perhaps more persuasive to doubters might be the fact that the supermarkets and a number of wine merchants take care only to hold tastings on fruit days. Not to say that all are convinced, of course. The following letter to Decanter magazine, which landed through my letter box only last month, is ample enough evidence of this:

I find it disappointing that otherwise rational and well-educated people are taken in by aspects of biodynamics. Take the biodynamic calendar for instance. This tells us that the same bottle of wine tastes differently on different days of the week, depending on the lunar cycle. Perhaps the moon really is made of cheese, and its aromas homeopathically permeate the cosmos in the same fashion as the buried cow horn in the vineyard. In 2016, should we not be embracing science and reason instead of superstitious claptrap?

Voltaire might have replied that doubt is not a pleasant condition but certainty is absurd. And is doubt not the source of knowledge?

Anyway, here we are in Margaux. Whereas the other three jewels of the Médoc, Saint-Estèphe, Pauillac and Saint-Julien, are contiguous (such a lovely word: so superbly succinct and of such singular meaning), there is then a gap before, heading south, you reach the fourth jewel, Margaux. It is a gap filled by the catch-all Haut-Médoc appellation and, in small part, Moulis and Listrac (on which, more below). And whereas the other three are fairly compact and homogenous, Margaux goes to the other extreme, being spread out over a much larger area and displaying far more heterogeneity.

I have rarely bothered with Margaux. It is the serial underperformer of the big four, maybe simply (and unfairly) because wine merchants cannot succinctly categorise such a wide range of producers or such a wide range of wines in each and every vintage. "Variable" is a word often used. The loss, though, will undoubtedly be mine. The wines are usually labelled as being the most feminine of the Médoc and the most perfumed. Unfortunately I cannot comment.

But I did buy this wine. This is, supposedly, the third wine of Château Margaux itself (you will recall, Château Margaux being one of the First Growths). The Château's second wine is Pavillon Rouge which commands a king's ransom itself but, in common with many (all?) of the First Growths, Château Margaux sells off a small proportion of its wine as unclassified Margaux (the appellation, not the château) to negoçiants. And this is meant to be it. Is it? I have no idea. The merchant tells me it is but whether I trust the merchant or not is another matter. I am also hampered by the fact that my palate has been affected by chemotherapy each time I have tried the wine. So really I am in the dark but, well, it is a nice idea (and the wine certainly seems well constructed, with a strong start, middle and end) and others have certainly expressed delight at the wine. It still seems young to me, all its nascent attributes still tightly coiled. I think it will blossom (maybe that famous Margaux perfume) given another couple of years.

Margaux, Marks and Spencer 2010

One way I thought I might try and gauge the pedigree of the Ulysse Cazabonne wine was by comparing it with this offering from Marks and Spencer which is the third wine, from the same vintage, of Brane-Cantenac, a Second Growth. Stephen has always been a fan of this wine (for such an iconoclast, he has an unusually soft spot for claret which continues to surprise me) but thinks it comes up well short of the Cazabonne. It would be welcome if my palate could improve sufficiently to allow me to make this distinction too. Whatever the conclusion, however, it will be a fun and idle experiment to conduct.

Château Giscours, Margaux 2015

So if I have never really bought Margaux before, and if the doctors continue to utter their prognoses, why this?

It was maybe 15 years ago that my father travelled out to Hong Kong to see a Chinese billionaire. The billionaire had expressed a willingness to make a large donation to St Antony's College Oxford, of which my father was at the time Warden. Fund-raising was an integral part of my father's job and, at the same time, the least favourite part of his job. And this trip, in its way, would simply reinforce my father's dislike of this aspect since the billionaire (under pressure from his third wife maybe?) changed his mind while my father was en route and decided against making the sizeable donation promised. But they would still meet and have supper together.

The billionaire was an avid wine enthusiast and, clearly guilty at his change of heart over the donation, was keen to treat my father. He poured my father a glass of wine and asked my father (who must, a little too enthusiastically perhaps, have expressed his own love of wine) to try and guess what it was.

They always say in wine tasting that you should play the wine rather than the man but I am not sure. My father played both. First of all, the man. A Chinese billionaire who has expressed such a love of wine as he has, and who is obviously feeling guilty at the withdrawal of the donation, is only going to serve the best. So aim high. Playing the wine, my father could tell straightaway that the wine was a claret. Furthermore he could tell it was a Left Bank claret, the cassis, capsicum and cigar box flavours being strong. So, playing the man once again, he restricted himself to the five First Growths. Here luck came into play. My father might have been able to distinguish the tobacco of Haut Brion from the other four but really his exposure to the First Growths was limited and so he really stood no more than a one in five chance of guessing the château. He went for Margaux. I forget why but luck was on his side.

The billionaire was hugely impressed. "But what vintage?" he asked, the final hurdle.

My father paused. He thought a little, he paused a little bit more. He was on safer ground playing the man but now he had to play the wine again, intellectual application replaced by sensory discretion. Not easy. He could tell from the age of the wine (not too tawny, not too ruby) that the 1980's would be a good guess, a decade of blessed vintages and the wines now in their prime. But which? Here sentiment took over and he went for his favourite vintage of them all, 1985.

1985, such a beautiful, wonderful vintage. A vintage about which the connoisseurs and commentators were initially a little bit sniffy. A cool June, a damp July, a cool August, saved by a perfect September. But did not the rain and the cold earlier in the summer wing the promising concentration with which the vintage would otherwise have been blessed? So nearly but not quite was the initial verdict. How they were proved wrong. 1985 has never done anything but give, give, give. An abundance of pleasure, of light, of fruit (yes, fruit!), of discreet structure, perfect balance and endless charm.

And my father was right. The wine was Margaux 1985. The billionaire was so impressed that he gave my father three bottles of Cheval Blanc 1982 (100 Parker points at one time in its majority) with which to return home. Not much use to St Antony's but a source of great happiness to my father and me. We shared two of the bottles and my father gave me the third, a singular act of kindness and generosity.

So what does any of this have to do with Giscours 2015? The answer is 1985. They say that 2015 in Bordeaux is most like 1985, a year of charm and greatness, lighter on its feet than the monolith years of 2005, 2009 and 2010. A year perhaps where minor imperfections serve simply to make the wine even more beautiful. How could I resist such a thought? How could I resist the gift that this wine might bring 20 years down the line? How could I resist the temptation, if I am not there to drink it, of not reaching into the future now and blessing you, my love and my little ones, with an experience as fresh and as life-enhancing as 1985 brought to my father in his time and me in mine? Maybe I am being hopelessly romantic but, really, thoughts like this are balm to my soul and make the world go round. A long cast, as long a cast as I can throw, into the future.

And why Giscours? A number of years ago I attended a tasting of the 2009 clarets somewhere in Middle Temple. The vast majority of them, grand names, all of them, I had never tasted before. A few of the big names disappointed and quite a few of the lesser names were surprisingly joyous. It reminded me what an iniquitous part fashion has to play in Bordeaux, how reputations become self-propelling and how difficult it is for those without vogue on their side to obtain the recognition they deserve. In any event, three wines stood out – Haut-Bailly from Pessac-Léognan, Cantemerle from the Haut-Médoc and Giscours from Margaux. For a change, Margaux was considered one of the top performers in 2015; the decision was straightforward.

Château Chasse-Spleen, Moulis-en-Médoc 2009
Château Poujeaux, Moulis-en-Médoc 2009

I will bracket these wines together for the simple reason that they are from the same appellation, the same vintage, in the old days they were both classified as Crus Bourgeois Exceptionnels, they are both, in my view, in the sweet spot of Bordeaux (I will explain) and I have tried neither. In fact, I have never tried Chasse-Spleen (attributed, apparently, to Byron who thought the wines from this château well-suited to chasing away the blues) but, in terms of pleasure delivered measured against price paid, I struggle to think of any claret which can match Poujeaux. And as the two are normally uttered in the same breath, well I will allow Chasse-Spleen in on Poujeaux's coat-tails. Moulis, incidentally, lies well inland from the Garonne but in an area where the gravel mounds, so beloved by Cabernet Sauvignon, rise once again, like vast whales breaching the surface of an ancient sea.

1997 was a vintage over-rated by the Bordelais and, in my view, under-rated by the critics. Over-rated by the Bordelais means, you guessed it, high en primeur prices. Under-rated by the critics on account of a cold and damp May and June, a humid July, a stormy August and, throughout, the threat of rot. Even a damp harvest to contend with. So long as the grapes are ripe, however, rain at harvest time (unless biblical) has never bothered me too much. It lends a certain lightness and approachability to the wines. We all obsess about wines being built for the long haul, with the structure to last aeons, never thinking if we the consumers share those same traits. So we sit patiently while the great vintages slowly stretch and unravel and time slips slowly away. Once again, this obsessive pursuit of the absolute deprives us of so many pleasures along the way.

I bought one case in 1997, Poujeaux. A "sleeper of the vintage" Robert Parker called it. For years I had no idea what "sleeper" meant. An outperformer is what it means and, my word, how wonderful it was. Friendly from the word go, generous, full fruit, gentle tannins, maybe lacking the austerity that normally comes with a great vintage's structure, every bottle was a delight. Polished, classy, thrilling.

I have tried other vintages of Poujeaux along the way and all these experiences have convinced me that, yes, the likes of Poujeaux and Chasse-Spleen sit in the sweet spot of Bordeaux, at the point where the curve of diminishing returns begins to plateau. Château Poujeaux has always trumpeted the occasion when Baron Rothschild mistook the 1953 Poujeaux for his own Lafite. Poor man, it is easy enough to mistake anything for anything, but it does show that a well-made wine from Poujeaux can be a fine example of claret for the most discerning palates.

All of which means, in my view, that you do not need to spend more on a case of claret than you will have to spend on a case of Poujeaux. The prices of these middle-tier wines have not been subject to the same absurd inflation as the classed growths and yet deliver 90%, or even 95%, of the complexity and return that you would hope for from more expensive wines. Which is not to say, of course, that I have heeded my own advice here. Man is inquisitive and acquisitive in equal measure and there are far too many choices in the sweet shop to restrict you to one or two favourites each time.

2009, as you will know by now, was a dream of a vintage. Approachable early with the structure to last, generous almost to a fault. A vintage of all things for all men. These wines will last as long as you want them to but I would be tempted to take a sneaky peak sometime after their 10th birthday.

Château Beaumont, Haut-Médoc 2005

There was a bit of a fuss a few years ago when Neal Martin, now chief Bordeaux taster for the Wine Advocate, suggested that there was no point buying Château Beaumont en primeur, that there was plenty of it for the world market, that the price of the wine would not markedly increase once it was physically available and that the cost of parting early with one's money, and then paying the costs of storage until the wine was ready, might actually render the wine more expensive by the time you came to drink it. All perfectly reasonable arguments that, frankly, could be applied to most wine bought en primeur nowadays. But especially to the likes of Beaumont which is (I have to use this word carefully because all things are relative and many words carry connotations which I certainly do not mean to carry here) a cheap wine by Bordeaux standards. Poor Neal Martin. He did not mean to create this stink nor did he mean to diminish Beaumont's reputation which is for a well-made reasonably-priced wine which speaks well of its origins and offers some of the gloss of its more illustrious neighbours. It is found in the Haut-Médoc to the south of Margaux and shares some of that appellation's lightness of touch, femininity and class. It is lovely stuff.

It is also the first wine I ever bought en primeur and even now I can remember the sense of anticipation that buying the case engendered and the delicious promise for the future. Because that is something that buying en primeur does bring and which is not to be enjoyed if you simply buy the wine when it is ready to drink. And as I have written before, it is easier to justify an investment in the future than a luxury for the present. This way us wine lovers hoodwink ourselves and the loved ones around us.

These few bottles of 2005 belonged to Dad. Despite being 2005, they must be drinking by now, not least because it is vinified to be accessible relatively early. A favourite of golf clubs and those who know better than many, it should slip down smoothly with little in the way of challenge or obstacle and with the sheen of a better pedigree.

Château Bernadotte, Haut-Médoc 2009

One bottle. Another Haut-Médoc but, this time, not from south of Margaux but rather from west of Pauillac. The château is in the same ownership as Pichon-Longueville, one of Pauillac's finest. It comes with a good reputation. I won it at Sunningdale, playing with Richard in the annual Boxing Day family competition. I drove like a god and putted like an idiot. In the way of all things me, I will always associate this bottle, this château, with poor putting, not great driving. How Richard kept his temper I do not know; it was such a truly inept display of putting. Still, the wine will deliver better. Cellartracker suggests something chunky which still has tannins to resolve. The vintage certainly has the stuffing for further ageing so I would leave it a little while. Foursquare perhaps, honest certainly, straight down the middle.

Château Cantemerle, Haut-Médoc 2009

"Wow, that looks interesting."

Unfortunately, Dominic knew, knows, too much about wine. The line drawing of a château surrounded by mature trees, on a beige background, was not Château Lafite, to which I think he was referring and hoping, but rather Château Cantemerle. A Fifth Growth, not a First.

The vintage was 1997, the occasion your 40th birthday party. We had moved the table from the kitchen into the playroom, leaving the kitchen free for the caterers. We had fillet of beef and the Cantemerle performed its role to perfection, the tannin in the wine building a platform for the food, the soft cassis and sandalwood of the Cabernet flattering the beef and the gentle measure of the wine imploring further consumption.

There were no rows (not like my 40th!), all was civilised, all was calm, all was pleasure, all was perfect. Cantemerle to a tee.

All was civilised. Wine is civilised. Wine is civilisation. I forever think of this when I drink Cantemerle. For what is wine other than a devotion to pleasure? And when does man have the space to devote time and effort to pleasure? When civilisation carves it out for him. For at least 8000 years man has understood and appreciated wine's miracle and, for most of forever, little pockets of peace will have existed allowing man to enjoy its gift. At times, war and turmoil will have obliterated the environment in which wine could grow and flourish but, like deep-embedded seeds, the promise of the future will have lain dormant and, like the green shoots of spring, the ability and the capacity to make wine will have resurfaced when circumstances changed.

Wine is civilisation. Cantemerle is civilisation. A quiet statement of pure and gentle purpose, not shouting, not straining, not striving to beat its neighbour, a faithful reflection of the blessed times in which we live and man's ability to devote the time and effort to beauty such as this.

Cantemerle lies within the Haut-Médoc appellation between Margaux to the north and the city of Bordeaux to the south. It is not as fashionable as many but has never failed, in my experience, to deliver all that is expected of a Left Bank claret. Just as with Poujeaux and Chasse-Spleen, Cantemerle lies in the very cross-hairs of what claret is about. There is no need to spend more and if you spend less, you will get less. Cantemerle is perfectly situated.

So why have I not bought more over the years? A perfectly sensible question to which there is no sensible answer. Logic dictates that I should have. But logic and wine do not always go hand in hand. Maybe I have not bought more for the same reason that, certainly in the wine world and almost certainly in the wider world, we must never cease from exploration and must never take our own advice too much to heart. There is a whole world out there and we must look to know it. So, as it is, we only have the 2009 to look forward to. But when should disappointment at not having something more or else ever be allowed to detract from the pleasure of having something at all?

GRAVES

Domaine de Chevalier, Pessac-Léognan 2002
Domaine de Chevalier, Pessac-Léognan 2004
Domaine de Chevalier, Pessac-Léognan 2005
Domaine de Chevalier, Pessac-Léognan 2008
Domaine de Chevalier, Pessac-Léognan 2009
Domaine de Chevalier, Pessac-Léognan 2012
Domaine de Chevalier, Pessac-Léognan 2015

After all that I have written, does it reveal me as a complete charlatan to record that we have never been to Bordeaux? I hope one day we do. We shall idle away a couple of days in Bordeaux itself, stroll along clean streets, loiter by the quayside, bathe in the reflection of its 18th Century grandeur. Then we shall make our way north along the Left Bank, the slow-moving ever-moving Garonne close by our side, the perfect counterpoint to man's hubris and man's plans along the shoreline. We might stop in at Cantemerle if they'll have us and rest under the cedars in the lee of the sleeping beauty château. We'll not venture far into the hinterland. Before the landscape becomes too brutal we'll take the car ferry across the river to Blaye, to a kinder landscape. We shall explore small producers there, more interested in their wine than its return, and we'll lose ourselves in the combes and woods of a more intimate world. We shall stretch as far as Saint-Emilion and find a small restaurant. Time will move slowly and we will watch a great bottle gently unravel before us.

Gratuitous wish fulfilment. In fact, I tell a lie. We did visit Bordeaux once, but no more than Mérignac Airport. And we saw rows of vines there, a few rows only, planted outside the arrival hall, the deep red roses at the end of each row set off by the bleached gravel in which the vines had been planted. Our journey was east, though, away to the Lot and the black wines of Cahors. I had broken my arm less than a week previously. We stayed in a small house set deep in a cacophony of nightingales and thought no more of cities.

Domaine de Chevalier. Have I saved the best till last? Quite possibly. And not a million miles from Mérignac Airport either, part of the ever-creeping suburbs that threaten the vineyards of Pessac-Léognan to the south of the city.

Graves: the third great region of Bordeaux, along with the Médoc and the Libourne. And probably my favourite. Wines in a lower key. They lack the austerity of the Left Bank and the flash of the Right Bank. They are wines where Merlot and Cabernet Sauvignon share equal billing. They are matt rather than glossy, monochrome and reflective rather than stark and bright. They are soft, filled with heady scents of ripe summer berries and tobacco leaf. They are perhaps more Burgundian than their peers, as much given over to the sensual as to the intellect.

I have long been attracted by Domaine de Chevalier, an outlier, on its own on the edge of the silent pines, well away from most of the châteaux, well away from the city. It had a great reputation once, the property capable of producing astonishingly beautiful, world-beating bottles that would rival anything from the area. But it went through something of a decline in the 1980's and early 1990's, especially as the vogue for open, fleshy, instantly accessible wines hit its straps. But the necessary hard work and investment was made and, really for quite a while, the world was left playing catch-up as the property pulled itself up and together (there is nothing a wine lover loves so much as thinking that he is on the inside track, that he has spotted a star before anyone else has cottoned on). And the wine can be scratchy and difficult when young, a struggle to appreciate, especially when lined up against some of the prima donnas of the region which preen and mew at the annual en primeur tastings. An awkward ugly duckling, shot through with honesty and truth, that in time emerges from its hibernation and bewitches everyone with the fineness of its tannins, the smokiness of its fruit and the balance of a ballerina. What a wine, what a stellar stellar wine it is.

2002: Kermit Lynch's magnum opus is *Adventures on the Wine Route* but he also put together *Inspiring Thirst*, a selection of pieces from his monthly newsletter. Even if you do not live in Berkeley California, near his wine shop, this newsletter is compulsory reading and you should check his website each month to ensure you do so. In one such piece, he rails against vintage charts and offers his own cut-out vintage chart as an alternative. And this is? A blank piece of paper.

This is a refreshing and constructive take on the issue. Vintage charts should be ignored. To begin with, you cannot tar a whole region with one mark and, on the back of it, either dismiss a whole region's efforts for the year or, at the other extreme, buy blindly on account simply of a great vintage. Similarly, to rely on a vintage chart is to take the winemaker out of the equation. The winemaker is the most important part of the equation (whatever terroirists might say). And the winemaker, like anyone, can have a good day or a bad day. A good grower in a good vintage can have a stinker (maybe he had a row with his wife the morning he made a critical decision) and a good grower in a bad vintage can play a blinder, helped perhaps by a twist in the general weather which helped his property and not his neighbour's.

None of this is to say that vintages are not different. They are, of course they are, and comparing a grower's wines from different vintages is part of the fascination and pleasure of wine. But the wine should be judged on what is in the bottle, not on the vintage. Barring egregious examples, vintages are no better or worse than each other, they are just different. And the same is true of the wines themselves – vintage variation will make them different to each other but, in the hands of a skilled winemaker, should not make them necessarily better or worse. Appreciate the different elements that nature brings each year and don't damn by comparison. End of lesson.

End of lesson. But have I learnt this lesson? You may well say I have not. The grand vintages in Bordeaux of the last 15 years have been 2000, 2005, 2009, 2010 and 2015, the most hyped, the most expensive. And which are the vintages I have bought?

Precisely these, with only the odd exception. Why have I not concentrated on the other, less fashionable vintages? I haven't had this problem in Burgundy, the Rhône, Germany, anywhere else maybe. So why in Bordeaux am I slave to fashion and vintage? Perhaps it is because no one else places quite so much emphasis on the vintage as the Bordelais each and every year at the en primeur circus. Maybe it is because if, from time to time I spend this much money on a case, I want to think at least I am getting the best the region can offer. Maybe it is because I am weak and, despite knowing better, am susceptible to hype. I stand accused, dear reader, and have no defence.

In any event, I think of this often when drinking Domaine de Chevalier's 2002. An unflattering vintage according to the vintage charts, an unflattering wine according to the wine scores but, for me, one of the finest bottles in the cellar. Balance, warmth, controlled pleasure, minerality, place, smoke, tobacco, hints of cassis. Vintage chart: 5 out of 10. Wine: 10 out of 10.

2004: this wine needs longer. It is drinkable, for sure, but has yet, in my view, properly to unfold. The palate is there, thicker textured than the 2002, but, along with the nose, remains relatively mute. Allow the wine time to do its business. Let the tannins plane down, let the palate stretch out, let the nose reveal itself and then the wine will sing.

2005: based on everything going, this should be a great wine that will last forever. I doubt it will be at fighting weight for a very long time. 2025?

2008: ah, this is what we want. An unfashionable vintage! Bright and cool, with a streak of acidity. The Graves region apparently did better than other areas, benefiting from earlier ripening grapes. This wine will be lighter than the likes of

2005 and 2009 and, who knows, maybe the better for it? Too young at present I suspect.

2009: a friendlier wine than 2005 would be my guess but, like 2005, all the stars aligned. Another for the long haul.

2012: maybe in the class of 2008: bright, fresh and on its toes. Keep an eye on cellartracker. A good year for Chevalier that, without the millstone of a "great" vintage around its neck, will deliver in a delightful fashion.

2015: like the Giscours, a long cast into the future. A punt which will come off or, failing that, my gift. A lighter, sappier take on 2005 and 2009 but with the same potential. I doubt claret will ever get any better than Domaine de Chevalier 2015. When the time comes, may we raise a glass to the gods and acknowledge the miracle.

"Time present and time past
Are both perhaps present in time future
And time future contained in time past."

TS Eliot

AFTERWORD

I

Have I become my own second son? I become ever more protective of the boy I once was.

"Drink to me, drink to my health, you know I can't drink any more." I have an image of a young boy, no older than 10 perhaps, leaning out over a verandah, the warm Lusitanian night enveloping him, the music filtering out through open French Windows, the boy looking for a moment's solitude and an early (for his young life) opportunity to understand what has just happened and to explore his reaction to it. The dawning of self. And I want to put my arms around him, to reassure him that all is well and that, despite a lifetime to come of it, there is no need to be hard on himself, that we are always hardest on ourselves, that we always imagine things to be worse than they are, that, really, everything is and will be alright.

The projector goes dark.

"Drink to me, drink to my health, you know I can't drink anymore." So, it is claimed, did Pablo Picasso say good night to his dinner guests in Mougins on the night of 8 April 1973, the night the grand old painter died. And so did his words work their way into the penultimate track of Wings' album, *Band on the Run*, released in the same year. And so, finally, did his last words work their way into my brain as my older siblings and I repeatedly listened to the album during the long Lisbon summers of 1977 and 1978.

Phrases. Sequences of words. Patterns of letters. They follow us around all our grown lives, subconsciously sitting at the back of our minds, only to resurface at the unpredicted time and resonate with a meaning not previously credited to them. "Drink to me, drink to my health, you know I can't drink anymore". I never thought the words would come back to me this way. X or Y? Who knows? All I do know is that I shall continue to drink these wines with you as long as each of us makes our journey around the sun. And each time we shall celebrate the blessing of each and every one.

II

One difficult day, when the only light at the end of the tunnel appeared to be the eternal peace which awaits us all, I sat in the garden with Father Gianni and he asked me to list the five things for which I have been most grateful in my journey across the years. I was surprised how quickly and easily the list came to me: family, friends, work, the natural world, wine.

Family and friends speak for themselves: no less than the reflection and sharing of life itself.

As for work, well it has lent purpose to my day, has put food on my table, has gifted me friends, has fed my mind and has given me worth. How often we have cursed the routine and obligation of it all, how little perhaps we have celebrated its contribution. *"Wherefore I perceive that there is nothing better than that a man should rejoice in his own works, for that is his portion."* So the Good Book tells us.

For the natural world, I have bored you enough about this elsewhere. But mark these words from *Hawk in the Sky*; might I not say precisely the same about wine? Perhaps I am a broken record.

"Knowledge is not a condition of pleasure but it certainly informs and feeds it. Just as my father learnt from his father and he from his father before him, so my father first made me aware of the natural world and then taught me its traits. This awareness and knowledge has created a foundation for pleasure...that I have carried silently and weightlessly... [and that] teaches me the plurality and variety of this thing called life."

In any event, the effect of Father Gianni's question to me, and my response, was instantaneous. All these things that had combined to make my life so rich and so pleasurable were still there. Immediately I realised that by fussing about the future I was denying the present and the blessings of now. I must live for now.

I haven't told you the full story of when I tried that first bottle from the half case of Rioja Alta's 2001. Sam, an old friend from work, and I agreed to meet for supper at the local tapas bar, a small restaurant with small tables, small chairs and small glasses that has been going for years and years and never gets it wrong. Invariably, we have always ended up drinking too much beer, too much manzanilla and too much Rioja.

Another work colleague, Jeremy, asked if he might come along as he had a special bottle to share. For almost 20 years, Jeremy's father, a keen wine collector, had kept a bottle of Pétrus 1970 on top of the fridge. Jeremy had repeatedly told him to store the bottle properly, on its side in a cool, dark place. But his father would have none of it: the bottle reminded him of an old friend who had given it to him and, besides, he most probably enjoyed being reminded of its existence each evening. When his father died, the bottle came to Jeremy. And when the bottle came to us (before the three of us went out to the tapas bar) it betrayed its age: the label was yellowed and half unstuck.

Pétrus – Pomerol's most famous and desired wine. Pétrus 1970 – a cool £2,200 a bottle. I uncorked the bottle gently (the cork crumbling as I withdrew it). When the cork came clear of the neck of the bottle we all tried a little (you too my love). Relief spread. It was not corked, first hurdle, and was not oxidised, second hurdle: it was going to be drinkable. I decided to bring along the Rioja Alta as a back-up. I had checked with the restaurant beforehand and they were happy that we brought these bottles along. £10 corkage a bottle.

At the restaurant we started with an obligatory beer and then a couple of copitas of manzanilla. Then we drank the Pétrus. It had improved for the air and the walk to the restaurant. At 47 years old it was, needless to say, mild, gentle but nevertheless with enough identity and enough to say to make it remarkable. We were seated at the table by the door and, each time new guests arrived, the label, half peeled from the bottle, would gently catch in the breeze.

Jeremy remarked that the wine was undoubtedly past its best. Maybe it was; maybe 10 years ago, or maybe if the wine had been better stored, it would have shown more vigour. But 10 years ago, the three of us would not have been gathered around this small table, unconsciously appreciating the quiet friendship that we had built up with each other over almost 20 years, acknowledging the blessing of drinking this extraordinary bottle over simple food and drinking to the memory of Jeremy's father.

We spend our lives concerned with what has gone before and what awaits us next, a constant rush of anticipation and worry, how things might have been better, how things might be worse. This is to waste time, this is to dwell in the past and to deny the present. The present is the whole moment; it is the source of the past and the seed of the future. It is the present that we must inhabit and that Pétrus, with its imperfections and all its perfections, was an integral part of the perfect present and the perfect moment.

And what can be more present than to pull a cork on a bottle of wine and by doing so to unlock coordinates, to unstopper time and to release place? An all-forgiving Chilean red to end a day and a half; a bottle too many of a clean rosé slipped behind the laughter of a weekend lunch with friends; a stubborn but ultimately gracious claret shepherding a Sunday roast; a keenly anticipated grand old Burgundy with fellow wine lovers; a quiet white with the one you love, to break bread and to start again.

This is the present. This is what is to be lived for. This is what it is to be now.

III

The first time ever I saw your face.

19 I was, maybe 20. 19 you were, maybe 20. How do I remember? Because the future was on the lookout, because we were young then and saw things differently, we were seeing things for the first time. The world was new. Opportunity and potential presented themselves everywhere. We were attuned to the chances, looked for them and took them more than we later would. Lessons to be learnt, steps to be taken, life's language to be heard, its idiom understood, our minds were open and our stories virgin soil. We were alert to everything. Images stuck and, even though we were not to meet for a good while afterwards, so it is that I well remember the first time I ever saw you.

You were walking through George Square talking to an equal stranger. You were wearing your brown leather jacket. I was maybe 10 paces behind you. You kept turning to your companion and I could see your profile. I was interested in who you were. And who were you speaking to? And what about? There before me, unknowing to all, lay my life pattern, you the chief seamstress. There, before me, were the seeds of Emily, Gus and Claudia, random cells cannoning through space and time, yet to collide and combine. 3 March 1990, 2 September 1995, 27 June 1998, 26 November 2002, 8 June 2005. The co-ordinates of my life. All lay before me, all lay before us.

At the top of George Square, you carried on up towards George IV Bridge. I will have turned right and walked past Appleton Tower, past the Pear Tree and the Partridge and out onto Nicholson Square. Your conversation now gone, silence will have defined me. I will have walked down Clerk Street and turned left into Rankeillor Street. I will have walked up to the front door of number 8, turned the key in the lock and quietly let myself in, all the while quite unwittingly and quite unknowingly waiting for the future.

And then, I like to think, I will have heard the pull of a cork and, going downstairs, have discovered my flatmates gathered at the kitchen table, talking and laughing over a bottle of wine. Maybe even a Muscadet.

MARK'S GLOSSARY

All my life I have spoken a deal of nonsense. And here I have spoken a whole deal of nonsense. But here, in this book, I can hide behind the defence of winespeak. Winespeak: the language of all the wine fools and all the wine lovers the world over. I said at the beginning how, once a bottle is corked by the winegrower, the rest is subjective, there is nothing absolute left. All rests in the reaction of the consumer. This goes as much for the enjoyment the bottle gives the drinker as it does for the language the drinker uses to describe the wine or his reaction to the wine.

So how much can one man's language on wine accurately convey to another the flavours, the emotions, the reactions he has experienced? Maybe not much. This glossary is called Mark's glossary for it is he, who has so kindly read these pages and offered me encouragement along the way, who suggested I list the words, or at least some of the words, that I have used, perhaps to add meaning, perhaps to add ridicule!

So here goes. Some may be obvious, some may be too personal to be of universal application, some will certainly be inaccurate but all are well-intended.

Acidity – I bang on enough about this when talking about the wines of the Mosel. But understand that acidity is one of the core balancing aspects of wine. Too little and the wine will be bland, heavy, fat; too much and you are running a razor blade over your tongue and your eyes will water. Acidity is key to all wine. It adds life and lift. Some grape varieties are naturally more acidic than others but the level of acidity can be moderated in the vineyard as well – as a rule, pick earlier for greater acidity (maybe at the risk of less ripe fruit or less ripe tannins), pick later for less acidity (this time at the risk of overripe fruit). It is like salt I suppose – a necessity in the right quantities, an evil if you get it wrong.

Alcohol – in my experience, you taste this two ways. First in the body of the wine. The greater the amount of alcohol the heavier (and, if white, the oilier) the wine is likely to feel; conversely, the less alcoholic the wine the lighter it will feel. And secondly it can carry its own flavour. If a wine is out of kilter, as I suggest the Domaine de la Mordorée Lirac 2007 might be, the alcohol does not seam with the fruit and the body of the wine but lingers as an aftertaste, slightly bitter, sometimes sweet, always heavy, pulling the wine down by its tail. The taste ends on a low note. Not to say that some wines cannot carry greater alcohol. Those Barolos we have, and I daresay some of the Chateauneufs – they are nudging 15%. If the fruit and structure are there, then the weight of the alcohol is carried along, adding texture and body, and the wine retains its harmony.

Ambitious – winemakers come in all shapes and sizes and so do winemakers' plans for their wines. Some veer towards minimalist intervention, hoping the grapes and then the wine in the bottle will work its magic in time and ultimately reflect the time and place in which they were born. Others believe that the potential of the site and its grapes can best be realised by lending every helping hand on the way to maximise the product's offering. This might be reducing the yield in the vineyard (fewer grapes will pack in greater flavour), it might be pressing the grapes as much as possible in the cellar to squeeze out every last ounce of identity, it might be lavishing new oak on the young wine to dress it in the smartest clothes, it might be one hundred and one things. An ambitious wine is one in this latter camp. You can taste it early. The wine will likely be darker than others from its appellation, the tannins will be softer so the wine can be broached earlier, the alcohol might be stronger, maybe even the bottle will be heavier. There is nothing wrong with an ambitious wine if it holds a true mirror up to its place of origin. Some do but in my experience an equal number do not (this may just be the fashion of the time) and they tend to be more expensive in any event. Sometimes it can be a case of simply trying too hard. The Luce Brunello di Montalcino is a classic example of an ambitious wine. Time will tell to what extent the ambition has exalted the spirit of place, to what extent it has diminished it.

Authoritative – how on earth can a wine be authoritative? A very good question. Clearly only in the reaction it provokes in the consumer. That Gonon St Joseph I see I have described as authoritative. It is, I suppose, a wine that is in balance and that, without having to shout, confidently and truthfully speaks of its identity, a strong statement of origin and maybe even breeding. It can stand anyone's scrutiny and not be found wanting. It is not merely a good example; it stands out from the crowd. A great thing if you can find it.

Awkward – see what I have said about Dauvissat's Chablis. Like all adolescents, merely a transient stage, when the key components of alcohol, fruit, tannins and acidity are out of balance and not yet knitted together. The child who has shot up and who has not yet filled out, the child who thinks grown-up thoughts but who does not yet know how to articulate them, the child yet to be comfortable with the social graces of adulthood. The wine will taste out of kilter, normally because the tannins, the structure of the wine, are too noticeable but sometimes because the fruit has gone into a sulk and hidden deep in the wine's core. That case of Prüm's Graacher Himmelreich 2011 is another classic case in point.

Balanced – there! I am no more than six words into the

glossary and I am now repeating myself. Goldilocks. Need I say more than that? The right amount of everything. The right amount of everything so that the wine does not overpower you (in dryness, fullness, alcohol, acidity, fruitiness, front-loading, back-loading, add a few and take your pick) but that brings you back for more. It is a core component of all the great wines of the world, an alpha and omega, a beginning, a middle, an end. It starts well with clear aromas betraying the wine's identity, it carries on in the middle, the palate supporting the flavours, maybe developing them further, but all on a platform that allows the wine's continued progression, and then finishes consistently with how it has gone before, a gentle landing creating a clear picture of the whole. A natural harmony.

Beethoven – OK, I grant that this is absurd. But we are back here in the land of Proust and his madeleines. For are the two senses of taste and smell not the most evocative of memory and connotation? In the late 1980's or early 1990's Nike ran an advert of Carl Lewis in the starting blocks, staring sideways at the camera, for all the part looking the Olympic champion he was save only that he was wearing a pair of red stilettos. "Power is nothing without control" ran the strapline. Beethoven has always been associated with power – the opening bars of his Fifth, the astonishing French horns in the final movement of the Eroica, the almost strangled high notes at points in his Missa Solemnis – but it is the consummate control which he could always exercise when he needed to which, to me at least, marks him out as the genius he was, maybe no more so than in his late string quartets. In any event, I am going out on a limb likening that Raymond Roure Crozes to Beethoven, but the wine's ability to make such a strong statement and at the same time in such a controlled way absurdly puts me in mind of the great man. It is me who is the fool for making this comparison but the comparison increases my pleasure of the wine and there is nothing wrong with that.

Bitter – we all know the flavour of bitter. In wine it may be caused by unripe grapes or unripe stalks being included in the fermentation process, it can be a sign of excess alcohol or it may be that the grape is naturally bitter. Many Italian grapes carry a natural and interesting twist of bitterness that adds greatly to the whole. That Aglianico is such an example. It adds definition.

Black – not that any wine is actually black but it can look that way. It may be a heavily extracted wine where the winegrower has pressed the grapes so much to squeeze all the colour out of the skin (all colour resides in the skin; the flesh of red grapes and white grapes is the same) or it may be that the grape has a naturally high level of pigment in the skin anyway. Malbec is a dark grape. We don't have any in the cellar but the black wines of Cahors, made from Malbec, are famous for the depth of their hue.

Blue – and not that any wine is actually blue either. One way of assessing the age of a wine is by tilting it, in the glass, against a pale background. The browner the rim, as a rule, the older the wine is and the purple (to begin with) or redder the rim the younger it is. When a wine is very young, odd as it seems, this purple can almost seem blue.

Body – in other words, I suppose, how mouth-filling is the wine? If the wine is full-bodied, you feel it envelop all of your mouth, it fills each corner with a (pleasantly) slightly heavy feeling; if it is light-bodied, then the wine's sensation is more akin to water than to milk (and none the worse for that).

Breeding – ah, now we get into controversy. The wine world, wine appreciation, winespeak has long been accused of elitism and the imposition of outmoded concepts of privilege and entitlement on what is essentially just grape juice. A way, some would argue, to keep the hoi polloi in their place. Feed them Blue Nun and Mateus Rosé and we will keep the good stuff to ourselves. So it is difficult to explain or even justify the use of the word breeding. I see I have used it to describe the Hermitages of Jean-Louis Chave, the wines of Hochheim, even the Faugères of Jean-Michel Alquier. So what do I mean? Something timeless (certainly in the case of the wines of Hermitage and Hochheim that have proved themselves, over thousands of years, as being the best sites for the best wines), something predictably great and, in the case of upstarts such as Faugères, something understatedly whole and complete and great in every way.

Brett – or, to give it its proper name, brettanomyces. Or, to you and me, a touch of the farmyard. As winemakers have scrubbed up their act, and more importantly their cellars, this unwanted yeast is found in fewer and fewer well-made wines. A good thing, well a good thing on the whole. Because in some cases the slightest touch of brett can add character and identity to a wine. Crystal clear and pure of fruit is all very well but sometimes a wine needs just a little more definition and origin than that and the faintest whiff of manure and straw can provide that. Just try the well-executed examples of Chateau Musar to understand that.

Bright – sometimes as much a state of mind as a quality in a wine. A glass of Tempier rosé in the sun with old friends and fresh laughter – is there any brighter moment beneath the firmament? Or it might be in the wine – I talk about it in the extraordinary Santa Roc Gigondas: what should be a serious statement of Southern Rhône heat has a vivacity quite belying its origins. Or that Rieussec 2008 – the acidity adds a spriteliness which lifts the heavy unctuous fruit into something almost playful.

Broad – this is different to body and mouth-filling. Broad denotes a wide spectrum of flavours that stretches across the tongue, a wonderful generous panoply. You can have a lighter-bodied wine that is broad (mature Jadot Beaunes are magicians) or you can have a heftier wine that is broad (Barolos, step forward). It is difficult to explain but the flavours get you in the middle of the tongue and the sides of the tongue as well, hence the feeling of breadth.

Classic – different to breeding. A classic example of a wine, without the extremes or idiosyncratic characteristics that some vintages will impose on a wine. The 2001 Vieux Télégraphe is such an example, born of a vintage without drama, an honest expression of what Vieux Télégraphe is, a beauty.

Clear – clear may be colour, clear may be flavour, clear may be purpose. I talk of Chateau Batailley 1996 being clear. It is a wine unsmudged by too hot a year (which would add a jamminess to the fruit), unadulterated by too heavy a hand in the cellar (allowing the grapes to express their flavours without impediment) and left in lovely balance. Clear in colour is essential in whites and clear in purpose? More difficult. See below.

Complexity – forgive me Jonathan for writing this, forgive me (and you were only talking to your sister!). The generosity of bringing round that bottle of Jaboulet's La Chapelle Hermitage 1997 does not deserve this. But similarly, Vicky, if ever you read this, thank you so much for opening that bottle of Chimney Rock Napa Cabernet Sauvignon 2012. Two remarkable bottles.

Jonathan: "OK, where's the corkscrew? Let's move onto the good stuff."

Vicky: "But we're just having this Chimney Rock; this is good."

Jonathan: "No, this will be better."

A while later:

Vicky: "Do you know, I think I prefer the Chimney Rock."

Jonathan: "That is because the Chapelle is more" and he markedly slows down here, "com-plex."

Vicky: "Complex? Oh?"

Jonathan: "Yes, the Hermitage is more complex and you do not have the palate to understand this complexity."

Vicky: "Oh."

Poor Vicky! Complexity. Another hot potato? No, not really. In truth, both wines had complexity, the Chimney Rock's nascent, the Chapelle's mature. Complexity means twists and turns. Not a monolith of flavour but a flavour that develops yes, over time, but more importantly over the palate when you drink it. It can take many forms but the experience takes you on a journey.

Concentrated – the product of good winemaking, the product often of old vines which produce fewer deeper-flavoured grapes than young vines. Concentration brings an intensity to the flavour, just as in Brocard's Vieilles Vignes bottling of his Chablis.

Cool – cool fruits are not warm fruits. They are not so

expansive on your tongue, they retain a little reticence, maybe they make you work harder to taste the depth of fruit in the wine. Sometimes it is the vintage (not as sun-blessed as others – Chevalier's 2008 will likely fall into this category), sometimes it is the vineyard (higher elevation, higher latitude, fewer direct hours of sunlight, for whatever reason just that little bit colder – reds from the Loire Valley, even the Pernand-Vergelesses). But in this age of excess, a little reticence can be very welcome.

Cultured – or should I say uncultured? I dare venture that Palazzino's La Pieve tannins are a touch uncultured. By this I mean not polished to marble smoothness, a little tough maybe but which may conceivably mellow out in time.

Dark – see Black.

Deep – I don't mean intellectual here. I mean an intensity of flavour that develops on your tongue and lingers long after the last swallow. Mature Dauvissat Chablis is deep. And a deep wine might encourage reflection, if the conversation of friends has not been a distraction and you realise you are sharing something special of God's gifts.

Definition – some wines just spill it all out. Nothing wrong with that, their purpose to provide quick easy pleasure, fruit-forward maybe so you get a hit of soft and instant pleasure and then the wine leaves you alone. Other wines won't do that. The wine will have a structure which can be as delicate as Meissen but which will nevertheless impose itself in its disposition. I have always thought Alquier's Faugeres has this definition, the finest filigree, the most delicate tracery of a Gothic window. Rightly or wrongly I have attributed it to the schist on which the grapes are grown. It is persistent and will gently remind you of its presence each mouthful.

Demanding – see what I have said about Côte-Rôtie and Vieux Télégraphe. It is often simply a matter of personal taste – the flavour of the wine might not be something you immediately take to (but learn to appreciate if you concentrate) or the structure of the wine might be such that it doesn't slip down quite so easily, at least not without food. There is no rhyme or reason as to which wines you should find demanding or not.

Disjointed – very similar to awkward, the component parts yet to stitch together. I wonder when that case of Jadot's Theurons 2005 will finally come round?

Dry – principally a dry finish, the sugar in the wine having been integrated into the fruit that has come before and the wine landing smoothly without any hint of previous sweetness. Particularly in Alsace, it is easy to confuse a dry white for something sweeter because the grapes, such as Gewürztraminer or Pinot Gris, which can pack such a punch of flavour in the middle palate, create an impression of lingering sweetness come the end of the sip that in fact is non-existent.

Dumb – well-made Chablis, in particular, can go through a dumb phase – think Piuze and Dauvissat, a stage when all the flavours of the wine go into shut-down leaving a mute, almost tasteless, liquid. The wine will then re-emerge, having metamorphosed, with a different flavour profile, a butterfly slowly emerging from its chrysalis.

Earnest – how on earth can a wine be earnest? Of course it can't. Here I am transposing the intentions of the winemakers into the end product. I like wines with a certain joy, something carefree. If the winemaker is trying to hard, I cannot help but convince myself that this excessive effort and industry has worked its way into the wine and so detracted from this joie de vivre. Utter utter nonsense I know. Kiwi Pinot Noir is one such an example. I have no doubt the wines are lovely but they have never flicked my switch precisely because so much effort is being poured into the growers' efforts that they should be world-beaters. As I have said elsewhere, the most exciting Kiwi grape for me is Chardonnay – without the pressure of forcing an argument, the wines are so bright, so intense, so filled with existence there is not a hint of earnestness about them.

Elegant – pretty much means what you would expect it to mean. Nothing that bashes you about the head, a wine at ease with itself, a wine of gentle understatement.

Extracted – the process by which flavour, tannins, colour and, I am sure, many other things are pressed from the grape skin, along with the juice, when the grapes are first brought into the cellar. The degree of extraction will often inform the body and weight of the wine and, of course, the ambitions of the winemaker.

Finish – a long finish is better than a short finish. A long finish carries the flavour of the wine long after the sip has been swallowed, the flavour sometimes continuing to develop like echoes off a cliff. It is the sign of a good wine – just like that Rioja Alta 2001.

Framework – read structure. The scaffold on which the wine is built which should, in time, melt away to leave a complete wine able to support its own weight, like that bridge across the Cam secured with no nails or screws.

Gamey – forever and a day Red Burgundy has been described as gamey but I wonder for how much longer. The wine merchants will want to continue to do so because Red

Burgundy goes so well with the fruits of autumn, the grouse, the pheasant, the woodcock, the pigeon, the berries, the smoke, the closing-in of the year. But in recent years, I have detected less and less game in good Burgundy – cleaner winemaking practices maybe. It is still there, sometimes a faint echo, sometimes, in the hands of an unreconstructed traditionalist, to the fore, but I do wonder if it is a disappearing feature. Gamey – I recall the first time my mother gave me venison. My goodness it was (what shall I say?) mature. There was something rotten about it, something really quite high, something over the hill, something feral even fecal. The taste of decay. That might sound revolting in a wine but, like that Chambolle Sentiers all those years ago that James D'Albiac fed me, it can take wine to another level if the stars align. And in the absence of that particular star of the firmament, you will find it in that case of Maume Gevrey.

Generous – bountiful, devoted to pleasure, not holding back on ceremony, pretence or convention. In whatever form, a wine which fills you with a feeling of goodwill and warmth, of the wholeness and goodness of this planet.

Glossy – a modern phenomenon but maybe not necessarily the sign of a modern wine. A wine which has been made in such a way as to be enjoyable now and not only when it has reached full maturity. In the days of yore, (serious) wines were expected to be laid down for many years before being broached. This meant they were tannic, unapproachable, not open for business. Nowadays some winemakers try to make these wines in such a way that they can be drunk young or old. I am not always convinced but these young wines are certainly more palatable than some of their forebears. So what is glossy? A bright colour maybe, softish tannins, velvety on the palate, a full rich flavour, sometimes showy, sometimes just unutterably smooth. That Alion will be glossy, some of those swanky clarets will be glossy.

Glycerol – what on earth I am doing using a word such as this? I am on dangerous ground here. Aah, I see. To describe those Seaview Chardonnays all those years ago which gave my vinous universe such a jolt. Oh, and even now to describe some of the texture of a good White Bordeaux. I do not know the origins of the chemical, the whys and hows as to its presence in wine but, to me at least, it has always added a certain viscosity, body and oiliness to a white wine. Sometimes good, sometimes bad. Sweet wines carry more of it and can carry it very well. I will stop before I get it too hopelessly wrong.

Green – some use green to denote youth in a wine, some will use it as a flavour profile (Loire reds can carry an element of greenness which, if intended, I find quite refreshing) but it is probably most commonly used to denote underripeness. And in my experience, if a wine is underripe (because the grapes were not able to ripen properly), it will never lose that greenness, a stalkiness that remains throughout its life. Think unripe tomatoes, even undercooked potatoes. The crunchy green of a Loire red can soften effortlessly with time into something captivating and, if you are using green to describe youth, well we all leave that behind eventually.

Harsh – as ever, sometimes the grape, sometimes the vintage conditions, sometimes the winemaker. I see I mainly use it in describing the difference between Left Bank and Right Bank wines in Bordeaux, mainly therefore to describe the difference between Cabernet Sauvignon and Merlot. Cabernet Sauvignon is certainly a tougher grape than Merlot when young. The tannins are more noticeable, the flavours maybe harder (green pepper, for example?) but then age weaves its magic and everything softens.

Heady – when you put your nose in the glass and your whole being is consumed by the sensation. It may of course be the alcohol (some grapes, such as Grenache, can purr past 15%) or it can be the sheer wealth of sensory overload, the rose-petal punch of Gewürztraminer.

Herbaceousness – a hint of green but not really a fault. A welcome antidote to sun-baked jam.

High-toned – it is disappointing that I used this word (step forward Rioja Alta's 2001) because it is one of those words that I have gone through life using but which I have never properly understood. What I am trying to say is that, if a wine is high-toned, it has elements to its bouquet and sometimes flavour which lift it out of the ordinary and make it fly higher and further. It can be delightful and I have only ever been meant it as a compliment.

Honest – used so often by me, for some reason particularly in describing the wines of Italy. Without pretence, a faithful mirror to a wine's origin, not trying to be something it cannot be.

Intellectual – see what I say about claret in general. A wine given over to thought rather than sense, to reason rather than emotion. That Léoville Barton 1994 – think as you drink!
Intensity – concentrated, deep, well-made. The difference between an enjoyable Chablis and a crafted Premier Cru Chablis where the experience, if you choose to concentrate, has so many more layers as flavours, even textures, twist and turn in the vacuums of our minds.

Length – simply, how long can you taste the wine on your tongue after you have swallowed it? The finest examples will linger longingly. Not that length is always what you need of course – laughter and the love of friends trumps length, every time.

Lift – something in the taste of a wine that refreshes parts other wines cannot reach. Not a dull hand or heavy statement, something spritely and refreshing, sometimes almost citrus. Think Mosel, happy Beaujolais, that wonderful Nuits-Saint-Georges from Gachot-Monot, that Volnay from Vaudoisey.

Liquorous – thicker-textured, heavier. The young Clos du Mont Olivet shows it but, in age, it shall lose most of that puppy fat and a generous texture should be all that remains of it.

Mature – a fine wine at its peak, when all the parts have come together, none at the expense of the other, the wine revealing its true identity, a wine with the cards on the table and there to be welcomed home.

Meaty – I am put in mind of Maume's Gevrey-Chambertin again. Yes, something savoury, quite dark, the sweetness of fruit ceding centre to drier flavours of umami and stock.

Minerality – oh the fun that people have had with this word, endless pages in the wine press about whether minerality even exists, whether the roots of the vine can actually carry minerals up into the plant and then the grape and then whether we can even taste such minerals. Does it matter? I know when a wine has a flavour of minerality. Maybe it is my mind playing tricks but the pleasure is all mine, it gives me a sense of place and connects me to the earth. The slate of the Mosel, the schist of Faugères, the Kimmeridge of Chablis, the high limestone of the Côte de Beaune, the gravel of the Graves. It does it for me, regardless of whether or not montmorillonites and other substances even exist to transport such traces into the grape. I will defend minerality to my dying day.

Modern – I have said enough myself about this elsewhere – see Ambitious, Extracted and Glossy for starters. A laudible desire, however, to bring winemaking up to an acceptable standard of consumer-friendliness. You may not want to see "modern" in the same sentence as "Hermitage" but it is all of us who benefit from tasting "modern" in a £5 bottle pulled off a supermarket shelf in a tired rush for home at the end of a long day.

Mouth-filling – ditto. See Body, Broad and Generous. An abundance of texture and flavour, let's leave it at that.

Nervy – on edge. Normally when the fruit and the acidity vie for the upper hand. A cold steel rail. Never the most relaxing wines but at least alive.

Neutral – for me, bland. For me, too many Italian white wines are too neutral, difficult flavours to pinpoint, difficult textures or identity to elicit, wines which speak of little but which may of course slake many a happy thirst.

Oaky – tomes have been written on this subject but the flavour of oak is often most noticeable as an overlay of vanilla, especially if the wine has been aged in new oak barrels or American oak (French oak is more subtle). If the wine has been well-made, the vanilla flavour will merge and disappear into the wine and, in its maturity, you will be little reminded of it. Of course, in wine designed to be drunk young, a healthy dose of gentle creamy flavour can work wonders in helping it slip down and so it is often employed for exactly this purpose.

Open – not closed! The wine has something to say, it tastes well, it has blended sufficiently to be an enjoyable experience, shedding off awkwardness, taciturnity, desultoriness. Come in; I may only just be open but nevertheless I am so.

Overblown – wines out of kilter, normally in terms of excess of fruit or alcohol, wines that lack balance, often top-heavy, wines that are a pastiche of what they should be. Egregious examples of New Zealand Sauvignon Blanc or Californian Zinfandel are often guilty parties.

Overripe – the product of a hot vintage (2003 in Europe is a good example) or sometimes the product just of a difficult grape to get right. Viognier, Grenache, Pinot Noir – they are all examples of grapes that tiptoe towards maturity and then seem to accelerate through it to overripeness if the winegrowers are not on their game. Much like peaches in the fruit bowl: maddening. In any event, this often comes from having thin skins. If grapes are overripe, the resultant wine can be too sugary or top-heavy or, if the sugar is fully fermented, too alcoholic. And they will lack the necessary acidity to keep the wine on its feet.

Oxidised – the taste of sherry, of nuts, of a creeping blandness and often enough accompanied by a darkening of the colour of the wine. Far more prevalent in white wines and, sadly, in highly-priced White Burgundy. Not much to be done with it other than the sink. Of course, where the oxidation is intentional, as in Sherry or Madeira, the wine is built around the oxidised flavours and tastes much fresher and complex and frankly becomes a world-beater.

Persistent – akin to a long finish. A flavour which will not go away.

Playful – what an absurd adjective to use. But I mean a wine to be enjoyed, not to be taken too seriously, to provide all the pleasure that is demanded of it but ultimately to play second fiddle to the occasion on which it is being drunk. That Castellinuzza Chianti (what a delicious wine) is a classic example.

Polished – not necessarily modern, just so cosseted. A lot of smart claret nowadays is just so polished, the tannins so fine as to be almost invisible, the gloss of the fruit so seductive as to be a second thought. The wine must be able to make a statement, there must be a friction in the mouth so the brain can be engaged and register its merits. Polishing a wine too much can detract from this – don't hide the wine's DNA, its bones and identity, beneath veneers of expensive polish.

Primary – a wine in the first stage of its drinking life. It is not too young, just the flavour of the undeveloped fruit will be to the fore and it will not yet have developed a complexity showing the wine's full potential or its full identity.

Purpose – hmm, another difficult one. Wholly utterly subjective but, for me, a wine which is clear in what it is, where it is from, what it wants to say (how can a wine want to say anything? Aah, us wine lovers are always listening for the siren call). A wine such as that bottle of Lamarche's Echézeaux from which we once so drank deeply, from a well of truth at such a difficult time. The wine had a core of immutable certainty and fixed singularity which it was impossible to deviate from and against which it was impossible not to lean and rest awhile. Shelter from a storm.

Red fruits – I have always loved using these words because really I do not know what I am talking about. And black fruits too! Even more difficult to pin down. Red fruits – strawberries, raspberries, maybe redcurrants – softer, gentler fruits. Black fruits – blackberries, blackcurrants, blueberries, all a little darker and more difficult to define. Red fruits – I do not know if I taste them or not but they bring me a gentle comfort. Rioja, mature Red Burgundy – soft red fruits...

Ripe – obviously when the fruit ripens but also, in today's sophisticated world, when the tannins are ripe. Physiological ripeness it is called – when the pips lose a certain green bitterness. This physiological ripeness adds a great deal to the modern texture of wine, to the extent that some winegrowers now wonder whether this tannin ripeness should be sacrificed to allow the wine to wear a lighter mantle.

Ruby – if a young red wine is blue (see above), purple will be next but then that might mellow into ruby (or garnet if I knew the difference) on its way to maturity (something more tawny).

Sappy – another favourite word for something lifted, something playful. Nebbiolo as interpreted by some Roero producers, Volnay in the good hands of Monsieur Vaudoisey.

Scratchy – similar to awkward, maybe. Young Domaine de Chevalier (long before the swan it becomes) is famously difficult to taste, all components out of kilter.

Seamless – an effortless tapestry of all the relevant parts to create an indivisible whole. Try that Gonon Saint-Joseph and tell me if you can pick it apart. I don't think you will be able to.

Secondary – after primary comes secondary. See what I have said about Dauvissat, his Chablis and how the flavours develop. And secondary also of course means the secondary market. Many of the world's best wines are on allocation or difficult to find when first sold on the open market. Those lucky owners will then squirrel them away and, when the time is right, either drink them or sell them on the secondary market by which time the stock may well have risen, because of scarcity, reputation or because they are now ready to drink. The profits can be remarkable (at the expense, I think, of a little bit of your soul).

Soft – need I say more than I have said before? I think not. The opposite of hard.

Sombre – again, a shameless imposition of human emotion onto a glass of fermented grape juice. A wine, I suppose, which provokes introspection and deeper thought. That Burgaud Morgon for example.

Stalky – I cannot pretend to understand the reasons for including or excluding the stems of grapes from the fermentation process; some winemakers swear by it, others abhor it. All I can say is thank you for all variety it brings, whichever decision is taken. Except when the stalks are not ripe, when greenness lurks within. This can work its way into the wine and bring a woody unwelcome unripeness to proceedings. Then I would say no thank you.

Structure – as above. The tannin scaffold beneath which the alcohol, the acidity and the fruit of a wine hang and develop.

Subtle – Muscadet, my beautiful Muscadet. No one would say you have a flavour which smacks between the eyes. Some might well say you are nothing more than neutral. But your identity is as strong as the sea air, the currents that bear it and the fruit that the sea brings. You are subtle. You must be looked for and the pleasure is all the greater for finding it.

Supple – is Arnold Schwarzenegger supple? No. Is a jaguar supple? Yes. Supple denotes hidden strength, cloaked beneath a coat of smoothness and elegance. Different to an iron fist in a velvet glove (often used to describe powerful Red Burgundy), there is something more powerful and potential at work. That Coursodon Saint-Joseph – hidden power and depths lurk within.

Tawny – blue, purple, ruby, tawny. The natural degradation of colour in a red wine as it passes through the ages.

Tension – all the fashion, especially in white wine. Gone, sadly for me sometimes, are the generous ripe flavours of butter and melon in Australian Chardonnay and White Burgundy to be replaced by something more challenging, the interplay of acidity and fruit. The drinker must not luxuriate but must think. Not as extreme as nervy, but is tension always what the drinker wants? I suspect not, in which case I find Chilean Chardonnay a happy hunting ground. The answer, as ever, must lie somewhere in the middle.

Tertiary – beyond primary, beyond secondary. When is a good wine at its best? Secondary or tertiary? When is the true character of the wine and its birthplace revealed? Each wine will be different and each taster will have a different opinion. Tertiary might represent the apogee before tertiary then heralds the gentle waning of a bright star. Flavours of game, maybe, of even softer fruits, the tannins melting almost completely as the wine slowly, gracefully, inexorably surrenders to age. Pétrus 1970.

Texture – the mouthfeel, nothing more, nothing less.

Thin – the product of overcropping or dilute grapes or unripe tannins. When the substance of the wine is not enough to support its structure.

Unchallenging – damning with faint praise? That would be unfair. Most wine is not designed to be an intellectual exercise or an obstacle course. It should be a source of pleasure. Some of the world's most wonderful wines can be undemanding – many, many truly delicious Spanish wines, even Château Batailley – because they are devoted above all to the principle of enjoyment. Long may that continue. If a wine is deemed undemanding, it is probably because the tannins are not too noticeable, the fruit is too easily smooth, the wine too easily drinkable. Nothing wrong with that.

Unripe – not enough sun! Green, thin flavours.

Velvet – I have always been nervous to use this adjective but I can think of nothing more appropriate for my beloved Mugneret Vosnes. We are back into the land of mouthfeel and texture. Not a sensation you would want in every wine you drink – a velvety white would cause a bit of a stir – but when it combines with all the other strings of the symphony, it strikes to the very core.

Warmth – a by-product of heat, not surprisingly. Heat creates sugar creates alcohol creates warmth.

Wider – very similar to Broad. A case of spectrum of flavours rather than texture.

Young – I have said enough now, my love, my little ones, my song now sung. You will be able to glean from other pages in this book what I mean by young. Young – just as we were, my love, just as once upon a time we were.